Living Stones in the Household of God

The Legacy and Future of Black Theology

edited by Linda E. Thomas

Fortress Press
Minneapolis

For
Dwight N. Hopkins,
my husband,
and
Dora Linda Thomas Hopkins,
my daughter

LIVING STONES IN THE HOUSEHOLD OF GOD
The Legacy and Future of Black Theology

Cover art: "The Past" by Anna Belle Lee Washington © SuperStock, Inc. Used by permission.
Book design: Beth Wright

ISBN 0-8006-3627-9

Manufactured in the U.S.A.

Contents

Part Four: Black Theology and a Persevering Faith

Preface

Linda E. Thomas

The idea of a book on the future of black theology arose from a conference I coordinated while on the faculty at Garrett-Evangelical Theological Seminary. In 1997, when I arrived at Garrett to teach theology and anthropology and direct the Center for the Church and the Black Experience (CBE), I knew I entered an institution that had a checkered history in relation to African Americans. CBE developed out of African Americans' struggle to have a voice and intellectual space in the institution. James H. Cone, the first African American to graduate with a Ph.D. from Garrett/Northwestern Graduate School, experienced explicit incidents of racism there. I also believed that the souls of black men and women made it possible for me to become the second African American woman professor in the institution's history. Thus, in my second year, I decided that CBE would invite James H. Cone back to his alma mater to honor him and to examine the future of black theology. The key questions for the conference were: What impact will black theology have on the church in the black church's third century? In what ways has black theology influenced all of modern theology? The chapters in this volume result from the conference participants' responses to these questions and include a cross section of perspectives based on black theology's global reach.

What is exciting about this book is that black theology is examined as public theology not only addressing the historically black churches but also in dialogue with various theologies—Asian, Native American, Latino/a and white—and the corresponding faith traditions represented by these theologies. The volume reflects the international impact of black theology and the ways various peoples around the world have engaged the theology for liberative purposes, while particularizing it for their own contexts. Black theology's method and practice have been so forceful that it contributes to a self-reflective process for many marginalized peoples developing their own theologies around the globe.

I was motivated to edit this book by a commitment to integrate theology and anthropology in my academic research. *Theology* is critical reflection about the God-human relationship, and *anthropology* is rational inquiry into and understanding of human beings and culture. Black theology then is critical reflection about the relationship between black humanity and God in culture. One might mistakenly think that black theology is concerned with the God–black human relationship in black culture only; on the contrary, black theology inquires into the God–black human relationship wherever black women and men find themselves. The social construction of race has a negative impact on black people globally and therefore is a central category in black theology's analysis of the God-human relationship. As such, black theology's main thrust is its tenacity as a discipline to examine the faith practices of black folks that move toward liberation grounded in Jesus Christ. Black theology's locus of concern has historically been black people and liberation in the United States, yet it is in dialogue with black people on every continent, especially those in Africa. Indeed, black theologians in other parts of the world have developed black theology to articulate the particular God-human relationship and cultural issues for their specific situations.

I would like to thank the scholars who helped to make this volume a success. I especially thank my husband, Dwight N. Hopkins, who helped with all stages of the project, especially its conceptualization. I want to thank my colleagues at Lutheran School of Theology at Chicago who encouraged me to complete the book. I especially thank President James Echols and Academic Dean Kathleen Billman, who provided funding for a research assistant to help with the editing of the volume, and Jamie Jazdzyk, whose enduring editing work helped improve the book's clarity. I also want to thank the faculty at Garrett, who were extremely supportive since the book's inception. I want to thank the CBE staff: Karen Mosby Avery, Abby Fyten, Marie Clark, and Nathan Dixon. Without their help the conference would never have taken place. Finally, I want to thank my teacher and mentor, James H. Cone, who weathered the storms, continues to fight, and has gifted the world with a theology that makes faith take risks as no other theology has done before.

About the Contributors

Edward P. Antonio is Assistant Professor of Theology and Social Theory at Iliff School of Theology, Denver, Colorado. He previously taught at the University of Witwatersrand, South Africa.

Lee H. Butler Jr., Associate Professor of Theology and Psychology at Chicago Theological Seminary, is author of *Loving Home: Caring for African American Marriage and Family* (2000).

Iva E. Carruthers is former chairperson and Professor of Sociology at Northeastern Illinois University, Chicago. She is also founder and President of Nexus Unlimited, Inc., a management training and consulting firm.

James H. Cone is the Charles A. Briggs Distinguished Professor of Systematic Theology at Union Theological Seminary, New York City. Among his pioneering publications in black theology are *Black Theology and Black Power* (1969), *Martin and Malcolm and America* (1992), and *God of the Oppressed* (1997).

M. Shawn Copeland is Associate Professor of Theology at Boston College and President of the Catholic Theological Society of America. Author of more than sixty articles and chapters, she is also co-editor of two volumes: *Feminist Theology in Different Contexts* (1996) and *Violence against Women* (1994).

Dwight N. Hopkins is Professor of Theology at the University of Chicago. He is author of *Shoes That Fit Our Feet* (1993), *Introducing Black Theology of Liberation* (1999), and *Down, Up, and Over: Slave Religion and Black Theology* (Fortress Press, 2000).

Yvonne Young-ja Lee holds a doctorate in theology from Iliff School of Theology, Denver, and is Pastor of Deer Park United Methodist Church in Bailey, Colorado.

D. Stephen Long is Associate Professor of Systematic Theology at Garrett-Evangelical Theological Seminary, Evanston, Illinois, and author of *Divine Economy: Theology and the Market* (2001).

Karen E. Mosby-Avery, a doctoral candidate at Garrett-Evangelical Theological Seminary, is Pastor of Good News Community Church (UCC) in Chicago.

Jim Perkinson directs the D.Min. program at Ecumenical Theological Seminary, Detroit, and is Associate Professor of Religious Studies and Philosophy at Marygrove College there. Apart from his many published theological articles, he is a hip-hop poet of increasing renown and has organized programs for teaching theology in urban environments.

José David Rodríguez is Professor of Systematic Theology and Director of Hispanic Ministries at Lutheran School of Theology, Chicago. He is co-author of *Teología en Conjunto: A Collaborative Hispanic Protestant Theology* (1997) and author of *Justicia en Nombre de Dios: Confesando la Fe desde la Perspectiva Hispano/Latina* (2002).

Rosemary Radford Ruether is the Carpenter Professor of Feminist Theology in the Graduate Theological Union, Berkeley. Among her two-dozen groundbreaking works in feminist theology are *Sexism and God-Talk* (1983) and *Women and Redemption* (Fortress Press, 1998).

Linda E. Thomas is Professor of Theology and Anthropology at Lutheran School of Theology, Chicago. She is author of *Under the Canopy: Ritual Process and Spiritual Resilience in South Africa* (1999).

George E. Tinker is Professor of American Indian Cultures and Religious Traditions. Among his works is *Missionary Conquest: The Gospel and Native American Genocide* (Fortress Press, 1991).

Emilie M. Townes is the Carolyn Williams Beaird Professor of Christian Ethics at Union Theological Seminary, New York City. Her many influential works include *Womanist Justice, Womanist Hope* (1993), *In a Blaze of Glory* (1995), and *Breaking the Fine Rain of Death* (1998).

Laceye Warner is Assistant Professor of the Practice of Evangelism and Methodist Studies at Duke Divinity School, Raleigh-Durham, North Carolina. She is co-author of *The Ekklesia Project: Missional Evangelism* (2002).

Jeremiah A. Wright Jr. is Senior Pastor of Trinity United Church of Christ, Chicago. A noted preacher, he has authored many volumes, including *What Makes You So Strong* (1993) and *Africans Who Shaped Our Faith* (1995).

Introduction

Linda E. Thomas

Black theology has created a vision of faith and purpose of life for black people in light of the situation of the black oppressed. It has provided the intellectual space for people of African descent to reflect critically on the nature of their faith and the God-human relationship. Through black theology, black people have grappled with what the "good news" means for them in light of the life and works of Jesus. In this volume we take a careful, sustained look at how the black theological legacy affects the black church, other Christian communities, the global religious scene, and the perennial challenge of transforming people's lives through faith.

Black Theology and the Black Church

If black theology is grounded in God's liberating action for the sake of people of African descent, especially the black poor, then the work of the black church must reflect God's work. This means that the black church must focus on liberation in its activities, actions, rituals, and practices. All of the affairs of the church ought to reflect God's transforming presence in the lives of black folks.

Black theology will assist the church in examining its liberatory work centered on the life of Jesus Christ. The black church must be responsive to the needs of the oppressed, outcast, and poor, just as Jesus was. Jesus changed and transformed people's lives in a radical manner, and he was killed because of his commitment to the humanity of the poor and the struggle for God's justice. Thus the struggle for justice is tied intimately to Christian identity. Black theology and the black church must be actively involved in the political struggle for justice. The church's actions, norms, and mission statements must reflect this commitment. Certainly the church of Jesus Christ can in the present age participate in a passionate struggle for justice.

The new millennium is witnessing a rising number of megachurches in the African American community. These churches bring together thousands of African American Christians, and the power that resides in them is tremendous. How do these megachurches harness their energy for the future of black theology and liberation? There needs to be a well-developed plan for liberation so that the theology and message of the church are clear to the local community, the nation, and the world. Megasized black churches have the talent and economic base to make a substantial contribution to lifting up issues that negatively affect black people. The question for these churches in the new millennium is, Will megasized black churches, especially neo-pentecostal and charismatic churches, embrace a liberatory black theology rather than one based simply on the ascendancy of individuals who aspire to prosperity?

Black Theology and the White Church

In *Black Theology and Black Power* (1969), James H. Cone, the father of black theology, criticized the white church. He wrote, "If the real Church is the people of God, whose primary task is that of being Christ to the world by proclaiming the message of the gospel *(kerygma),* by rendering services of liberation *(diakonia)* and by being itself a manifestation of the nature of the new society *(koinonia),* then the empirical institutionalized white church has failed on all counts."

While there have been various responses from white theologians to this comment, one of the questions for this volume is, What is the relationship between black theology and the white church? Even in the United States, where people of color will soon outnumber whites in the population, white people still have institutional power to control those who have historically been minorities. What then is the future relationship of black theology and the white church? Black theology will continue to exist whether or not it has a relationship with the white church. Thus one might ask whether the white church is an audience for black theology. And if so, what does the white church do as a result of what it hears and learns? Black theology is not accountable to the white church, but can the white church change racism without having a conversation with black theology?

Evangelical white Christians have been attracted to Cone's early christological stance in black theology. However, Cone's dialogue with third-world theologians shifted his christological stance. In 1975, Cone began to do theology no longer assuming that Jesus is God's only revelation. This shift made evangelicals curious to know how black theology thinks about Jesus and black suffering. Some white theologians have taken black theology seriously by posing significant and interesting questions as a result of critical engagement with the discipline. Black theology's future will involve similar questions not only from white theology but also from evangelicals of all persuasions.

Black Theology and Global Religions

In the new millennium, black theology must continue its conversation with global communities about Christianity and other religions. This is especially important because much of the conflict in the global arena is about or affected by religious belief systems. If black theology has a global commitment to the liberation of the oppressed, then understanding the religion and culture of non-Christians who are black, poor, and oppressed is critical. This means continuing the dialogue with African theologians and also with African scholars in general. While black theology is not responsible for articulating a theology on behalf of black people in other parts of the world, it has a responsibility to share the faith experience of black people in the United States and to respond to issues such as poverty, AIDS, and war in Africa.

The crucial conversation that black theology has had with the Ecumenical Association of Third World Theologians must continue. Taking seriously the concerns of the Women's Commission of this organization is especially important because black theology's response to gender oppression of black women needs a more forceful response from black male theologians.

The Centrality of the Christian Faith and a Liberation Imperative

Black theology in the future will maintain a firm tie to the Christian faith. After all, the majority of black folk in the United States are interlocutors with the God of Jesus Christ. Since faith is a reflection of religious beliefs within particular cultural contexts, and because black people live in predominantly white Christian societies, Christianity will continue to be the religion that large numbers of black people practice. There are historic reasons for this. Whenever and wherever dominating forces have oppressed people, the latter have often adopted some form of the religion of their oppressors. The oppressed are not powerless, however, and there has never been a total embracing of the dominant religion. There has been adaptation; that is, components of the dominant religion were selected and commingled with the religion that the oppressed practiced prior to domination. Black theology records the religion and practices of the black church, whose members are the descendants of enslaved Africans. These ancestors created a religion that selected portions of white Christianity as well as African religious and cultural attributes. This is the religion that black theology will reflect when it is centered in liberatory Christian faith, for two reasons: First, even if some black theologians see Jesus as one of several revelations for liberation sent by God, a significant number of black people believe that Jesus is God's sole revelation for salvation. Second, freedom is a historic and present theme among black people, who want all the privileges that come with citizenship of the United States or any nation. The work of black theology is to challenge unequivocally the historical, structural, and cultural subordination of black people within societies dominated by white supremacist rule. Its work in the future is therefore liberation.

The Legacy of James H. Cone

The work of James H. Cone has made an indelible mark on the discipline of theology. Since 1968 he has written a black theology whose theme has been the empowerment of the poor. Not only has he created a new discipline but also he has sustained the discipline with his own writings and texts written by his students and others. This creates a legacy that makes Cone a leader of liberation theologies globally. Cone's theology has had many challenges from the white church, the black church, and womanist scholars. Yet its endurance is due largely to its resilience to criticisms in all of these sectors as well as to its adaptability.

After three decades, what issues will drive the future of black theology? What will a second, third, and fourth generation of black theologians and womanists write in this discipline? As long as there are black women, men, and children who are poor, black theology will have a central theme on which to reflect and write critically. The African American church will continue to have great influence in the African American community. Its moral authority, resources, and tradition of seeking justice will maintain its role as the central institution for black faith expression. The black church is black theology in action, and if it keeps a focus on the poor and justice, then it can work for liberation.

In the future black theology will focus on gender justice. This means that black women, especially the poor, will exercise their full humanity before God and men. It will speak to issues of women's overworking in areas of church life (the kitchen) and being spared leadership on principal church boards and committees. Black theology will not shy away from dealing with gender justice at work and at home. At work black women are to receive equal pay for equal work. At home it will not be assumed that women will do all the household work if men are present, nor will women hold the position that fathers do not play a major role in child care. Black theology will be a household theology in which men live out a new definition of what it means to be a man. This means that black men will recognize that their maleness gives them privilege despite their blackness. Just the freedom to walk around at home and away from home and not to be concerned about being verbally and physically assaulted is a privilege.

The future of black theology will also have to deal with sexual orientation in the black community and the church. Black heterosexuals enjoy privilege by virtue of their sexual orientation; this societal structure oppresses and fractures the lives of black lesbians, gays, bisexuals, and transgender persons. In addition, black theology will articulate the reasons that it is unjust for heterosexuals to use the Bible to condemn homosexuals while at the same time expect verses that sanction slavery to be thrown out, put aside, or reinterpreted.

The future of black theology will articulate the importance of treating black children as full human beings. The future of black humanity is embodied in black children. They must be nurtured from their earliest days. Black parents must have quality child care that is free or affordable. Children must have free health care. Children must be the investment of choice for the black church as it relates to education and housing. In the future and for the future, black theology must be a theology of liberation for black children.

Part One

Black Theology and the Black Church

1 / Calling the Oppressors to Account

God and Black Suffering

James H. Cone

God is not dead—nor is He an indifferent onlooker at what is going on in this world. One day He will make requisition for blood; He will call the oppressors to account. Justice may sleep, but it never dies. The individual, race, or nation which does wrong, which sets at defiance God's great law, especially God's great law of love, of brotherhood, will be sure, sooner or later, to pay the penalty. We reap as we sow. With what measure we mete, it will be measured to us again.[1]

This 1902 statement by Francis Grimké, an ex-slave and Princeton Theological Seminary graduate, is an apt summary of the major themes of justice, hope, and love in African American religion from slavery to the present. These themes were created out of the African slaves' encounter with biblical religion (via the white missionaries and preachers) as they sought to make meaning in a strange world. To make meaning in any world is difficult, because human beings, like other animals, are creatures of nature and history. We can never be what we can imagine, but to be slaves in a foreign land without the cultural and religious support of a loving family and a caring community limits human possibilities profoundly. Because Africans were prevented from freely practicing their native religion, they merged their knowledge of their cultural past with the whites' Christian religion. From these two sources, Africans created for themselves a world of meaning that enabled them to survive 246 years of slavery and one hundred years of segregation—augmented by a reign of white terror that lynched more than five thousand black people.

The black religious themes of justice, hope, and love are the product of black people's search for meaning in a white society that did not acknowledge their humanity. The most prominent theme in this trinity of divine virtues is the justice of God. Faith in God's righteousness is the starting point of black religion. African Americans have always believed in the living presence of the God who establishes the right by punishing the wicked and liberating their victims from oppression. Everyone will be rewarded and punished according to their deeds, and no one—absolutely no one—can escape the judgment of God, who alone is the sovereign of the universe. Evildoers may get by for a time, and good people may suffer unjustly under oppression, but "sooner or later . . . we reap as we sow."

The "sooner" referred to contemporary historically observable events: punishment of the oppressors and liberation of the oppressed. The "later" referred to the divine establishment of justice in the "next world" where God "gwineter rain down fire" on the wicked and where the liberated righteous will "walk in Jerusalem just like John." In the religion of African slaves, God's justice was identical with the punishment of the oppressors, and divine liberation was synonymous with the deliverance of the oppressed from the bondage of slavery—if not "now" then in the "not yet." Because whites continued to prosper materially as they increased their victimization of African Americans, black religion spoke more often of the "later" than the "sooner," more about justice in the next world than in this one.

The theme of justice is closely related to the idea of hope. The God who establishes the right and puts down the wrong is the sole basis of the hope that the suffering of the victims will be eliminated. Although African slaves used the term *heaven* to describe their experience of hope, its primary meaning for them must not be reduced to the "pie-in-the-sky," otherworldly affirmation that often characterized white evangelical Protestantism. The idea of heaven was the means by which slaves affirmed their humanity in a world that did not recognize them as human beings. It was their way of saying that they were made for freedom and not slavery.

> Oh Freedom! Oh Freedom!
> Oh Freedom, I love thee!
> And before I'll be a slave,
> I'll be buried in my grave,
> And go home to my Lord and be free.

Black slaves' hope was based on their faith in God's promise to "protect the needy" and to "defend the poor." Just as God delivered the Hebrew children from Egyptian bondage and raised Jesus from the dead, so God will also deliver African slaves from American slavery and will "soon" bestow upon them the gift of eternal life. That was why they sang:

> Soon-a-will be done with the trouble of this world;
> Soon-a-will be done with the trouble of this world;
> Going home to live with God.

Black slaves' faith in the coming justice of God was the chief reason they could hold themselves together in servitude and sometimes fight back, even though the odds were against them.

The ideas of justice and hope should be seen in relation to the important theme of love. Theologically God's love is prior to the other themes. But in order to separate love in the context of black religion from a similar theme in white religion, it is important to emphasize that love in black religion is usually linked with God's justice and hope. God's love is made known through divine righteousness, liberating the poor for a new future.

God's creation of all persons in the divine image bestows sacredness upon human beings and thus makes them the children of God. To violate any person's dignity is to transgress "God's great law of love." We must love the neighbor because God has first loved us. And because slavery and segregation are blatant denials of the dignity of the human person, divine justice means God "will call the oppressors to account."

Despite the power of black faith, belief in God's coming justice and liberation was not easy for African slaves and their descendants. Their continued suffering created the most serious challenge to their faith. If God is good, why did God permit millions of blacks to be stolen from Africa, to perish in the middle passage, and to be enslaved in a strange land? No black person has been able to escape the existential agony of that question.

In their attempt to resolve the existential and theological dilemma that slavery and segregation created, African Americans in the nineteenth century turned to two texts: Exodus and Ps. 68:31. They derived from the Exodus text the belief that God is the liberator of the oppressed. They interpreted Ps. 68:31 as an obscure reference to God's promise to redeem Africa: "Princes shall come out of Egypt, and Ethiopia shall soon stretch forth her hands unto

God." Despite African Americans' reflections on these texts, the contradictions remained between their sociopolitical oppression and their religious faith.

A free black woman named Nellie, from Savannah, Georgia, expressed the challenge black suffering created for faith: "It has been a terrible mystery, to know why the good Lord should so long afflict my people, and keep them in bondage—to be abused, and trampled down, without any rights of their own—with no ray of light in the future. Some of my folks said there wasn't any God, for if there was he wouldn't let white folks do as they do for so many years."[2]

Throughout the twentieth century African Americans continued their struggle to reconcile their faith in the justice and love of God with the persistence of black suffering in the land of their birth. Writer James Baldwin expressed the feelings of most African Americans: "If [God's] love was so great, and if He loved all His children, why were we, the blacks, cast down so far?"[3] It was Martin Luther King Jr., a twenty-six-year-old Baptist preacher, who, empowered by black faith, confronted the evil of white supremacy and condemned it as the greatest moral evil in American society. He organized a movement that broke the backbone of legal segregation in the South. From the beginning of his role as the leader of the yearlong Montgomery, Alabama, bus boycott (1955–56) to his tragic death in Memphis, Tennessee (April 4, 1968), King was a public embodiment of the ideas of love, justice, and hope. The meaning of each was dependent on the others. Though love may be placed appropriately at the center of King's faith, he interpreted love in the light of justice for the poor, liberation for all, and the certain hope that God has not left this world in the hands of evil men.

Martin King took the American democratic tradition of freedom and combined it with the biblical tradition of liberation and justice as found in the Exodus and the biblical Prophets. Then he integrated both traditions with the New Testament ideas of love and hope as disclosed in Jesus' cross and resurrection. From these three sources King developed a radical practice of nonviolence that was effective in challenging all Americans to create a beloved community in which all persons are equal. While it was Gandhi's method of nonviolence that provided the strategy for achieving justice, it was, as King said, "through the influence of the Negro Church" that "the way of nonviolence became an integral part of our struggle"[4] against the evil of white supremacy.

As a Christian whose faith was derived from the cross of Jesus, Martin King believed that there could be no true liberation without suffering.

Through nonviolent suffering, he contended, blacks would not only liberate themselves from the necessity of bitterness and a feeling of inferiority toward whites, but also prick the conscience of whites and liberate them from a feeling of superiority. The mutual liberation of blacks and whites lays the foundation for both groups to work together toward the creation of an entirely new world.

In accordance with this theological vision, King initially rejected Black Power because of its connotations of revenge, hate, and violence. He believed that no beloved community of black and whites could be created out of bitterness. Only love, which he equated with nonviolence, can create justice. When Black Power militants turned away from nonviolence and openly preached self-defense and violence, King said that he would continue to preach nonviolence even if he became its only advocate.

He took a similar position regarding the war in Vietnam. In the tradition of the Hebrew prophets and against the advice of his closest associates in black and white communities, King stood before a capacity crowd at Riverside Church on April 4, 1967, and condemned America as "the greatest purveyor of violence in the world today."[5] He proclaimed God's judgment against America and insisted that God would break the backbone of U.S. power if this nation did not bring justice to the poor and peace to the world. God, King believed, was going to call America to account for its violence in Vietnam and in the ghettoes of U.S. cities.

During the crises of 1967–68, King turned to his own religious heritage for strength to keep on fighting for justice and for the courage to face the certain possibility of his own death. "It doesn't matter with me now," King proclaimed in a sermon the night before his assassination, "because I've been to the mountaintop . . . and I've seen the Promised Land."[6] It was the eschatological hope, derived from his slave grandparents and mediated through the black church, that sustained him in the midst of the trials and tribulations in the black freedom struggle. He combined the justice and love themes in the Prophets and the cross with the message of hope in the resurrection of Jesus. Hope for King was based on his belief in the righteousness of God as defined by his reading of the Bible through the eyes of his slave foreparents. The result was one of the most powerful faith responses to the theodicy question in African American history.

Centuries ago Jeremiah raised the questions "Is there no balm in Gilead? Is there no physician?" He asked these questions because he saw the good people suffering so often and the evil people prospering. Centuries later our slave foreparents came along, and they too saw the injustice of life and had nothing to look forward to, morning after morning, but the rawhide whip of the overseer, long rows of cotton, and the sizzling heat; but they did an amazing thing. They looked back across the centuries, and they took Jeremiah's question mark and straightened it into an exclamation point. And they could sing, "There is a balm in Gilead to make the wounded whole. There is a balm in Gilead to heal the sin-sick soul."[7]

Martin King's approach to evil did not satisfy all blacks. There is another side in black religion that is rooted in blackness and its identity with Africa and its rejection of America and Christianity. From the time of its origin in slavery to the present, black religion has been faced with the question of whether to advocate integration into American society or separation from it. The majority of the participants in the black churches and the civil rights movement have promoted integration, and they have interpreted justice, hope, and love in light of the goal of creating a society in which blacks and whites can live together in a beloved community.

While integrationists emphasized the American side of the identity of African Americans, black nationalists rejected any association with the United States and instead turned toward Africa for identity and hope for coping with suffering. Nationalists contended that blacks will never be accepted as equals in a white racist church and society. Black freedom can be achieved only by blacks separating themselves from whites—either by returning to Africa or by forcing the U.S. government to set aside a separate territory in the United States so blacks can build their own society.

The nationalist perspective on the black struggle for justice is deeply embedded in the history of black religion. Some of its proponents include Martin Delaney, often called the founder of black nationalism; Marcus Garvey, the founder of the Universal Negro Improvement Association; and Malcolm X, the late activist and a member of the Nation of Islam. Black nationalism was centered on blackness and saw no value in white culture and religion.

The most persuasive interpreter of black nationalism during the 1960s was Malcolm X, who proclaimed a challenging critique of Martin King's philosophy of integration, nonviolence, and love. Malcolm advocated black unity instead of the beloved community, self-defense in lieu of nonviolence, and self-love in place of turning the other cheek to whites.

Malcolm X rejected Christianity as the white man's religion. He became a convert initially to Elijah Muhammad's Nation of Islam and later to the worldwide Islamic community. His critique of Christianity and American society as white-dominated was so persuasive that many blacks followed him into the religion of Islam, and others accepted his criticisms even though they did not become Muslims. Malcolm pushed civil rights leaders to the left and caused many black Christians to reevaluate their interpretation of Christianity.

> Brothers and sisters, the white man has brainwashed us black people to fasten our gaze upon a blond-haired, blue-eyed Jesus! We're worshiping a Jesus that doesn't even *look* like us! Now just think of this. The blond-haired, blue-eyed white man has taught you and me to worship a *white* Jesus, and to shout and sing and pray to this God that's *his* God, the white man's God. The white man has taught us to shout and sing and pray until we *die*, to wait until *death*, for some dreamy heaven-in-the-hereafter, when we're *dead,* while this white man has his milk and honey in the streets paved with golden dollars right here on *this* earth![8]

During the first half of the 1960s, Martin King's interpretation of justice as equality with whites, liberation as integration, and love as nonviolence dominated the thinking of the black religious community. However, after the riot in Watts (Los Angeles, August 1965) some black religious activists began to take another look at Malcolm X's philosophy, especially in regard to his criticisms of Christianity and American society. Malcolm X's contention that America was a nightmare and not a dream began to ring true to many black clergy as they watched their communities go up in flames.

The rise of Black Power in 1966 created a decisive turning point in black religion. Black Power forced black clergy to raise the theological question about the relation between black faith and white religion. Although blacks have always recognized the ethical heresy of white Christians ("Everybody talking about heaven ain't going there"), they have not always extended their race critique to Euro-American theology. With its accent on the cultural heritage of Africa and political liberation "by any means necessary," Black Power shook black religious leaders out of their theological complacency.

Separating themselves from Martin King's absolute commitment to nonviolence, a small group of black clergy, mostly from the North, addressed Black Power positively and critically. Like King and unlike Black Power advocates, black clergy were determined to remain within the Christian community. This was their dilemma: How could they reconcile Christianity and Black Power, Martin King and Malcolm X?

Under the influence of Malcolm X and the political philosophy of Black Power, many black theologians began to advocate the necessity for the development of a black theology. They rejected the dominant theologies of Europe and North America as heretical. For the first time in the history of black religion, black clergy and theologians began to recognize the need for a completely new starting point in theology, and they insisted that it must be defined by people at the bottom—not from the top—of the socioeconomic ladder. To accomplish this task, black theologians focused on God's liberation of the poor as the central message of the gospel.

To explicate the theological significance of the liberation motif, black theologians began to reread the Bible through the eyes of their slave grandparents and started to speak of God's solidarity with the wretched of the earth. As the political liberation of the poor emerged as the dominant motif, justice, love, and hope were reinterpreted in its light. For the biblical meaning of liberation, black theologians turned to the Exodus, while the message of the Prophets provided the theological content for the theme of justice. The gospel story of the life, death, and resurrection of Jesus served as the biblical foundation for a reinterpretation of love, suffering, and hope in the context of the black struggle for liberation and justice.

There are many blacks, however, who find no spiritual or intellectual consolation in the Christian answer to the problem of theodicy. After nearly four hundred years of black presence in what is now known as the United States of America, black people still have to contend with white supremacy in every segment of their lives. This evil is so powerful and pervasive that no blacks can escape it. But poor blacks bear the heaviest brunt of it. The persistence of racism makes the creation of meaning difficult for blacks inside and outside of the church.

Is God still going to call the oppressors to account? If so, when? Black churches seem to have no meaningful answer to these questions. They simply repeat worn-out religious clichés: "All things work out for the good for them who love the Lord." "God will make a way out of no way." "By and by when the morning comes. . . ." "We'll understand it better by and by." Black suffering in America and throughout the world, however, seems to be a blatant contradiction of that faith claim. Black suffering is getting worse, not better, and we are more confused than ever about the reasons for it. White supremacy is so clever and evasive that we can hardly name it. It claims not to exist, even though black people are dying daily from its poison.

No people are more religious than blacks. We faithfully attend churches and other religious services, giving reverence and love to the One who called us into being. But how long must black people wait for God to call our oppressors to account? How long is it going to take for black people to get justice in America?

Theology's task is to give reasons for the Christian hope in the face of horrendous human suffering. How can Christians hope in the face of unspeakable evil? No one wants a hope that has not been tested in life's great agonies.

"Suffering precedes thinking," wrote Ludwig Feuerbach. It creates thought, forcing people to search their faith for meaning and purpose in a world of deep contradictions. If the massive suffering of black people does not cause them to think deeply and critically about the reasons for their absurd predicament, then what will shake them out of their spiritual complacency? What will it take for blacks to stop preaching pie-in-the-sky as an answer to worldwide black suffering? Whether in Harlem, New York, Chicago's South Side, or Nairobi, Kenya, "O LORD, how long shall I cry for help, and you will not listen? Or cry to you 'Violence!' and you will not save?" (Hab. 1:2).

There is no easy answer to this theological problem, no easy way to deal with the absurdities and indignities of American life. We must reflect theologically, probing the depth of our faith in our effort to deepen it. This is an urgent and necessary task, because an uncritical faith cannot sustain you through a life filled with trouble.

Black and womanist theologians have no satisfactory answers for the theodicy question either—at least, not for those blacks, who like Job, "will not put away [their] integrity" or "speak falsehood" (Job 27:5, 4) about what is happening to them in this world. We can write about God's justice and love from now to the end of time. But until our theological discourse engages white supremacy in a way that empowers poor people to believe that they can destroy the monster, then our theology is not worth the paper it is written on.

Most black churches preach a cheap spirituality, a "cheap grace," to use Dietrich Bonhoeffer's classic language. It doesn't cost us much, except a little time on Sunday. Our preachers are well trained in the art of proclamation. They can open up the doors of heaven without leaving earth, giving people a transcendent entertainment that surpasses anything on New York City's Broadway.

Martin Luther King Jr. described "the existence of evil in the world . . . as the great enigma wrapped in mystery."[9] There is no intellectual or theoretical answer that will ease the pain of police brutality and the daily insults to black humanity woven into the fabric of this society and its churches. The Christian answer to suffering is both practical and spiritual. We solve the mystery of evil's existence by fighting it. And faith is real only to the degree it endows us with the courage to fight.

On the one hand, suffering challenges faith, causing us to doubt and question faith's credibility, its authenticity in a world of trouble and sorrow. "Nobody knows the trouble I've seen. Nobody knows my sorrows." On the other hand, faith challenges suffering, refusing to let trouble have the last word, the final say about life's meaning and purpose. "Nobody knows the trouble I've seen, Glory Hallelujah!" The "Glory Hallelujah" is faith's stubborn tenacity, grounded in its political struggle against the perpetrators of evil.

In 1903 W. E. B. DuBois said: "The problem of the twentieth century is the problem of the color-line—the relation of the darker to the lighter races of men in Asia and Africa, in America and the islands of the sea."[10] That message is as true today as it was when he uttered it. There is still no justice in the land for black people. "No justice—no peace" proclaimed blacks to whites during the 1992 Los Angeles riot and the years that followed. "No love—no justice" was Martin King's way of proclaiming to all who would listen. King's words are what whites want to hear when there is a racial disturbance that protests the limits of black patience with white supremacy. But African Americans want to know whether there is any reason to hope that the twenty-first century will be any less racist than the previous four centuries. Is there any reason to hope that we will be able to create a truly just society where justice and love flow freely between whites and blacks and among all peoples of the earth? Let us hope that enough people will bear witness to justice and love so as to inspire others to believe that with God and the practice of freedom fighters "all things are possible."

2 / Doing Black Theology in the Black Church

Jeremiah A. Wright Jr.

Introduction

The doing of black theology in the black church depends on the geographical location of the pastor and the people. It depends on the psychological location of the minister and his or her members. It depends on the cultural location of the clergy and the congregation, and it depends on the theological location of the leadership of the church and the membership of the church.

Geographical location is important. Churches that are located geographically in northern urban centers, major metropolitan areas, and cities in which there is a cross fertilization of ideas and ideologies from universities, seminaries, and other faiths like the Black Hebrew Israelite Nation, the Nation of Islam, Orthodox Islam, and the Kemetic Institute are more likely to be engaged by the issues raised by black theology than churches in other locations.

Those churches are more likely to be successful in doing black theology than are pastors and churches located geographically in rural areas or Bible Belt regions where the prevailing paradigms for doing theology are Robert Schuller, Charles Stanley, Fred Price, T. D. Jakes, and Creflo Dollar. There are glowing and glaring exceptions in some southern urban and southern rural areas, like Zan Holmes at St. Luke United Methodist Church and Freddy Haynes at Friendship West Baptist Church, both in Dallas, Texas. Also, one would have to mention John Kinney at Ebenezer Baptist Church in Beaver Dam, Virginia, and Arthur Jones at Bible Based Fellowship in Tampa, Florida. Zan Holmes and Freddy Haynes, incidentally, are in the same town as the conservative Dallas Theological Seminary. They are, moreover, in the same city as Tony Evans, who says there is no such thing as a

13

black church, and the Potter's House, pastored by T. D. Jakes, who publicly admits to having obtained all of his degrees—bachelor's, master's, and doctorate—through the mail. Yet over 20,000 people have flocked to his church in under three years.

Zan Holmes hosts Dr. Cain Hope Felder and other black theologians annually. In addition, Holmes has an African-centered ministry in the heart of the ghetto in Dallas. Freddy Haynes has an annual *Sankofa* conference that focuses on the *Maafa,* and he invites such persons as Dr. Asa Hilliard and Dr. Julia Hare. Furthermore, Freddy Haynes's congregation is constructing a community on sixty acres of land that features an African American church museum, an African-centered seminary, an assisted living facility, an African-centered Christian school (grades kindergarten through 12), a football field, a baseball field, tennis courts, and a shopping mall.

Dr. John Kinney, of course, is a former Ph.D. student (in philosophical theology) of James Cone and the dean of the School of Theology at Virginia Union University. He pastors a rural church twenty-five miles north of Richmond, Virginia, whose members have come to appreciate African-centered theology and ministry.

The *psychological* location of the minister and the members is the second factor I have isolated in terms of whether doing black theology is possible in the black church. If an African American pastor does not situate himself or herself as black psychologically, or members engaged in the hour-long ritual of racial denial on Sunday morning do not see themselves as black, then they are more than likely to continue that deception in their ministry throughout the week, and the issues black theology addresses will go untouched, unaddressed, and unrecognized.

Closely related to psychological location is the factor that I call *cultural* location; by using this term I am interpreting what Molefi Asante defines as our location or our centeredness. If a people do not know where they came from, then they will be forever heading in the wrong direction. That is how Asante puts it.

Here is how Chancellor Williams expresses the same idea: "'What happened to the people of Sumer?' asked the traveler of the old man. 'For legend has it that they were Black.' 'Ah,' said the old man. 'They forgot their story and so they died!'"[1]

Any people who forget their story will die, and the large number of African Americans who have forgotten their story is overwhelming. The large number of African Americans who are or have been assimilationists and acculturationists have forgotten their story. Furthermore, the large number of African American clergy and congregations who do not see themselves as African American but perceive themselves rather as multicultural or (as Cornel West and Mike Dyson argue)[2] as *hybrids* have lost their cultural center. They have forgotten where they came from and have forgotten their story. The likelihood of their doing black theology in the black church is practically nonexistent.

The *theological* location is the fourth factor I will isolate. For example, "health and wealth" theology is anti–black theology. So, too, "prosperity theology" is antithetical to black theology. "Name it and claim it" and "call it and haul it" theologies are diametrically opposed to the tenets of black theology. A growing number of black congregations live on this theological boulevard. They have erected mansions there and have no desire to move to another location.

Plus, *where* the pastors were trained (and if the truth be told, the reality for most of our pastors in the African American community is not *where* they were trained, but *if* they were trained!) plays a major role in the theological location of a pastor and a people. Earning a Master's of Divinity from Union Theological Seminary in New York City, the School of Theology at Virginia Union, Howard University, the Lutheran School of Theology at Chicago, or the Interdenominational Theological Center is not the same as getting a Master's of Divinity from Dallas Theological or Southwestern Baptist Seminary, where, until five years ago, James Cone's name was not on anybody's bibliography.

At a school like Southwestern, without Cone's work being included as a part of the students' reading regimen, you could forget finding names like Cain Hope Felder, Jacquelyn Grant, Kelly Brown Douglas, Emilie Townes, Deotis Roberts, or Gayraud Wilmore. So, where those clergy who attend those schools come out theologically—where they are located theologically—becomes a major factor in terms of whether or not any black theology will be done in the congregations that they serve.

Trinity United Church of Christ: A Paradigm Shift

Now, having said that, by way of introduction, let me share with you one congregational model for doing black theology. Let me share with you both its successes and its failures.

As a defining moment, 1968 is the date that Cone uses in his book *Risks of Faith: The Emergence of a Black Theology of Liberation, 1968–1998.*[3] Similarly, there is a journalist in the city of Chicago, Lou Palmer (who is a graduate of

Virginia Union), who says that 1968 is the year that Negroes turned black. When Dr. King was killed, the Negroes in Chicago turned black. When King was murdered, Negro churches turned black. Many of them—and Trinity United Church of Christ in Chicago is included in that "many"—changed and turned black. Trinity is the congregation I serve, and it is the model that I want to share with you.

An interesting footnote, before talking about that congregation, is one of the things that has amazed me since the emergence of black theology. That is, when you look at the signatories of the 1969 National Committee of Negro Churchmen's "Black Power" statement and you examine the leading proponents of black theology and the congregations tending to support that paradigm shift from Negro to black, those black congregations are in predominantly white denominations. Look at the signatories and the leading voices in black theology over thirty years ago. For instance, Gayraud Wilmore is a United Presbyterian. During 1968 and 1969, Black Methodists for Church Renewal (BMCR) was established. Significantly, BMCR is a caucus in a white denomination.

United Black Christians and the Commission for Racial Justice represent caucuses in another white denomination. Also, Albert Cleage, a United Church of Christ minister, wrote *The Black Messiah* and *Black Christian Nationalism*[4] and founded the Shrine of the Black Madonna. The National Black Episcopal Caucus, the Black Lutherans, the Black United Presbyterians—all of those folk leading the fight for black theology are in white denominations.

The National Baptists, Inc., the National Baptists unincorporated, the Progressive National Baptist Convention, the African Methodist Episcopalians, the African Methodist Episcopal Zionists, and other historically black denominations are for the most part (with some exceptions) missing from the list of clergy who "signed on" to this notion of black theology.

Let us return to Trinity United Church of Christ in Chicago and the transformation of its paradigm. The years 1969 to 1979 at our church entailed a shift from Negro to black. There was a dynamic development in terminology, theology, and sociology.

First of all, getting black folks to stop saying "Negro" and "colored" was a challenge during those crucial and creative years. My mother still says "colored people." Some older African Americans still use that terminology.

Second, having a witness *among* the poor and having a ministry *to* the poor is one thing, but making the poor folks members of your congregation is something else altogether. It is not until you sit down at the table as equals with poor black folks that you can really be serious about talking or doing any black theology. Failure to have the black poor at the table with you as equals means you are doing missionary work. That sociological shift for us was a very difficult thing. We lost members when we started doing that. Not everyone can handle it when you actually start doing what you've said you want to do on paper.

Some of the early successes (1969–71) were the Joint Educational Development (JED) ministry and its educational efforts. JED came out in those same years with a new paradigm for constructing and implementing a curriculum. Once again, however, this was an attempt in which predominantly white denominations started trying to address the perspectives of their black constituencies. They wanted to do Christian education from the black vantage point. The historically black denominations made no efforts to include black theology in their curriculum or in their denominational outlook.

At Trinity, Dr. Yvonne Delk teamed up with the former Executive Minister, Rev. Barbara Allen, and we ended up rewriting our entire church school curriculum from the black perspective. That effort evolved into our Center for African Biblical Studies (CFABS). CFABS is our Bible Study program. Our church runs between twenty-five and thirty-two Bible classes every week during each of the four twelve-week terms per year.

The paradigm shift resulted in some failures; for instance, some members left, while today some members *still* don't want to hear anything about being black. For them it is anathema. It offends white folk, they claim. They have a Rodney King–like "Can't we just all get along?" mentality! Many suburban-living blacks feel like William Julius Wilson—"We've settled all that stuff about race."[5]

Our new member classes were changed in 1972. We intentionally started calling them Black and Christian Classes because of what happens when new members are taken into the church. When new members are received into our church, the congregation stands and says: "We then welcome you to a part with us, in the joys, the hopes and the labors of the United Church of Christ. We promise to walk with you in Christian love and sympathy and to promote, as far as in us lies, your growth in the Christian life. There is no task more sacred than the liberation of Black people. God has called us to that task, and hearing God's Call, we say, 'Here am I. Send me!' We therefore declare that we are Unashamedly Black and Unapologetically Christian!"

There are a lot of churches that don't want to "offend" their white members. What happens at Trinity is not going to happen in some other churches. Our congregation voted to make that "shift" under the former pastor, Dr. Reuben Sheares, before I arrived. They voted in 1971 to adopt the motto "Unashamedly Black and Unapologetically Christian."

In 1979, when African American women scholars began to be published in greater numbers and womanist theology emerged, we then found ourselves in a different ball game altogether. I never will forget the first time the Rev. Dr. Jacquelyn Grant[6] preached at our church. I introduced Jackie, and she stood up and said, "Shall we bow our heads in prayer? Mother God . . ." All the eyes in the sanctuary opened.

One summer I led my Saturday night Bible class study in an investigation of Delores Williams's *Sisters in the Wilderness*,[7] and people in that class were not happy. Thus many members were not comfortable with the womanist perspective. We can see how black theology has been successful in gaining acceptance in some powerful instances, but it is not flying in any great way in many local churches—at least not in ours. We are supposed to be an advanced, progressive church, yet many of the members have negative reactions to the developments of black theology.

Take Kelly Brown Douglas's *Sexuality and the Black Church*,[8] for example. Kelly states it is clear that we have to be against racism, sexism, militarism, and heterosexism. STOP! With "heterosexism," you have just lost a significant number of folks in the congregation. Why? Because in the black church we have many deeply homophobic members. You can talk all the profound theory you want to talk, but there is a deep homophobia in the church that is still real.

Because of our progressive theological stance against various "isms," we are told that as a congregation we are too political. We have been involved in the Free South Africa Movement since 1975. We were involved in that struggle long before it became a media event and the Rev. Jesse Jackson found out where South Africa was and who Nelson Mandela was. When Dennis Brutus, an exiled South African during the apartheid era, was a professor at Northwestern University in Evanston, the Rev. Thanda Ngcobo, a South African, was one of our members. She was the first minister ordained in our church. Elkin Sitholi was a South African ethnomusicologist with whom we also became closely involved. We had been educating the members since our initial relationships with Elkin and Thanda about Soweto, the Sharpsville Massacre, and the entire Free South Africa Movement.

We put a sign out in front of the church that proclaimed, "Free South Africa!" A lot of people were critical of the sign; some of our own members had problems with that theological statement. Now that Nelson Mandela is out of prison, everyone knows Dr. Allan Boesak and Archbishop Desmond Tutu and the fall of apartheid. Everyone now claims to be supporters of the anti-apartheid movement and the new South Africa. But ask them about Stephen Biko or the Black Consciousness Movement if you want to see the lack of depth in their understanding about the struggle in South Africa.

Addressing theological issues (for example, racism, sexism, militarism, and heterosexism) as a congregation is a touchy kind of thing. We will have a substantive agenda and special political forums (we don't allow politicians to come in and speak during the worship service). We invite politicians to come and talk about their political stances on certain issues during these forums, which are like town hall meetings. Yet, with our political discussions, our panels, our issue forums, and our Health Advisory Board with its workshops throughout the year on hypertension, homosexuality and heterosexuality, HIV/AIDS, sexually transmitted diseases, etc., the largest number of members who will attend any of those gatherings is 200 to 250 people in a congregation our size (7,500 active members). Invite the Thompson Community Singers, on the other hand, and you will have three thousand people in attendance.

Having said for nine years that we are "Unashamedly Black and Unapologetically Christian," in 1981 the congregation decided to put together a Black Value System (BVS). I am very proud that the congregation initiated and implemented the project; I had nothing to do with this process. The BVS was composed by the members of the church. I attended none of the meetings, had no input, and made no suggestions. They came up with a document titled "What Does It Mean to Be Black and Christian?" We wanted people to understand what it is they had joined when they became members of our congregation. We didn't want them to become scared and think that they had joined the Black Panther Party. What does it mean when you say you are "Unashamedly Black and Unapologetically Christian"?

The members came up with twelve aspects of the motto that embrace an intentional theological stance. Our deacons, while they are in training, have to memorize the Black Value System. We also have a Christian Education Department that implements these values in Bible classes and new member classes. The twelve values are:

1. A commitment to God
2. A commitment to the black community
3. A commitment to the black family
4. Dedication to the pursuit of education
5. Dedication to the pursuit of excellence
6. Adherence to the black work ethic
7. Commitment to self-discipline and self-respect
8. Disavowal of the pursuit of "middleclassness"
(Here is a big problem when it comes to black theology and black congregations: A whole lot of black folks think they are middle-class when they are actually middle-income. If most members of most black churches miss two paychecks, they are going to be over in the soup line. That whole notion that we are middle-class prevents us from being conscious and centered on doing any type of black theology.)
9. Pledge to make the fruits of all developing and acquired skills available to the black community
10. Pledge to allocate our financial resources, including a portion of those resources for supplying and supporting black institutions
11. Pledge allegiance to all black leaders who espouse and embrace the Black Value System
12. A personal commitment to embrace the Black Value System and to measure the work and validity of all activity in terms of positive contributions to the general welfare of the black community and the advancement of black people toward freedom

In 1981, the congregation wrestled with what it means to be black and Christian and what is the meaning of black theology as a congregation involved in ministry. While adoption of the Black Value System was one step, it has also been augmented by retreats that focus on those values, classes that teach those values, and ministries that carry out those values.

In addition to the ministries that embrace a black theological perspective, having theologians at our church on a year-round basis has also helped our congregation's efforts to *do* black theology. Over the years we have hosted such notables as Na'im Akbar, Asa Hilliard, Robert Franklin, Walter Fluker, Jacquelyn Grant, and Prathia Hall Wynn. We have also had Jacob Carruthers, Renita Weems, Henry Mitchell, Ella Mitchell, Bobby Wright, Dwight Hopkins, and Linda Thomas. Iva Carruthers has been a long-standing member of Trinity. Other speakers include Charles Adams, John Bryant, James Forbes, Michael Dyson, Cornel West, Bettye Parker Smith, Ayanna Karanja, Gloria Wade

Gayles, and Molefi Asante. That mix of folks who come from different places on the theological spectrum yet are committed to the black community helps our congregation keep a clear focus while wrestling with the changing and emerging definitions of what it means to do black theology.

For twenty years, we have had a Black Liberation Workshop once a month at the church. But again even when we pursue these discussions by choosing a book each month, sometimes the book chosen for discussion becomes so controversial that a big fight takes place among different perspectives within the church (for example, E. Lynn Harris's books).[9]

In spite of all the negatives, however, we still have had (and continue to have) our share of successes. One example is our Rites of Passage Programs—*Isuthu* for African American males and *Intonjane* for African American females. Another is our *Umoja Karamu* service, which is now packed like an Easter Sunday service or a Freddy Haynes's revival where the sanctuary is standing room only. We have been celebrating *Umoja Karamu* since 1975; it is the feast of unity celebrated on Thanksgiving Day. The feast's service was written by Dr. Ed Simms and funded by the Board for Homeland Ministries of the United Church of Christ—an example of a predominantly white denomination funding the creation of a black celebration. *Umoja Karamu* looks at who we are as an African people from before slavery to the present. It is a high point in the life of the congregation. Similarly, as a church body since the 1970s, we have been celebrating Kwanza for the days that fall between Christmas and New Year. We further reflect our African heritage with our African Dance Ministry and our Africa Ministry, which evolved out of our congregational trips to Ghana, South Africa, and, this year, to Ethiopia and Côte d'Ivoire.

We have been celebrating for many years Martin Luther King's birthday and Malcolm X's birthday. We do not let white folks pick and choose our heroes; we commemorate both King and Malcolm. Our church staff are off from work (with a paid holiday) on both days.

Our Sojourner Truth Cultural Institute has good and bad news. I will explain the theory and practice. Just like the Jewish people have had synagogue schools for centuries, where they teach their students their history, culture, and heritage, we started a similar institution with our Sojourner Truth Cultural Institute. The problem, however, is that in major metropolitan areas you cannot have after-school programs in the city for kids who have to come from the suburbs to attend. Their mothers and fathers are still at work when the children get out of school, and the students have no way of traveling into the city. For the kids in the city, moreover, there is another problem. Those students, in order to get to church, have gang turf boundaries to cross. The attendance at that after-school program, therefore, has always been very poor. Because some things that look good on paper do not work in the reality of a black congregation in inner-city Chicago, we ended up shifting it to another day of the week like Saturday, when most of the youth are at the church.

One of our members, Dr. Colleen Birchett, has been working on the development of a black curriculum for the African American church. Such a comprehensive curriculum will reach all age groups—kindergarten through adult. Already she has several of the units completed. Dr. Birchette was the editor of *Inteen* for over a decade, and she has a Ph.D. in curriculum development.

Our prison ministry is another success as it pertains to black theology. Gayraud Wilmore introduced this "chapter" of black theology almost a decade ago. This is not just a prison ministry where you go into the prisons, worship, "open the doors of the church," and then leave the prison after a Sunday worship service. On the contrary, in this prison ministry your members are in the prisons every week, and they are also working with the prisoners' families. The flip side of that, however—that is, a failure—is what happened when we adopted a woman who was on death row. She went all the way through the criminal justice system and was released, but when she came to our church, she would not join because, as she said, she felt like "y'all don't want me here."

When we speak about changing the sociology of our church and getting new members, we have the whole alphabet of professional degrees—A.B., B.S., M.D., D.D.S., Ph.D., M.B.A., C.P.A., and A.D.C. We firmly believe that all those letters behind your name have nothing to do with the church. They pertain to how you make a living, but not how you make a life. Indeed, the church is the center of how you make a life. However, there are some of our members who are from the projects and some, like our former prisoner, who come to church and are made to feel like they have leprosy. If you don't have expensive clothes or drive the latest car, you are made to feel (by some members) that you do not belong. Even though the former death row prisoner came to Trinity and felt uncomfortable, our prison ministry continues its ministry with the inmates and their families—despite our "losses."

Our domestic violence ministry, our drug and alcohol abuse recovery ministry, our three child-care programs (active for twenty-five years for families of unemployed and unemployable, low-income families) are all added instances of "the word" of black theology becoming flesh. Our reading and math tutorial programs are also examples of what it means to do black theology. Even more exciting is our program that runs forty weeks a year, in which Trinity members go into the schools and spend the whole day at school.

That is *doing* black theology. It is not setting a program and saying "Here is what we think ought to happen." It is the members actually putting their bodies on the line by going into the schools forty weeks a year for the entire school year and staying there with poor black kids all day long.

All of these types of ministries have developed out of our commitment to *do* black theology rather than just talk about it. We have tried to be a congregation in the midst of the black community and really committed to that community. As a footnote, please remember that if you are a pastor out in Cedar Rapids, Iowa, Fargo, North Dakota, Maine, or New Hampshire, those geographical locations are not going to afford you this "Chicago" kind of geographical setting. Our setting is also affected by the strong nationalist communities in Chicago. And please remember that there are more than one kind of black nationalist. Within Chicago, you have Haki Makdubuthi, Conrad Worrill, and Dr. Bobby Wright (deceased). Those nationalists are not thinking about belonging to or attending anybody's church or serving alongside any type of spiritual leaders whatsoever. Dr. Jacob Carruthers and the Kemetic Institute are in Chicago along with Maulana Karenga, who comes into town at Oliver Harvey Community College of Chicago two or three times a year. Furthermore, Chicago has the Nation of Islam with Louis Farrakhan and the headquarters for the Black Hebrew Israelite Nation. You will find too Noble Drew Ali's Moorish Science Temple. This heavy black nationalist presence affects both the members of our church and their children. It affects the members because they work with these folks from other faiths, and it affects their children, who are recruited into the Nation of Islam when they are in elementary school.

This black nationalist reality is not going to take place in Maine. That is the geographical footnote that I was talking about. Yet, given the particularity of Chicago and other major inner cities, a fertile ground exists for developing and deepening the actual doing of black theology as part of ministry for the new millennium.

Testimony as Hope and Care
African American Pastoral Care
as Black Theology at Work

Lee H. Butler Jr.

> My salvation was found in black music combined with a
> disciplined program of reading black literature and other
> writers concerned about human suffering. I immersed
> myself in the writings of Baldwin, Wright, Fanon, Camus,
> Sartre, and Ellison as well as the new black writers emerging
> from the context of the Black Power movement. When I
> compared Baldwin, Wright, Ellison, and LeRoi Jones (now
> Amiri Baraka) with Barth, Tillich, Brunner, and Reinhold
> Neibuhr, I concluded that I was in the wrong field. How
> could I continue to allow my intellectual life to be con-
> sumed by the theological problems defined by people who
> had enslaved my grandparents?[1]

Introduction

I have attended several events in recent years where Dr. James H. Cone has
been honored. Many who spoke their love and appreciation for Dr. Cone
identified his "red book," *Black Theology and Black Power,* as the inspira-
tional volume that undergirded their transformed position for faith and
praxis. Although my mother gifted me with the "red book" when I was in
junior high school, it has been the "grey book," *My Soul Looks Back,* that has
had the greatest impact upon my development as an African American pastoral theologian.

Pastoral care is the ministry of sharing responsibility for the well-being of
another. As such, it is attentive to the developmental and predictable crises of
the human experience. When life seems to be shaken and without a stable
foundation, pastoral care offers support and stability. During crisis moments,

the pastoral caregiver symbolizes the presence of God and declares the assurance that the person in crisis has not been abandoned by God in their time of uncertainty and need. Most often perceived to be a ministry that springs into action during the time of loss, there is also a social justice dimension to the practice of pastoral care that attends to human suffering that results from societal oppressions. This dimension of pastoral care exercises the liberating aspects of the gospel and seeks to restore people to human life.

The discipline of African American pastoral care reframes the challenges of black life to bring hope out of despair, inspire joy where there is sorrow, and heal the brokenhearted. The practice of African American pastoral care expresses the dynamic relationship between story, testimony, and the Spirit/spirit to bring courage and renewal out of the pain and suffering wrought by this world. In *My Soul Looks Back,* Dr. Cone participates, through the act of testifying, in the caring traditions of the African American community. In this text, he says,

> Testimony is a spiritually liberating experience for the believer wherein he/she is empowered by God's Holy Spirit to stay on the "gospel train" until it reaches the kingdom. Although testimony is unquestionably personal and thus primarily an individual's story, it is also a story accessible to others in the community of faith. Indeed, the purpose of testimony is not only to strengthen an individual's faith but also to build the faith of the community.[2]

Dr. Cone's statement is not merely sharing his individual experience, but testifying to a community that is the source of his identity as a *human* creation of God. When suffering black folks ask the question "How long, O Lord?" the pastoral caregiver, through the resources of faith and spirituality, helps sufferers to answer, "Soon I will be done with the troubles of this world."

Although the praxis of black theology is not necessarily African American pastoral care, all African American pastoral care *should be* black theology at work. I do not mean to suggest that African American pastoral care lacks a clear theory, method, and practice but that the tenets of African American pastoral care are consistent with those of black theology. In fact, pastoral care is interdisciplinary, and African American pastoral care engages black theology as a critical methodological partner. Drawing from the same roots as black theology, African American pastoral care has always been concerned for black suffering and the hope of freedom.

Themes and Issues

Because black folks have always been attentive to the causes and effects of evil and suffering, the theodical question is one that has been a resident of the black psyche for as long as we have been self-aware. From the primordial "ouch" to our present existential woes, we, the people of the sun, have sought to be attentive to the evil and suffering we have experienced under the sun. During the days when it seemed as though the life-denying forces would prevail against us, we conjured a sustaining hope through a song, a prayer, and loving-kindness. We have a long heritage of caring for the souls of black folks. As an academic discipline, however, African American pastoral care has a short tradition. Many practitioners, as Dr. Cone has stated, "continue to allow [their] intellectual life to be consumed by the theological problems defined by people who had enslaved [our] grandparents."[3] Even if we allow others to select the issues to be engaged, we cannot allow others to articulate the context of our experience.

We must always be prepared to define the details of our reality. An appropriate agenda for our future requires an accurate description of our present condition, which is dependent upon an accurate assessment of our past. Therefore, ministry for the new millennium demands that African American pastoral theologians become more astute about the traumatic legacy of African Americans, understand the nature and complexity of African American relationships, and promote healing as a requirement for our continued survival.

I agree with my senior colleague Dr. Homer Ashby of McCormick Theological Seminary, who says African Americans must continue to struggle, but not continue to struggle to cross over Jordan into the Promised Land. Ashby suggests that we have crossed the river. With our backs to the sea, we must now defend ourselves against the enemies that are encamped around us to the north, east, and south. He states, and I agree, that this description of our reality calls for new strategies for declaring who we are and why we must survive. While we must maintain a posture of defense against the forces that would consume our lives, we must know our context and location in order to best defend ourselves. This suggestion is similarly supported by C. T. Vivian of Atlanta, who says that today "civil rights issues are left-hand issues. We've got it down to where the lawyers could handle it." We must, therefore, clearly define the right-hand issues. Freedom continues to be important, but the specific issues that constitute the struggle for freedom are not the same as days gone by. The six critical care issues for African America's future are:[4]

African American Identity

Identity has been a very significant struggle for blacks in America from the moment we landed on these shores in 1619. As a process, identity seeks to establish a consistent sense of self. Rather than being inconsistent and fragmented by the various roles and tasks we must fulfill in life, a clear sense of identity helps to maintain our stability and integrity as relational beings. The issues of identity are primarily attended to by answering the question, Who am I? Because the African self is not grounded in individuality, however, our attending has reshaped the question to be, Who are we? Although individualism is an American norm, our communal sense of being has been the primary influence upon our identity formation.

Important to our identity struggle in America has been our efforts to maintain our self-understanding as human beings. Whereas we could have developed deep, isolating psychoses that would fracture the self, making individualism normative of our being, our identity has been informed and nurtured by a spirituality that maintains there is no separation between blood and non-blood relations, public and private life, physical and spirit world, church and community. A human being's identity says a great deal about what it means to be alive and defines our relationships with those around us and with God. Answering the question "Who are we?" through declaring our humanity means that we have direct contact with God and a responsibility to and for one another.

Although I believe it is important that we continue to be attentive to the identity question as we have in the past, today, there are more important ways for us to ask the question. For example, who are we as *African* Americans? African American culture is a unique cultural experience because it is the combination of our distant African past and our more recent American past. If we deny our African heritage, we revive the image of America as the "melting pot" and doom ourselves to identity confusion. The denial of our African heritage will result in an "incognegro" way of living.

Another very vital question is: Who are we as *Africans* in the face of American slavery? This question moves to the core of a struggle to distinguish slave and enslaved. Throughout human history, all peoples have experienced some form of slavery. Even in America, the indenture system was a slave system that included Europeans. Yet Africans are the only group in America that are identified and self-identified as slave. Slavery was our circumstance, not the essence of our being. We will take a major step toward freedom when we liberate ourselves to say that we are Africans who were *en*slaved rather than slaves who left Africa.

The Black Body

African Americans have an *anthropodical* understanding of our bodies. That is to say, we have some peculiar ideas about our physical nature as an evil nature. The ideas we have about our own black bodies make it difficult for us to be "at home in our own skin." If we are not conscientious, our dark bodies can feel like jailhouses of shame and ostracism.

America's social systems are regularly described in terms of polar opposites. The contrasting colors of black and white, symbolizing life's eternal struggle of evil against good, have been established as the defining features of God-human interactions. White and white bodies have been equated with God and good; and black and black bodies have been equated with anti-God and evil. Together, color and body declare who is acceptable and can belong and who will always be rejected and outcast. Through spiritual pronouncements based on racialized sexual differences, our black bodies are seen and experienced as the unholy, unclean incarnation of evil in America. Consequently, we sacrificially escape our bodies through overspiritualizing our minds.

Spirituality and Sexuality

African American spirituality, which is rooted in African spirituality, promoted our survival through generations of hard times by an insistence that we maintain our self-understanding as whole and holy human beings. Generally speaking, spirituality is the active integration of our humanity resulting in a singularly directed effort to be in communion with God and others. It is the human spirit moving and being drawn toward God's Spirit. African spirituality has a multilayered, communal understanding of reality. From this perspective, the world is filled with spirits, and God's Spirit is an inescapable presence in the world. Because God is in everything and everyone, the most mundane activity is regarded as a spiritual activity. This is why African spirituality declares there is no separation between the sacred and the secular.

We are living in an era that promotes affirmative action as no longer being necessary, and the work ethic has been revitalized to illustrate that poverty is the result of laziness. Both affirmative action and the work ethic combine to say that America believes in fair play and a level playing field. While the picture being propagated presents equal opportunity, our lives are dominated by the powerful memory of "separate and unequal." Inequality still looms large in our everyday lives. Many people continue to regard African Americans as inferior and believe we should be separated from other "races." Similarly, spirituality and sexuality are also seen as separate and unequal. Spirituality is seen as superior and sexuality as inferior. Just as the work ethic is used to argue that poverty is a result of laziness, the most prominent spiritual ideas associate spiritual poverty with expressions of sexuality. The poor in spirit are thought to be those who are the most sensual. We have been seduced into believing that our "holy dance" is always up and down, never side to side or in and out. We have denied our humanity by separating our spiritual lives from our physical lives.

Individuality versus Communality

African America is an oral culture organized around the principle of communality. A person has no existence outside the context of community. All life is seen through a spiritual interconnectedness, and our whole being is organized around a spirituality of interdependence. If one attempts to address crises or traumas within the African American community from an individual rather than a collective care approach, the community will continue to destabilize until it self-destructs. Here I am suggesting that part of the genocide of the African American community is not the result of self-hatred as many have assumed. Our genocide is the result of masking communality with the face of individuality. We no longer recognize our reason for being.

In order to be a responsible caregiver within the African American community, one must have communality as the starting point. Many problems we perceive to be individual problems are actually collective problems. The fact is, African Americans have problems when we split off from the community. The ideal here is not what has dominated American culture, that is, "Pull yourself up by your own bootstraps." Our hope lies in the African concept of "lift as we climb." It means I am related to everyone and everything that contains life, and there is life all around us.

Life and the Forces of Death

The preservation of our humanity as Africans in America was once a high priority. Although difficult to maintain in the face of the inhumane treatment we received, our commitment to life was stronger than death. The destructive forces of the Middle Passage, slavocracy, Reconstruction, segregation, and neo-racism progressively represent our history of protracted traumas. Each historical period sought to destroy our self-understanding as human beings, but we have been determined to remain human in opposition to the pain. In fact, our entire experience as Africans in America has been a struggle to maintain human contact. Unfortunately, our preserving acts have sometimes resulted in negative consequences. There have been times when we did not plan to be hurtful to one another, but we were. Our ability to live together with tender sympathy for one another has been diminished by our fear that another will see our kindness as weakness. Fearful of abuse, we build walls of defense rather than sharing with one another in openness.

We have a long history of experiencing the lack of compassion, abuse of power, destruction of hope, and devastation of our lives from without and within the community. We grieve a past marked by blood, terror, and tears. We have been terrorized into believing that it is better to use a person than it is to care for one another. We live in a society whose contempt for us chained our lives by saying we were crazy outside of slavery, terrorized us just for the "fun" of it, experimented on us without our consent, secretly sterilized us, and limited our opportunities in the name of social order. Essentially, there has been a blatant disregard for our humanity. It is impossible to live under this kind of pressure and not be affected. Although individualism is not the foundation of our survival in the United States, our relationships are moving toward the survival of the fittest individual. We must not allow individualism to be the basis for our survival in the future. If one person is going to survive, then our entire family and community must survive.

Health and Healing

Within the African American church community, there is an overwhelming tendency to encourage an absence from the body in order to have a holy

experience with the Lord. This condemnation of the body has been conflic-
tive for Africans in America. Historically, we were reduced to being a bodily
people only. Our bodies have been exploited in every way possible: for labor,
for sex, and for science. Whereas spirituality has been the strength of our
survival, rarely have we been seen as spiritual people, except in extremist
ways.

Good health is a physical and spiritual matter. When good health is challenged, healing is required to restore one to health. An unhealthy body is one
that has experienced some sort of breakdown in one or more of the body's
systems. An unhealthy spirit is one that has experienced some sort of breakdown in the flow of life energy or the lines of communication between the
person, God, and others. If the body is unhealthy, it affects the health of the
spirit. If the spirit is unhealthy, it affects the health of the body. Healing
restores the body and the spirit to a harmonious relationship. Put simply,
healing is the process of being restored to a life of relationships.

If we are going to obtain and maintain healthy relationships, we must first
be healed. There are two situations that intersect and promote unhealthy
relationships. They are punishment and feeling "less than." As to the first, for
generations we have heard, "I punish you because you are unable to take care
of yourselves." That was the message of the landholder to the enslaved. We
have heard, "I punish you because I love you." That is the message of the par-
ent to the child. We have learned these lessons too well and have come to
believe that punishment is the way to show how much we care. And for the
second, an unhealthy person feels "less than" and is likely to withdraw from
full participation in relationships. Our entire existence in the United States
has been a fight against the many "less than" messages. Sometimes we have
been successful, but the relational problems we have suggest that more often
we have been unsuccessful.

There are many different ways the "less than" feeling can express itself and
affect our health. Feeling "less than" can encourage self-hate. Self-hate can
lead to self-destruction and violent aggression through attempting to elimi-
nate the source of the hatred. Much of our "less than," which gets expressed
as the punishment of self-hate, is a condition of shame. The shame we feel,
in turn, encourages us to hide in despair. As long as we have a feeling of less
than, we will never have relationships in which we experience *more* than punishment and pain. Healing transforms relationships and restores a person to
life. When our wounds are healed, our relationships are open, trusting, and
loving.

32   Lee H. Butler Jr.

Conclusion

African American pastoral caregivers must be attentive to the blood of our people. "We have come over a way that with tears has been watered. We have come treading our path through the blood of the slaughtered."[5] To point to the blood of Jesus and declare him as the way-maker while ignoring the bludgeoned, bloody bodies of black folks is to deny our humanity and make us invisible. African American pastoral care as black theology at work means we are actively engaged in binding the victim's wounds, healing the brokenhearted, and setting the captives free to testify.

4 | Black Theology and the Black Church

Karen E. Mosby-Avery

Black theology has been defined as "a theology of liberation."[1] James H. Cone has powerfully declared that black theology is a theology that places God clearly on the side of those who are oppressed. God is invested in the liberation of the poor and the oppressed. God acts in history by moving God's people toward freedom and moving against everything that obstructs that freedom.

> There is no liberation without transformation, that is, the struggle for freedom in this world. There is no liberation without the commitment of revolutionary action against injustice, slavery, and oppression. Liberation then is not merely a thought in my head; it is the sociohistorical movement of a people from oppression to freedom.[2]

According to Cone, God's liberating and transforming work is to be mirrored in the work or mission of the Christian church. Just as Christianity cannot be separated from Christ,[3] God's freedom work, most decisively exemplified through the life and ministry of Jesus, cannot be separated from the understanding of what it means to be Christian and what it means to be the church.

Cone's most consistent critique of the Christian church, including the African American church, is that it has not mirrored God's liberating work on behalf of the poor and the oppressed. "Black churches permitted their preachers and members to be involved in the political struggle for justice, but never made it a requirement for their Christian identity."[4] African American churches, Cone contends, have contributed to the oppression of the poor along with white churches by their "permissive silence"[5] and by their refusal to fight for freedom and against injustice.

A perusal of the plight of the world's poor and the Christian community's lack of resistance to this plight validates Cone's critique. In the face of poverty, homelessness, and the widening of the gap between the "haves" and the "have-nots," there has not been a sustained, organized response from Christian churches. Instead, we find further support for Cone's critique in the continual growth of "Word churches," which purport to focus primarily on the teaching of God's word exclusive of any call to social justice. Similarly, we perceive the expanding receptivity to "prosperity theology," which focuses primarily on the attainment of wealth as a God-given right and thereby implies that there is something wrong with those who do not attain it. Cone's work does not attempt to present a "twelve-step" program for how African American churches can return to God's work of liberation of the poor and transformation of the society that perpetuates oppression. However, through the tenets of black theology, he does offer directions for getting back on course.

The congregation I serve is located in a racially diverse and economically poor neighborhood on Chicago's far north side. The congregation includes the "have-nots," who must contend with five-day eviction notices, affordable housing being replaced by condos, raising children in shelters, minimum-rather than living-wage jobs, and the litany continues. Admittedly, Cone's work is not the conversation at the tables of the church's soup kitchen. Nor do people debate the relevance of black theology in the new millennium. However, when I think of what has brought about change in people's lives and what has brought about change in the community, I must affirm the truth of what we have learned from Cone and black theology.

Of the many benefits we have gained from black theology, there particularly stand out three actions related to how the African American church can more effectively join with God in liberating the oppressed.

Affirming the God-Declared Dignity of Individuals

Speaking of the riots in the 1960s, Cone wrote: "The rebellion in the cities is not a conscious organized attempt by black people to take over; it is an attempt to say *yes* to their own dignity even in death."[6] African Americans and other people of color, especially the poor, need to be reminded of who God says we are.

Bombarded by words and actions and laws that negate their basic humanity, the poor are left with little to help them envision an alternative reality and wage resistance against their current reality. Unlike many African American slaves who resisted annihilation by developing a faith of resistance in the face of the systematic attempt to destroy their spirits, the poor today seem to have lost their connection with history, the assurance of being created in God's image, and the existential implications of being created in God's image. "Because black people believed that they were God's children, they affirmed their *somebodiness*, refusing to reconcile their servitude with divine revelation."[7] Without this basic sense of "somebodiness," the poor today are ill-equipped to survive.

The African American church has historically been the place where African Americans have been nurtured, strengthened, and reminded of who and whose they are. But somewhere we stopped connecting who and whose we are with what we are supposed to be doing in the world.

Resisting Evil, Injustice, and Oppression

Cone wrote:

> If we are created for God, then any other allegiance is a denial of freedom, and we must struggle against those who attempt to enslave us. The image of God is not merely a personal relationship with God, but is also that constituent of humanity which makes all people struggle against captivity.[8]

The African American church has to reclaim a definition of Christianity and a definition of "child of God" that includes social justice. If we hear nothing else from Cone and from black theology, we must hear the exhortation to be agents of change in the world: "In Christ, God enters human affairs and takes sides with the oppressed. Their suffering becomes his, their despair, divine despair. Through Christ the poor are offered freedom now to rebel against that which makes them other than human."[9] Cone's words imply that we cannot continue to bear the name Christian, especially African American Christian, if we will not join God in eliminating marginalized people's suffering, if we will not join Christ in rebelling against injustice.

Determine Our Course toward Liberation

Over the years many people have entered the community where I serve and brought their energy, their money, and their agenda for what the community needed. Most often, this agenda did not solicit input from the people in need. There is this prevailing notion that poverty is synonymous with ignorance. Those who have never been oppressed, have never been poor, or have forgotten what it was like to be oppressed and poor often think that somehow they have a better grasp on what needs to be done than the people indigenous to the oppressed situation.

One of the things that black theology does is remind us of where the starting point is. The starting point for black theology is the experiences and stories that are the basis of black faith. Likewise, the starting point for liberation of the poor is the experiences and stories of the poor. The African American church and the white church cannot set the agenda for the liberation of the poor without dialogue with the poor. If the church is unwilling to stand among the poor and take the risk of the incarnation, which was the risk of God being with us, it will not be in a position to effect long-lasting change.

In the early 1980s, I read *God of the Oppressed* for a class at Garrett-Evangelical Theological Seminary (Evanston, Illinois). I remember feeling that finally someone understood what I was feeling. Someone gave voice to what I believed. Almost two decades later, I return to James Cone as a pastor having the same feelings that I had as a student. The prophetic nature of Cone's work allows it to continue to be insightful and instructive. When I read his words today, it is as though I hear Jesus saying, "Let those who have ears hear."

5 / Womanist Theology, Epistemology, and a New Anthropological Paradigm

Linda E. Thomas

The dynamism and influence of James H. Cone's theology leave a legacy that demands that the black church globally cultivate an emancipatory Christianity as it relates to African American women. In honor of Cone's life and work as well as to draw a direct link between his work and the liberatory works of African American women in the black church, I will use womanist theology and epistemology to create an anthropological paradigm for the black church in the new millennium.

Womanist theology is the valiant voice of African American Christian women in the United States. Employing Alice Walker's definition of womanism in her book *In Search of Our Mothers' Gardens*,[1] black women in America are calling into question their suppressed role in the African American church, the community, the family, and the larger society. But womanist religious reflection is more than mere deconstruction. It is, more importantly, the empowering assertion of the black woman's voice, regardless. To examine that voice, this essay divides into three parts. First, I look at the overall state of womanist theology. The development of womanist theology denotes a novel reconstruction of knowledge, drawing on the abundant resources of African American women since their arrival in the "New World," as well as a creative critique of deleterious forces seeking to keep black women "in their place." Next, I sort through a womanist reconstruction of knowledge. In an intentional manner, I unpack the contours of the knowledge formation claims that undergird womanist theology. And last, based on womanist theology as an instance of new knowledge and on an analysis of epistemological presuppositions, I advance a new anthropological paradigm of religion for the continued development of womanist theology.

Womanist Theology in the United States

Womanist theology is critical reflection upon black women's place in the world that God has created and takes seriously black women's experience as human beings who are made in the image of God. The categories of life black women deal with daily (that is, race, womanhood, and political economy) are intricately woven into the religious space that African American women occupy. Therefore the harmful and empowering dimensions of the institutional church, culture, and society directly affect the social construction of black womanhood. Womanist theology affirms the positive and critiques the negative attributes of the church, the African American community, and the larger society.

Womanist theology's goals are to interrogate the social construction of black womanhood in relation to the African American community. Everyday interactions among African American women create the space for an energetic claiming of the life stories of African American women and their contribution to the history of the United States and the African diaspora. An additional way of achieving this goal is to engage in a critical conversation with black (male) theology so that a full theology for the African American community can emerge from that dialogue. Likewise the pursuance of the black family's sanctity ranks high on the womanist's theological agenda. Another goal of womanist theology is to unearth the ethnographic sources within the African American community in order to reconstruct knowledge and overcome subordination. And finally womanist theology seeks to decolonize the African mind and to affirm our African heritage.

Womanist theology engages the macro-structural and micro-structural issues that affect black women's lives and therefore, since it is a theology of complete inclusivity, the lives of all black people. The freedom of black women entails the liberation of all peoples, because womanist theology concerns notions of gender, race, class, heterosexism, and ecology. Furthermore, it takes seriously the historical and current contributions of our African forebears and women in the African diaspora today. It advances a bold leadership style that creates fresh discursive and practical paradigms and "talks back"[2] to structures, white feminists, and black male liberation theologians. Moreover, womanist theology asserts what black women's unique experiences mean in relation to God and creation and survival in the world. Thus the tasks of womanist theology are to claim history, to declare authority for ourselves, our men, and our children, to learn from the experience of our forebears, to admit shortcomings and errors, and to improve our quality of life.

Womanist theology assumes a liberatory perspective so that African American women can live emboldened lives within the African American community and within the larger society. Such a new social relationship includes adequate food, shelter, clothing, and minds free from worries so that there can be space for creativity.

Womanist theology draws on sources that range from traditional church doctrines, African American literature, nineteenth-century black women leaders, poor and working-class black women in holiness churches, and African American women under slavery. In addition, other vital sources include the personal narratives of black women suffering domestic violence and psychological trauma, the empowering dimensions of conjuring and syncretic black religiosity, and womanist ethnographic approaches to excavate the life stories of poor women of African descent in the church.

Womanist theology, moreover, grasps the crucial connection between African American women and the plight, survival, and struggle of women of color throughout the world. Womanist theology intentionally pursues and engages the cultural contexts of women who are part of the African diaspora. To enhance the networking among women of color all over the globe, the methodology of anthropology, a key discipline within the social sciences, aids womanist theology in this engagement. Anthropological methodology encourages womanist religious scholars to embrace the cultural, symbolic, and ritual diversity dispersed throughout the religious lives of women of color on this earth.

Womanist theology takes seriously the importance of understanding the "languages" of black women. There are a variety of discourses deployed by African American women based on their social location within the black community. Some black women are economically disadvantaged and suppressed by macro-structures in society. Other African American women are workers whose voices are ignored by the production needs of the capitalist world order. Some other voices are dramatically presented in the faith speech of black women preachers. And still other articulations are penned in the annals of the academy. Womanist theology showcases the overlooked styles and contributions of all black women whether they are poor, and perhaps illiterate, or economically advantaged and "Ph.D.'ed." Womanists bring forth the legacy of our grandmamas and great grandmamas and carry their notions in the embodiment of life that we create daily. This language of black women is understood by black women; it accentuates intragroup talk. It is a language of compassion, and yet it is no-nonsense. The words and actions of this language oppose sexism, racism, classism, heterosexism, and abuse of any of

God's creation. It is a language that respects the natural environment in the fullness of creation.

The method of womanist theology validates the past lives of enslaved African women by remembering, affirming, and glorifying their contributions. After excavating analytically and reflecting critically on the life stories of our foremothers, the methodology entails a construction and creation of a novel paradigm. We who are womanists concoct something new that makes sense for how we are living in complex gender, racial, and class configurations. We learn from the rituals and techniques our foremothers originated to survive in hostile environments and from how they launched new perspectives, reconstructing knowledge of a liberative approach for black women's lives. This self-constituting dynamic is a polyvalent, multi-vocal weaving of the folk culture of African American women.

In addition to unearthing the sources of the past in order to discover pieces to create a narrative for the present and the future, womanist methodology comprises active engagement with marginalized African American women alive today. Ethnographic methodology necessitates our entering the communities of these women, creating focus groups and utilizing the women's life experiences as the primary sources for the development of questions that establish a knowledge base from everyday people. These questions are then refined by the womanist scholar as she reflects on the initial conversations with her focus groups. Further refining takes place when the womanist scholar conducts a pilot study in which she ascertains whether the questions asked fit the context of poor black women and where she also learns the nuances needed for the sensibilities of the culture in which she is operating. Employing the context and knowledge base derived from the focus and pilot groups, she launches a larger and more comprehensive ethnographic research study by living among the people, thereby encountering their symbolic cosmology. In this living and learning process, these women evolve into the womanist scholar's teachers. The task thus becomes the production with integrity of the story of these poor people's lives and the reflection of their polyvalent voices. They have created space for the scholar in their communities, and now she creates space for their stories in their own words reflected in her publications. The womanist ethnographer entrusts to the reader these narratives for interpretation, assuming that many truths will emerge, transformation will occur, and readers will learn from those not usually given voice. Furthermore, the African American female scholar risks becoming emotionally connected to these people's lives as she reenters the community on a regular basis and understands that she has familial obligations to the people about whom she writes. Thus womanist theology is a longitudinal theology.

Names associated with the emergence of womanist theology in the United States are Katie G. Cannon, Emilie M. Townes, Jacquelyn Grant, Delores S. Williams, Cheryl Townsend Gilkes, Kelly Brown Douglas, Renita J. Weems, M. Shawn Copeland, Clarice Martin, Francis Wood, Karen Baker-Fletcher, Jamie T. Phelps, Marcia Y. Riggs, and Cheryl A. Kirk-Duggan. We are university, seminary, and divinity school professors. We are ordained and lay women in all Christian denominations. Some of us are full-time pastors; some are both pastor and professor. We are preachers and prayer warriors. We are mothers, partners, lovers, wives, sisters, daughters, aunts, nieces, and we comprise two-thirds of the black church in America. We are the black church. The church would be bankrupt without us; the church would shut down without us. We are from working-class as well as middle-class backgrounds. We are charcoal black to high yellow women. We love our bodies; we touch our bodies; we like to be touched; we claim our created beauty. And we know that what our minds forget our bodies remember. The body is central to our being. The history of the African American ordeal of pain and pleasure is inscribed in our bodies.

Womanist theology associates with and disassociates itself from black (male) theology and (white) feminist theology. The point of departure for black theology is white racism. Since white supremacy is a structure that denies humanity to African American people, black liberation theology examines the gospel in relationship to the situation of black people in a society that discriminates on the basis of skin color. Within black theology, the exodus story is a hermeneutical device used to draw a parallel between the oppressed Israelites and the oppressed African American community. Consequently, the liberation of the Israelites represents symbolically God's freeing of black people. First-generation black (male) theologians did not understand the full dimension of liberation for the special oppression of black women; this was their shortcoming. To foster the visibility of African American women in black God-talk, womanist theology has emerged.

Unlike black theology with its emphasis on race, feminist theology addresses the oppression of women, though primarily white women. The project of feminist theology did not deal with the categories of race and economics in the development of its theological discourse. As important as the work of feminist theology has been, its shortcoming is its lack of attention to the everyday realities of African American and other women of color. It is therefore not a universal women's theology and does not speak to the issue of all women. In a related fashion, too often white feminist theology creates a paradigm over against men; it is an oppositional theological discourse between females and males. In contrast, womanist theology recognizes patriarchal systems as problematic for the entire black community—women, men, and children. Moreover, certain feminist theological trends disregard the institutional church as a patriarchal space anathema to women, thus advising women to abandon the ecclesiastical mainstream. For African American women however, the black church has been the central historical institution that has helped their families survive. Womanist theology, at the same time, would critique the black church, particularly black male pastors' inappropriate relations with black female members.

Womanist theology concurs with black theology and feminist theology on the necessity of engaging race and gender in theological conversation. But womanist theology demands a God-talk and God-walk that are holistic, seeking to address the survival and liberation issues of women, men, children, workers, and gays and lesbians, as these relate to local and global economies and the environment.

A Womanist Perspective on Reconstructing Knowledge

Womanist theology is in the midst of reconstructing knowledge not only for the broad "mainstream" parameters of knowing but even for black male and feminist theologies. Thus as womanist scholars of religion advance a new epistemology of holistic survival and liberation, a more intentional understanding of reconstructed knowledge processes is warranted.

Admittedly, reconstructing knowledge is like tearing down a formidable edifice that has been built over an extensive number of years. The structure was designed by architects who had a clear vision of what the end product would be like and used only the most advanced technical devices for its erection. The architects guaranteed that the materials used would be permanent and indestructible. The building is, of course, our minds, and the architects are those who historically have represented patriarchal, white European cultures. A womanist, in her reconstruction of knowledge, must not only be a diligent craftsperson but also develop an approach using the kind of technology that can dismantle the seeming indestructibleness of the original building materials.

Human beings acquire knowledge through culture, most often obtaining it through the culture into which we are born. We procure knowledge in the same manner that our lungs receive oxygen. It is a conscious and unconscious process that systematically and deliberately pervades our minds and senses. Amassing knowledge is the process of becoming persons who know the things that are essential for living. And for white patriarchal culture in the North American context, it is knowing how to dominate. For most people of color in the United States, it is knowing how to survive in white culture.

The people with whom we interact and the environment in which we mature, especially during our formative years, determine the kind of knowledge we acquire. Hence, to get a sense of the attitudes and assumptions that were and are the bricks of the building that houses our knowledge, we have to revisit who and what has influenced our lives from the earliest days. I call this foundational period our encounter with our "culture of origin." Therefore the culture of origin of excluded voices becomes an important aspect for reconstructing knowledge.

As Margaret Andersen and Patricia Hill Collins suggest, the primary question that must be asked in considering the reconstruction of knowledge is: "Who has been excluded from what is known and how might we see the world differently if we acknowledge and value the experiences and thoughts of those who have been excluded?"[3] The knowledge we acquire from formal institutions is the ideas, philosophies, and histories of the privileged; more specifically, it is information about people who wrote down their histories and their ideas. Chroniclers of the human historical record did not consider people with oral traditions to be essential for cultivating the Western mindset. Even when non-Western people, such as the Aztecs, had written texts, they were ignored. Thus, the knowledge we have gained is knowledge by and about the privileged. How do we know this is the case? Let us turn once again to Andersen and Collins, who ask:

> How else can we explain the idea that democracy and egalitarianism were defined as central cultural beliefs in the nineteenth century while millions of African-Americans were enslaved? Why have social science studies been generalized to the whole population while being based only on samples of men? The exclusion of women, African-Americans, Latinos, Native Americans, gays and lesbians, and other groups from formal scholarship has resulted in distortions and incomplete information not only about the

experiences of excluded groups but also about the experience of
more privileged groups.[4]

Our knowledge base has been exclusionary, and now the building that
houses our knowledge is being meticulously dismantled, a dynamic that will
eventually fashion a more diversified and inclusive edifice, even if it takes several generations. Scholars of all persuasions and backgrounds are committed
to adding diversity to the way that knowledge is constructed. Thus, scholars
adhering to a transformation and reconstruction of a knowledge paradigm
are discovering and accenting those marginalized ways of knowing that have
been suppressed and dominated by the discourses governing our societies.

What are the dominant cultural themes with which we are living? We
may believe that the culture with which we are most familiar is the dominant
one, but that is not always nor necessarily the case. Renato Rosaldo in *Culture and Truth: The Remaking of Social Analysis* examines a university in California that reviewed its first-year core curriculum.[5] Many faculty, who had
been teaching for several years, assumed that the course "Introduction to
Western Civilization" would naturally be continued without any revisions.
When faculty members with alternative pedagogical perspectives began to
raise questions about whether Introduction to Western Civilization was the
best course to prepare first-year students to live in a rapidly changing world,
many who sought to maintain the status quo were surprised. They asked,
Why shouldn't that which had worked over many years be continued? In
response, those who proposed a revamped curriculum argued that change
was necessary because what was assumed to work may have worked for
some, but not for all.

From such a highly charged intellectual debate, we can discern how marginalized and locked out voices are speaking up in a forceful manner. Consequently a radical shift must take place in our thinking because monovocal
myth is being dislodged and a truth of inclusivity is being restored. Reconstructing knowledge means tearing down myths that have paralyzed communities, and re-creating truths that have been buried in annals containing
vast sources of knowledge. In brief, I am talking about inclusive knowledge
construction. Inclusive construction of knowledge denotes exploring sources
that culturally may be vastly different from our own epistemological points
of departure. It may be knowledge based on human experience as well as theory, and it decidedly involves inclusion of the ideas, theories, orientations,
experiences, and worldviews of persons and groups who have previously been

excluded. When such views are included, we infuse the Eurocentric and male construction of knowledge with other vitally important constructions. The normative Eurocentric male construction of knowledge, while construed to be universal, is but one perspective now undergoing supplementation and correction.

Womanist theologians bring to the center the experience and knowledge of those marginalized by a complex layering and overlapping of race, gender, and class experiences of all groups, inclusive of those with privilege and power. Thus, as we explore this multiple effect dynamic, we pose the question: If historically suppressed voices were central to our thought processes, would our conception of the world and analytical sensibilities be any different? If we pursue such epistemological dynamics as the personal/experiential or theoretical/scholarly, what influence would this endeavor have on the reconstruction of knowledge?[6] Womanist theologians, in a word, retrieve sources from the past, sort and evaluate materials, and thereby construct new epistemologies that effect change in the space and time occupied by black women.

A New Paradigm for Womanist Theology

The overwhelming majority of contemporary womanist religious scholars relies primarily on written texts, such as fiction, biography, and autobiography. I agree with the usage of these crucial sources and methodological approaches; however, I argue that we should examine further our procedural tools of analysis. Not only should womanist scholars include historical texts and literature in our theological constructs and reconstruction of knowledge, but we should also embrace a research process that engages poor black women who are living human documents. This is a very appropriate way to access the direct speech (the primary textual narrative) of subordinated African American women in our midst. That is to say, we must view books written about poor black women as secondary sources and employ anthropological techniques to collect stories and publish ethnographies of women who are still alive. The direct speech of marginalized black women invites a community of readers to participate in the interpretive process. For instance, by providing the unedited testimonies of poor African American women, we allow readers to glean for themselves that which is important for them. Such a hermeneutical undertaking removes the monopolizing interpretive power of the ethnographer.

Moreover, such an approach would utilize what Amilcar Cabral of Guinea Bissau called "a return to the source,"[7] which positions culture as an integral component of the history of a people and which also explores the dynamic between culture and its material base (that is, its class position). The level and mode of production determine dominant cultural forms. Thus, he asserted: "A people who free themselves from foreign domination will not be free unless they return to the upwards paths of their own culture."[8] From this perspective, culture is a historically contested resource struggled over by those working for or against social change to justify their respective standpoints.[9] This definition supports the earlier notion of knowledge being distributed and controlled. Therefore, if womanist scholars would collect data out of the context of the poor and working-class culture of living black women, womanists would act as intentional agents in the control and distribution of knowledge. Such a project would be greatly enhanced by a critical interchange of and solidarity with the narratives of similar women on the African continent as well as others in the third world or "two-thirds world."

A womanist anthropology of survival and liberation is a new paradigm for the twenty-first century. This novel model deploys a self-reflective sensitivity about the historical factors giving rise to oppressed voices—specifically for my purposes, the production of political economy and its impact on marginalized African American women. An interpretive anthropological approach (that is, the intentional assertion of poor and working-class black women's voices) therefore augments an analytical methodology for the womanist scholar that invokes the African American woman's perspective and clarifies how diverse cultural productions of everyday life influence the decisions and practices womanists make and implement in their lives.[10]

For womanist scholars who wish to employ the ethno-historical approach, some anthropological theories may be applied to the historical text that conveys knowledge about the womanist subject. The histories of poor and working-class black women arise out of specific contextual locations. Interpretive anthropological conceptual frameworks, therefore, guard against ahistorical methods and magnify the particular textures of these women's social and cultural locations. This process of theoretical application to primary data will enable the womanist religious scholar to access the subject's systems of cultural meaning in order to let as much of the subject's life story in historical context as possible emerge.[11]

In addition to the interpretive anthropological approach, with its accent on specificity of cultural location, an anthropological concern for political economy is warranted. Within the historical contexts of poor and black women, the womanist religious scholar must interrogate the nature of the power and resource configurations present—that is, who has influence derived from ownership and distribution of wealth. At the same time, we must not be provincial in our analysis, for local economies themselves are contextualized and implicated in global political economies. It is imperative for womanist scholars to "find effective ways to describe how [marginalized African American women] are implicated in broader processes of historical political economy."[12]

Ideally the womanist religious scholar is an indigenous anthropologist, that is, one who reflects critically upon her own community of origin and brings a sensitivity to the political, economic, and cultural systems that affect the poor and working-class black women being studied. At the same time, she gives priority to the life story of the subject in a way that underscores the narratives of a long line of subjugated voices from the past to the present.

Conclusion

Womanist theology is the positive affirmation of the gifts God has given black women in the United States. It is, within theological discourse, an emergent voice that advocates a holistic God-talk for all the oppressed. Though centered in the African American woman's reality and story, it also embraces and stands in solidarity with all oppressed subjects. In a word, womanist theology is a theory and practice of inclusivity, accenting gender, race, class, sexual orientation, and ecology. Because of its inclusive methodology and conceptual framework, womanist theology exemplifies reconstructed knowledge beyond the monovocal concerns of black (male) and (white) feminist theologies.

Such a reconstructed knowledge (an epistemology of holistic inclusivity, survival, and liberation) serves as a heuristic for the broader notion of re-creating knowledge and thereby offers some elements for a theoretical conversation. Womanist epistemological insights suggest the importance of commencing with all who have been left out of reflection upon a society, both its past and its present.

The current state of womanist theology and its implications for larger reconstructed knowledge conversations are advanced further with an imaginative womanist anthropological paradigm. Here we note the importance of secondary materials about African American women but underscore the decisive role of fieldwork among poor and working-class black women living today. Out of an emphasis on their historical and cultural specificities and the impact of political economy, a creative model emerges where the voices and meaning of the anthropological subjects themselves move to the foreground. Simultaneously, the power of the womanist religious scholar as researcher does not impede the presentation of data that invites the reader of ethnographic work to enter the interpretive dialogue with the voices of marginalized black women.

Part Two

Black Theology and the White Church

6 / A White Feminist Response to Black and Womanist Theologies

Rosemary Radford Ruether

In a recent Master's of Theological Studies program evaluation, a Euro-American woman, seeking to critique feminist theology from a womanist perspective, wrote the following introduction to her project:

> As an early movement, Feminist theology, like the larger Feminist movement, defined "women's experience" in a questionable way. Those engaging in the stated discourse were representative of a limited group of women, namely White Bourgeois Academics. Therefore the lives that were being put forth to challenge male co-option of theological discourse were as exclusivistic as those they were attempting to dismember. While Feminist theologians were claiming to insert the lives of women into a central discursive position, they neglected to radicalize the structures that would have allowed room for others. White women with class and academic privilege found it easy to make their claims from a position which valued those privileges. However they neglected to acknowledge those who were not offered the same privileges due to their race, class or sexual identity.[1]

This student then goes on to describe how womanist, lesbian, and third-world voices critiqued this exclusivism and opened up the model of feminist theology to a diversity of voices. She herself wants to work out of this larger critical perspective.

This statement constructs what has become a kind of formulaic "confession" of the sins of white feminist theology, which goes on to claim to have learned better. The assumption is that there was some cohort (usually unnamed) of feminist theologians who "in the beginning" (when?) ignored class, race, and third-world contexts. A "new wave" of women from a variety

51

of contexts was needed to critique this false "universalism" and demand a model of theology based on pluralism. I do not doubt that this was the way some women of African American, lesbian, and third-world background experienced a situation in many theological schools, universities, and perhaps areas of the women's movement at a some particular times. What I want to point out here is that this scenario deeply violates and indeed erases my own experience and that of a cohort of other feminist theologians who began our work in the late sixties and early seventies.

Perhaps it is important to point out here that there was not one but two quite different contexts in which the feminist movement arose in the mid- to late sixties. One was the movement among women lawyers, government workers, and writers, from which the National Organization of Women arose. This movement was open to issues of class, but was not particularly sensitive to race and at least some leaders, Betty Friedan in particular, were threatened by the lesbian movement, which she spoke of conspiratorially as the "lavender menace." A second movement arose out of the civil rights, New Left and Black Power movements. It is this context in which I found my own roots to speak about gender issues, beginning with my first talk in 1968, which I titled "Male Chauvinist Theology and the Anger of Women," echoing the militant language of Black Power.

The scenario of white feminists oblivious to class, race, and global contexts undoubtedly reflected realities of some contexts in the sixties. This may have become more common by the mid-seventies as feminism became more of an establishment discourse in academe and even in theological education. But my own experience was almost the opposite of this scenario. As someone who immersed herself in the civil rights movement in the early sixties, went through a trial by fire as a volunteer for the Delta Ministry in Mississippi in the summer of 1965, and then committed myself and my family to live in a predominantly black neighborhood in Washington, D.C., and to teach at a black theological school, Howard University School of Religion, between 1965 and 1976, I became steeped in a critique of racism, class hierarchy, and American neocolonialist interventionism in those years.

It was not race, class, and global awareness but gender analysis that was not welcome in the circles that had mentored me in critical consciousness in the 1960s. My mentors in the civil rights and antiwar movements were white and black leftist radical males, many of them clergy. Black theology and third-world liberation theology were being founded at that time. I drank in their critique of American classist, racist, and militarist society. Among my first books was a collection of essays written between 1968 and 1971, *Liberation Theology: Human Hope Confronts Christian History and American Power.*[2] The essays addressed black theology, Jewish-Christian relations, Christian anti-Semitism, communitarian socialism, the white left in America, and Latin American liberation theology. Two early essays concerned feminist and ecological theology. My essay on black theology was based on the early work of James Cone, while my essay on Latin American liberation theology cites the first book of Gustavo Gutiérrez, at that time not yet translated into English.

The working assumption of these essays, as in all my subsequent work, is that liberation theology is multidimensional and needs to be looked at across a wide range of diverse contexts. It was in the late sixties that I first began to add questions of gender to what was then, in the circles in which I moved, an established race, class, and anticolonial discourse. At the Howard School of Religion, where I taught from 1965 to 1976, there was little openness to black theology. The faculty were mostly older African Americans who had struggled in the 1940s and 1950s to establish a middle-class respectability. They preferred to be called Negroes (capital N) and shuddered at the word *black,* which they saw as close to a racist insult. I was the first faculty member to introduce Cone's writings at the seminary at that time, although one of my colleagues, Dr. Deotis Roberts, would begin to develop a black theology that was consciously more conservative and "reconciling" than Cone. My early article on black theology mentioned above was an effort to respond to this critique coming from my colleagues and to defend Cone's views, rooted in a positive reading of Black Power.

Gender was not mentioned at all in this article. At a historically black seminary, gender was a touchy subject from a white woman, but also from black women. There were few younger black women at the seminary when I first arrived. Women students were mostly older participants in a secondary degree program offered to urban pastors without a college education. I began to develop my first work in feminist theology during a leave of absence I took in 1972–73 to teach at Harvard Divinity School of Religion. This work was developed the next year in a series of lectures at Yale Divinity School. I did not try to teach a course on feminist theology at Howard. In one course on contemporary ethical issues I introduced one lecture on gender and asked a black male friend sensitive to questions of gender in the black community to give it.

There were no available black women to discuss gender issues in terms of theology at Howard at that time, but if there had been, they would have had a hard time being heard. I realized this in asking a black male to speak on gender. At that point critical perspectives on gender relations could hope to get a hearing among black males, the majority of my students, only if they came from another black male. This collaboration between a white feminist and a black male was, I think, an effective one in that context. Linda Thomas and Dwight Hopkins, in their joint course on black and womanist theologies, are a good example of a collaboration between a black woman and a black man in the current context in which a womanist discourse has been established side by side with black (male) theology.

Young black women were beginning to enter Howard School of Religion in the early 1970s and to express an interest in gender questions. In 1975 a latent tension over the issue exploded. A young black woman did her master's thesis on a gender critique of theology in the black church. Our faculty was a small one (eight members), and it was customary to have a hearing of theses with the whole faculty. This young woman was roundly ridiculed by the acting dean of the faculty, with the others passively backing him up. I intervened to defend her, and the hostility was turned on me. The acting dean called me to his office and threatened to fire me. In his view my defense of this woman student had insulted the faculty (himself). At that time I had no tenure at the school, so I was vulnerable to dismissal.

This attack did not worry me too much, because I was privy to two pieces of information. I was on the search committee for a new dean, and we had decided to hire Dr. Lawrence Jones from Union Seminary. It was evident that things would change at the seminary when he came. The new generation of black scholars who identified with a black theological perspective would doubtless be arriving. Second, Garrett-Evangelical Theological Seminary was inviting me to take the position of Georgia Harkness Professor of Applied Theology, where feminist theology was to be defined as central to my work.

Garrett had already made a strong commitment to having a significant number of black students and faculty and to doing theological education in the context of the church and the black experience. James Cone had received his master's of divinity from Garrett and his Ph.D. from the joint Garrett–Northwestern University program in the fifties and sixties and was deeply critical of Garrett's lack of attention to race issues in theology. But Garrett heeded his call in the early seventies and attempted to make the black perspective in theological education a major commitment. Then-President Merlan Northfelt was sensitive that any feminism introduced at Garrett should be compatible with this commitment to black people. He gave the black faculty a major role in the search and sent two leading black faculty to interview me in Washington, D.C. I was chosen for the position at Garrett in large part because of my experience at Howard and the fact that I had developed my feminist theology in the context of a dialogue with issues of racism.

I also had become convinced that it was time for me to leave Howard, precisely because, as a white woman, I could not initiate the discussion of gender issues there. The new era at Howard School of Theology, which I was confident Dr. Jones would develop as dean, needed to bring a new generation of African American women theologians and scholars to Howard to develop this discussion in a black church and seminary context. This is very much what has happened at Howard since my time there, especially helped by leading womanist theologians, such as Kelley Brown-Douglas.

By the late seventies and early eighties feminism was becoming an established area in an increasing number of theological schools, and women were being hired who had done some work on gender issues. Some of these feminist scholars had emerged, like myself, out of the civil rights struggle and had race and class as a integral part of our view. This was the case with Beverly Harrison at Union Theological Seminary (New York) and Letty Russell at Yale. Others had come from a purely academic route and had not had the same experiences of the civil rights movement. This included Mary Daly who came to Boston College in 1968, after completing a theology and a philosophy doctorate in Europe.

Daly was developing a radical feminist theology that would eventually lead her to rejection of Christianity altogether. But she had not shared the civil rights experience (being out of the country during most of the 1960s) and was hostile to discussion of race and class differences among women, which she saw as diverting from a unitary view of all women as equally "oppressed." Her insensitivity to the black experience in her use of certain symbolism, such as speaking of "castrating" the patriarchal God, led to a critique of her work by leading black feminist poet Audre Lorde.[3]

By the mid-eighties an emerging cadre of black women theologians who claimed the term *womanism* were adopting a "hermeneutic of suspicion" toward white feminists, assuming that they were oblivious to issues of race, unless clearly proved otherwise. In November of 1984 I was asked to give a plenary address at the American Academy of Religion on feminist theology, a recognition of its arrival on the academic scene. In my address, published in *Christianity and Crisis* on March 5, 1985, I tried to make very clear that, as a white woman, I could not speak for women as a whole. I wrote:

I need to acknowledge at the outset that I speak from a white Western Christian context. Theology should overcome patterns of thought within it that vilify or exclude persons by gender, race and religion. But this does not mean that we seek a theology that is universalistic in the sense of encompassing all cultures and religions. Such universalism is in fact cultural imperialism—an attempt by one religious culture to monopolize not theology but salvation, to claim that it alone has authentic access to the divine. Christian patriarchal theology has typically been imperialistic, claiming that white male Christian experience is equivalent to universal humanity.

Feminist theology, by contrast, must be consciously pluralistic. Despite similarities among patriarchal patterns, a Christian feminism will be different from a Jewish feminism, or a Buddhist or a Muslim feminism. Moreover, an Asian Christian feminist or an African Christian feminist or an American black Christian feminist will also have distinct problems and will come up with different syntheses. Pagan feminists, who seek to break with all patriarchal religious contexts and to rediscover an ancient female-centered religion or to create one today, pose yet a different problematic.

Feminist theology, then, needs to be seen as a network of solidarity that exists among feminist communities engaged in the critique of patriarchalism in distinct cultural and religious contexts, rather than one dominant form of feminism that claims to speak for the whole of womankind.

Several feminists, including Carol Christ and Delores Williams, were asked to give comments on this article in a subsequent issue of *Christianity and Crisis*. Unfortunately the editors had scrambled some of the paragraphs of the article, which misrepresented the sequence of my argument. Specifically they put my claim that all feminists need to be able to claim imagery of the divine as "goddess" out of context. They also inserted into my article a large reproduction of a marble head of Athena. This image had nothing to do with anything I said in the article. Delores Williams focused on this image of Athena and my defense of speaking of God as "goddess" and attacked the article as a typical example of white feminists oblivious to class, race, and imperialism. She claimed that I was seeking to establish an idea of God as a "white Goddess," failing to include the perspective of black feminists.[4]

In the May 13, 1985, issue of *Christianity and Crisis* I replied to Williams's (and others') comments on my article, pointing out the errors in the magazine's presentation of my article. I said that Williams had misread my article. Her attack on it:

> was based on a total unwillingness to take seriously what I said explicitly at the outset of the essay: I affirm a plurality of feminist theologies both in various Christian racial and cultural contexts and in various inter-religious contexts and I reject any dominant form of feminist theology that claims to speak for the whole of womankind.

Unfortunately Williams's polemic had been received in literature on the development of feminist theology as a confirmation of the "story line" of white feminists oblivious to class, race, and imperialism, until called to account by womanists and other feminists of color. Several recent books and articles cite Williams's comments as a example of this "story line," lumping me with Mary Daly, and typically failing to read either my original article or my reply to Williams in *Christianity and Crisis*, much less my other books and articles that focus on class, race, intercultural, and interreligious dialogue.[5]

Let me make clear that I do not think that white feminists, such as myself, are innocent of racism just because we have consciously adopted a certain rhetoric of pluralism. Race and class bias are deeply embedded in the context in which we all work in the United States (and elsewhere). No matter what my words are, and my words reflect my deep convictions on which I have attempted to live and act for thirty-five years, I still live in a context of race and class privilege that is automatically accorded to me no matter what my personal views may be.

A hermeneutic of suspicion that racism is not being recognized adequately is always appropriate on the part of womanists toward white feminists. White feminists also must constantly be aware of their own race and class privilege and question how they are collaborating with this. Ultimately this is not simply about individual "politically correct" words, although this is a part of cultural change, but of deep systematic economic and cultural changes that create a more egalitarian society. Economically the United States is more deeply split by the gaps of wealth and poverty today than in the late sixties.

The words that I wrote in the article published in *Christianity and Crisis* in 1985 express my views more deeply today than ever. We need more and more plurality in feminist theologies done in every racial, ethnic, religious, and cultural context to explicate the issues of women in as many contexts as possible, as well as a solidarity between this expanding diversity that can help midwife real social and cultural transformation toward justice and mutuality. One of my great delights is the increasing emergence of feminist theologies in many different contexts: womanist, Mujerista, Asian-American, and lesbian theologies in the United States, as well as diverse feminist theologies in Africa, Asia, Latin America, and the Middle East. Buddhist, Hindu, Jewish, and Muslim women are doing feminist theology in their distinct religious contexts. I have been deeply involved in the last twenty years with both first–third world dialogue between Christian feminists and interreligious feminist dialogue.[6]

This pluralism is coming to be assumed, although we are still learning how to collaborate and not be used to undercut one another. Moreover, feminists in Asia, Africa, and Latin America have experienced something of the same resistance of male leftists to their thought that I and others experienced in the late 1960s and 1970s. Most of the African, Asian, and Latin American feminist theologians began their theological reflection in the context of liberation theologies in their regions. They had deeply incorporated a critique of issues of class, race, and colonialism, committing themselves to a theology in solidarity with the oppressed. But when they sought to bring gender into this discussion their male leftist colleagues ridiculed them. They insisted that feminism is a "white, bourgeois, first-world issue" and was not appropriate in third-world contexts. As a result of this treatment, third-world feminist theologians in groups such as the Ecumenical Association of Third World Theologians insisted on having their own women's commission, where they could contextualize feminist theology in their own situations. As these women stated at a founding meeting in Geneva in 1983, "We have to decide for ourselves what feminist theology means for us. It is not for First World women to tell us how to do it, nor is it for Third World men to tell us feminism is not our issue."[7]

First- and third-world women, as well as men and women across class, race, and gender divisions, have still to learn how to work together effectively on a liberating agenda in theology and praxis in a way that is fully open and mutual. Questioning of feminists in privileged contexts continues to be appropriate, but it needs to be based on some careful effort to understand one another's actual histories. Constructing a story line about white feminism that fails to respect some of our actual experiences is not helpful. Pluralism was not invented in 1990.

7 / What I Learned from James Cone and Black Theology

D. Stephen Long

How has black theology affected the white church? What has the white church learned from black theology, and what *should* it learn? Let me discuss four significant lessons that at least I, as a member of the white church, have learned from black theology. I pose these themes as an invitation for others to judge if I have learned these lessons well, what I have not yet learned, and how these lessons might contribute to a fruitful conversation about the nature of theology.

First is the lesson of audience. Black theology both assumes and does not assume the white church. It develops theology without concern for the criteria by which the white church and white theologians seek to judge theology, and thus it is free from any oversight by the white church. But at the same time this very distinction—a black theology free from white oversight—posits a counterposition, that of the "white church" over and against which it primarily makes sense.[1] The first lesson I have learned comes in the form of an open question, a question that cannot be answered definitively because in its content and form black theology makes the question necessary: To what extent is the white church an audience for black theology?

The second lesson is the lesson of Christocentricity. In its early formation black theology was one of the most Christocentric theologies among theologies in the North American context. This Christocentricity seemed to be a feature not so much of the personal convictions of the theologians who produced it, many of whom were educated in mainline educational institutions that were suspicious of any Christocentrism. But it was a necessary feature of speaking to and out of the black church. This lesson also ends with a question, for James Cone's work itself has moved away from this Christocentricity. This raises the question whether black theology now approximates a form of "European" cosmopolitanism.

The third lesson is theology's direct political relevance. Black theology was a theological politics that eschewed sociological mediation in an effort to unite nature and grace (theology and politics) without any mediating science. Theology was directly related to political and economic realities. This is perhaps most evident in Cone's *The Spirituals and the Blues,* in which Cone critiques reading the spirituals through the sociologist's category of "compensatory." This category, he argued, is the "sociologist's tool for tucking theology into a corner." Cone recognized that subordinating theology to sociology meant that theology would be "policed" into insignificance.[2] Black theology did not need socioanalytic mediation for it to be political.

Fourth, black theology extended the theological conversation; voices that had not been heard were granted a privileged position. Because these voices had not been granted access to the institutions that produce dominant cultural products—such as seminaries and universities—alternative forms of theological production were identified and drawn upon as resources for theology. This is the lesson of theological resources.

Lesson of Audience

The very fact that we understand the designation "white church" reveals perhaps the most significant impact black theology had on the church. I was neither raised nor baptized into any institution explicitly named "the white church"; yet through Cone and others, that designation has been disclosed. More familiar ecclesial divisions—Catholic/Protestant, low church/high church, established/free church—were further complicated by a more pervasive North American political distinction: black/white. Cone not only told us that there were "white" churches, but he explicitly told us that those churches were species of heresy, in which baptism introduced us more clearly into a cultural discourse (whiteness) than into a redeemed messianic community. He spoke and wrote with a bluntness and theological particularity that insured the point could not easily be missed.

Cone's work is significant precisely because he breaks through the bourgeois sentimentality that too often masquerades in and through the language of contemporary theological education, where the language of the white church dominates the language of pluralism, inclusion, diversity, and dialogue. Cone transgresses the boundaries this language establishes, boundaries that seem to invite the production of a civic and civil theology. In the midst of that language Cone tells us:

The time has come for white America to be silent and listen to black people.

All white men are responsible for white oppression.

Theologically, Malcolm X was not far wrong when he called the white man "the devil."

To love the white man means the black man confronts him as a thou without any intentions of giving ground by becoming an it.

Any advice from whites to blacks on how to deal with white oppression is automatically under suspicion as a clever device to further enslavement.

The task of black theology is to take Christian tradition that is so white and make it black, by showing that whites do not really know what they are saying when they affirm Jesus as the Christ.[3]

Cone's work is neither sentimental invitation for dialogue nor liberal pleading for inclusivity. For those of us in the white church there is no way out of the judgment these statements render. The liberal move of inclusivity does not work; one cannot incorporate Cone's work into some generic cosmopolitanism. One cannot co-opt it through some vague call for an invitation to dialogue. And although I assume most of us understand the sentiment and would express the desire put forth so charitably by Rodney King, "Can we all just get along?" the reality of the black/white division seems to be so pervasive that such sentiments detract from a proper social analysis of the conditions that make black suffering normative in the United States. Cone confronts us with this reality and gives us no room to affirm his work and avoid that reality. In fact Cone lets us know that far from seeking reconciliation, establishing community, or working on a common project, the relationship between blacks and whites in America can best be described as a low-intensity conflict. He boldly states: "The asserting of black freedom in America has always meant war. . . . There is no place for the white liberal in this war of survival."[4] There may be particular truces where blacks and whites can work together without violence, but in North America the political and cultural narrative that perpetuates this low-intensity conflict seems to be always present. Any appeal to the one, holy, catholic, and apostolic church that overlooks this low-intensity conflict will ring as hollow as asserting a unified church in Northern Ireland.

When reading Cone's work, white folk seem caught on the horns of an uncomfortable dilemma: either liberal self-loathing or conservative denial. This dilemma finds expression in such statements as "Yes, my white ancestors and I are personally responsible for the untold misery of black suffering," or "Why bring that history up to me? I didn't own any slaves." Even though there is partial truth in both responses, neither of them is satisfying. The first response can still be a veiled way for white culture to control the situation: Look at what *we* did; now *we* must fix it. The second is simply to live from amnesia—something quite possible in the modern era, but not a viable option for the baptized who are only sustained through remembrance.

The problem with both liberal self-loathing and conservative denial is that they leave the power asymmetry unchanged. White folk still get to control the discourse. By coupling black theology with the Black Power movement, Cone left no place for such control. As he put it, "Religiously or philosophically Black Power means an inner sense of freedom from the structures of white society which builds its economy on the labor of poor blacks and whites."[5] At one level, the status of the white church in Cone's work is that of spectator; we are positioned such that we must listen and discover what it means to be out of control. It is a position to which the white church is not accustomed.

The status of spectator to which black theology positions the white church could tempt it to misunderstand its role, imagining it has no place in the conversation.[6] It can too easily lead to the sentiment that it is a "black thing" we cannot understand, and therefore we can affirm it but we need not listen. This leads to an indifference toward black theology on behalf of white theologians; an indifference that occurs when white theologians refuse to engage black theology either through a patronizing affirmation or through a not-so-benign neglect. But even though black theology places white responses under suspicion, it still recognizes that our fates are inextricably linked. As Cone noted, "when blacks assert their freedom in self-determination, whites too are liberated."[7]

Black theology should not be read such that it tempts the white church toward a paternal or malignant indifference. Instead it discloses how the health and salvation of our communities are necessarily linked. And this also seems to be a lesson Cone teaches. For even when he tells us, "all white men are responsible for white oppression," he seeks to expose white supremacy not for the purpose of condemnation alone but to issue a prophetic call. For he goes on to say, "insofar as white do-gooders tolerate and sponsor racism in their educational institutions, their political, economic and social structures, their churches, and in every aspect of American life, they are directly responsible for racism."[8] The preposition that begins that sentence comes as a challenge and not merely a universal indictment. "Insofar as"—to the extent that we merely look the other way, refuse to speak—then, says Cone, we are responsible. And those of us who are white know that it is almost impossible at some moment in our lives not to have looked the other way, not to have refused to speak. And Cone tells us what is at stake. "Racism is possible because whites are indifferent to suffering and patient with cruelty."[9]

On the one hand, Cone's theology is not intended for a white audience; at least not a white audience prepared to do anything other than listen. On the other hand, Cone's work demands a white audience. He has done something revealing; he has broken the silence that exists between the black and white communities in the United States by saying in public what often is said, or assumed, in private. Like Malcolm X's prophetic utterance, "I came to tell the white man the truth about himself or die trying," Cone has revealed for public consumption a black strategy for survival in white America.[10] That is a risky venture, which finally can only have been motivated by a severe charity. What seems initially to have generated this move to make public the things that were silent is the freedom in Christ proclaimed in the black church.

Lesson of Christocentricity

The interests of those who are white may appear on the surface to be not well served by taking stock of what Cone has to say. As C. Eric Lincoln has said, white interest in black suffering is always limited by that time when whites "return to mind the stores of privilege" from which we come. But for the baptized seeking to be faithful, Cone's words cannot be easily dismissed. The first time I read them they angered me. I thought they unfairly characterized all white people and forcibly separated me from the Jesus I thought I knew and loved. But as an evangelical Christian I could not easily dismiss Cone's theology because of the Christocentric basis from which he worked. And thus the caricature of black theology I had heard—that it was a leftist politics dressed in Christian garb—was insufficient to keep me from reading black theology seriously. It was obviously not a politicized theology, but a theological politics.

Early on, Cone sought to focus black theology on Jesus Christ and not culture or nature. Thus he wrote, "Black theology is Christian theology because it centers on Jesus Christ."[11] And he was clear in that early work that Jesus Christ was the central norm for theological reflection. "In Christian thinking the man Jesus must be the decisive interpretive factor in everything we say about God because he is the plenary revelation of God."[12] This Christocentrism contributed to black theology's over-againstness in the culture of North American theology. It established a fruitful church/world distinction. "To be free in Christ is to be against the world," wrote Cone, and this leads to a sense that something both cosmic and particular is at stake in Christian claims.[13] The particularity of those claims resulted in inscribing opposition to racism into the heart of the Christian mystery. "God in Christ has freed us. . . . The battle was fought and won on Good Friday and the triumph was revealed to men at Easter. . . . There is a constant battle between Christ and Satan and it is going on now. . . . The demonic forces of racism are real for the black man."[14] One cannot participate in Christ's resurrection without opposing the principalities and powers Christ came to vanquish. To participate in Christ's resurrection entails opposition to the demonic forces of racism.

That Jesus gave theology its norm in black theology meant that other norms were displaced. In his early theological proposal Cone followed Karl Barth in rejecting any natural theology or *analogia entis* as mediating between God and creatures.[15] He even indicted North American theologians for their addiction to a natural theology. Cone argued that their self-interest prevented them from taking Barth's criticisms of nature and culture seriously.[16] In other words white theologians had too much stake in the structures of North American culture to embody the kind of ecclesiology and Christology present in persons like Barth and Dietrich Bonhoeffer. The white church and its theologians primarily functioned as chaplains in service to the power structures that rule America—government, military, corporations, hospitals. Cone rejected any natural theology that sought to subordinate Christology to a larger overarching metaphysical vision, a vision that so easily led the church into this accommodation with North American culture via its chaplaincy role. Cone called us to a more radical obedience: "The white American Church has no history of obedience; and without it, it is unlikely that it will ever know what radical obedience to Christ means."[17]

Later, Cone seems to have at least qualified if not repudiated this Christocentrism as one more form of Eurocentric exclusivity. In fact, Cone argued that Asian theologies have persuasively challenged using language such as "uniqueness," "finality," or "absoluteness" with respect to Jesus; such language is now viewed as a species of "Christo-fascism." This caused Cone to reconsider his earlier Christocentric focus. "Since 1975 a radical development has taken place in my christological reflections. No longer can I do theology as if Jesus is God's sole revelation. Rather he is an important revelatory event among many."[18] Can the radical ecclesiological vision he advocated be sustained without his earlier Christocentrism? Can there be a Christocentric vision that is not fascist? Must Christ as the center now be replaced with a more cosmopolitan account of religion, in which Christianity is subordinated to a more overarching vision of "revelation in general," of which Christianity is a particular species? But if this is the direction black theology is moving, how can it continue to offer an objection to European philosophy and culture? For hasn't European philosophy and culture, at least since Immanuel Kant, advocated a similar cosmopolitan vision? So the second lesson I learned from black theology ends with a question: How should we think of Jesus in light of black suffering, and how should we think about black suffering in light of Jesus?

Lesson of Theology's Direct Political Relevance

Cone's early work was criticized for drawing too heavily upon European theologians. He has stated that Barth's work was the best he could do with his graduate education but it was still inadequate for his purposes.[19] His 1972 publication, *The Spirituals and the Blues*, represents a more adequate presentation of his theology, for in it he incorporated new resources into his theological vision. Many seminarians have re-presented the form of this theology—a theological aesthetics drawing upon the poetic expression of people who did not have access to seminary education, but still produced signifying creations to explain who God is and pass on that sacred knowledge.

One overlooked fact that I find intriguing about *The Spirituals and the Blues* is its suspicion of sociological categorization. The book is not a "sociological" analysis in the disciplinary sense of that term. Cone critiques the sociological categorization of the spirituals because he argues such categories tend to overlook the genre of the spirituals as *theological*. So in opposition to Benjamin Mays's reading of the spirituals as "compensatory," that is, an expression of a political and sociological lack overcome through poetic production, Cone notes that the term *compensatory* is not a theological category. And he suggests it may be a "sociologist's tool for tucking all theology into an insignificant corner."[20] Such a brilliant insight distances black theology from other forms of liberation theology preoccupied with questions of method and the appropriate tools for social mediation. Precisely because black theology was not dependent upon such a sociological mediation, it has not been thrown into the crisis other forms of liberation theology have been with their (at least tacit) accommodation of sociological theories, such as dependency theory.

Cone's *Spirituals and the Blues* is an example of a theological politics in which a theologian without the aid of a sociological method explores a poetic creation, disclosing that theology itself can provide political and social readings. This potentially avoids the problematic notion of the "social" that has developed in Western thought. As John Milbank has argued, the notion of the social as an autonomous, self-contained object of study arose within a particular history marked by Christian heresy and a return to paganism. The heresy was in conceiving God in terms of pure power; in the relationship between God and creation, this concept gave rise to the notion of autonomous "facts" that are self-contained. The "paganism" arose because the notion of power and antagonism are written into the ontological structure of the social, which can then be rationally mediated via science. The key architect for this scientific study of the social is Max Weber. But Weber, Milbank argues, "is really saying that . . . sociology is primarily about economic rationality, formal bureaucracy and Machiavellian politics." The result is that Weber (and Ernst Troeltsch) "create a sociology which is nothing but a spurious promotion of what they study—namely the secular culture of modernity."[21] Sociology functions then as a way to "police the sublime," that is to say to render what counts as reasonable with respect to language about God in terms acceptable to sociology. Cone did not develop his critique of sociology in the same terms that Milbank has done, but I find Cone's work in *The Spirituals and the Blues* to be a confirmation of Milbank's thesis. From the perspective of reading the spirituals as theological resources, Cone intuits that sociology is inadequate. It seeks to "tuck theology into an insignificant corner" and then decide itself—in terms solely of a power the sociologist can control (that is, the language of compensation)—what constitutes an adequate depiction of religion. For this reason, I find Cone's *The Spirituals and the Blues* particularly helpful in thinking theologically about politics and economics without allowing our *theological* thought and practice to be determined by the sociologist's policing of the sublime.

Lesson of Alternative Theological Resources

This leads to the fourth and perhaps most important lesson to be learned from black theology: for marginalized voices to contribute to theology resources other than classical texts, they need to be incorporated into theology. Perhaps these resources will primarily be aesthetic; they will be the songs, prayers, hymns, and poems of persons who produced great theological "literature" without access to the mediation of theological thought provided by corporations such as denominational and other religious publishing houses, university presses, and so forth. A theological politics might be best exemplified precisely in the aesthetic irruption of alternatives to the dominant culture. Cone found this in spirituals and blues music: "Black music is social because it is black and thus articulates the separateness of the black community. It is an artistic rebellion against the humiliating deadness of western culture."[22] Such an aesthetic approach to theology refuses to view Jesus merely as an object of study, but instead expresses the reality of the risen crucified Savior in the lived practices of a concrete people. Cone reminds us:

> The spirituals are silent on abstract theological speculations about the person and work of Christ. There are no theories about the *ousia* or Being of the Son in relation to the Father. . . . Jesus was not the subject of theological questioning. He was perceived in the reality of the black experience, and black slaves affirmed both his divinity and humanity without debating the philosophical question, "How can God become human being?"[23]

That the experience of black slaves seems to affirm something quite similar to Nicea and Chalcedon without the slaves' direct knowledge of those debates and decisions might lead us to reaffirm the conciliar wisdom of creedal Christianity rather than dismissing it as abstract speculation. For what the creeds affirm—God is found in flesh and not abstraction from it—appears to have given people the ability to sustain hope in the midst of the "most execrable villainy" ever practiced. The more we affirm God's fleshliness, the more those burdened in the flesh can truly speak of God.[24]

Conclusion and Further Reflections

Cone's work seeks to reveal the pathology present in Western culture, a pathology that has normalized and routinized black suffering. And he identifies that pathology with the European language of "freedom and equality." "Underneath the European language of freedom and equality," writes Cone, "there is slavery and death."[25] Cone is by no means the first person to identify

that which European theology, philosophy, and culture so highly prize—
freedom and equality—as the very seeds of the pathology that lead European
culture into an inevitable drift toward nihilism. Marx identified a similar
phenomenon. And in 1887 Friedrich Nietzsche wrote:

> What I relate is the history of the next two centuries. I describe
> what is coming, what can no longer come differently: the advent
> of nihilism. This history can be related even now; for necessity
> itself is at work here. This future speaks even now in a hundred
> signs, this destiny announces itself everywhere for the music of
> the future all ears are cocked even now. For some time now, our
> whole European culture has been moving as toward a catastro-
> phe, with a tortured tension that is growing from decade to
> decade: restlessly, violently, headlong, like a river that wants to
> reach the end.[26]

Nietzsche can be faulted for failing to see that this nihilism had already
deeply marked European culture for three centuries through the development of global trade routes that made possible the Middle Passage and routinized black suffering. This nihilism was already present in the genealogy of
modern racism and the new "scientific" basis upon which slavery was enacted
in the "New World."[27] This new world was predicated upon an unlimited
will to power masquerading as freedom. Those who bore the burden of this
new world are the same ones whose voices rise up in song to speak against it
in black theology. This is a wonderful gift not only to the white church in
North America but to the worldwide church. It is an antidote that frees us
from the pathology present in Western culture and philosophy. Still, two
questions remain. First, can the category of "liberation" ever be an adequate
term to oppose the pathology that has rightly been identified as embodied in
Western notions of freedom? Second, is this pathology still evident in black
theology in the neo-Lutheranism of Paul Tillich, which has not received (as
far as I know) the same criticisms Barth's work received in the later developments of black theology?

Tillich drew upon Martin Luther as the exemplar par excellence of the
"courage to be."[28] The will's affirmation of life in the face of anxiety expressed
for Tillich the essence of the Christian faith. Cone developed this similar
ontology as he sought to incorporate the notion of Black Power into Christian theology. Black Power, wrote Cone, "means the complete emancipation

of black people from white oppression by whatever means black people deem necessary." Cone clarified this meaning of Black Power by drawing upon "Paul Tillich's analysis of the 'courage to be,' which is 'the ethical act in which man affirms his being in spite of those elements of his existence which conflict with his essential self-affirmation.' . . . And as Tillich goes on to say, 'He who is not capable of a powerful self-affirmation in spite of the anxiety of non-being is forced into a weak, reduced self-affirmation.' "[29] But it was not Malcolm X who first coined the term "by whatever means necessary." That expression seems to have first been advocated by Martin Luther in his justification for secular violence. It was, after all, Luther who first put forth the idea of using violence "by whatever means you can" for the sake of the neighbor's liberty as an alien work of charity.[30] Such an understanding of violence was fully developed in Carl von Clausewitz's rationalization of war. It certainly contributed to the notion of total warfare that dominated European history in the twentieth century.

"By whatever means you can" signifies something different from the social location of black slaves who do not control the means of violence as did the Prussian authorities for whom Clausewitz wrote. And perhaps that is sufficient to deny any residual Western pathology that correlates freedom and violence in the work of black theology. But this brings us to the question Cone himself has posed in his *Malcolm and Martin and America.*

In his early work *Black Theology and Black Power* Cone argued that Martin Luther King Jr.'s approach was "the least threatening to the white power structure."[31] Some two decades later Cone is still explaining the relationship among Malcolm, Martin, America, and the church. He writes:

> Malcolm was right to insist that African-Americans should take their freedom "by any means necessary," refusing absolutely to let white exploiters shape the ethics of resistance to exploitation. . . . Malcolm felt that this point especially needed to be made to white people. What right did white people have to tell black people the methods that they should use to fight against white racism? Since whites themselves were not nonviolent when they perceived their humanity was being violated, why should they expect blacks to be nonviolent? Martin, however, was right in his claim that nonviolent direct action is *resistance* and not passivity or cowardice. Indeed it was the only creative way that an African-American minority of ten percent could fight for freedom and at

the same time avoid genocide, the logical consequence of racism.[32]

While it would certainly be understandable that out of black suffering something like the Irish Republican Army developed, and while there have been attempts to do so, such a force is not yet present on the political scene in the United States. This may have more to do with the minority status of blacks in the United States as compared to Catholics in Northern Ireland, but this fact is intriguing. Could this also have something to do with the Christocentrism in the black church and a theological politics that avoids at all cost the effort to reproduce the master narrative of a deceived "master" race that sought initially to impose its will by all means available? I have now in part transgressed the lessons learned in black theology and have posed questions, which must be placed under critical suspicion. Because of baptism, I think such transgressions are inevitable by white theologians, clergy, and laity. Because of black theology, such transgressions can be identified as such.

8 Reconsidering Evangelism

Lessons from Black Liberation and Womanist Theologies

Laceye Warner

The implications of black liberation and womanist theologies for evangelicalism are profound and provocative. As a middle-class Euro-American evangelical Protestant woman and historian in the field of evangelism, I am concerned about the inconsistencies between the content of black and evangelical theologies. James Cone and others writing within black liberation and womanist theologies present important observations and critiques that address these inconsistencies in the wider Christian tradition. Such statements are also pertinent for white evangelicalism in particular.

> The white church has not merely failed to render services to the poor, but has failed miserably in being a visible manifestation to the world of God's intention for humanity and in proclaiming the gospel to the world. It seems that the white church is not God's redemptive agent but, rather, an agent of the old society. It fails to create an atmosphere of radical obedience to Christ. Most church fellowships are more concerned about drinking or new buildings or Sunday closing than about children who die of rat bites or men who are killed because they want to be treated like men.[1]

Euro-American Christians in the United States often seem to resist the painful difficulty of remembering the sins of racism in their many embodiments. Despite the discomfort experienced, confrontation of these past and present wrongs and responding to the accountability called for by Cone and other black liberation and womanist theologians are necessary. This discomfort is demonstrated in the overwhelming silence[2] with regard to the implications of racism within evangelical scholarship that necessitates a critical response from scholars.

> Unfortunately, American theology from Cotton Mather and Jonathan Edwards to Reinhold Niebuhr to Schubert Ogden, including radicals and conservatives, have interpreted the gospel according to the cultural and political interests of white people. They have rarely attempted to transcend the social interests of their group by seeking an analysis of the gospel in the light of the consciousness of black people struggling for liberation. White theologians, because of their identity with the dominant power structure, are largely boxed within their own cultural history.[3]

Acts of repentance on the part of white evangelicals for participation and silence in social injustices of racism, classism, and sexism are essential for faithful discipleship and effective reflection and practice of ministry. One aspect of that repentance and conversion is the reconsideration of scriptural sources for theology and ministry to overcome culturally limited interpretations and therefore to embody the gospel more effectively and reclaim the integrity of the church's ministry in the world.

Because evangelical voices vary across a broad spectrum, this paper will focus its discussion upon the implications of black liberation and womanist theologies for the theology and practice of evangelism. Jacquelyn Grant describes an underlying theme of oppression within evangelistic and mission-oriented tasks of the church through history.

> In the area of Christian foreign missions . . . conversion to Christianity implicitly meant deculturalization and acceptance of the western value system on the part of Asians, Africans, and Latin Americans. Upon conversion, one had to withdraw from indigenous ways of imaging the divine reality, and embrace foreign, western ways that often served to undergird oppressive religious, social and political structures.[4]

Similar themes, though subtle, still seem to pervade evangelicalism as demonstrated by the relative silence on issues of race, class, and gender in evangelical theology generally and the field of evangelism in particular. Here I will explore in two sections the implications of race for the theology and practice of evangelism. The first section will examine broad themes within the literature addressing evangelistic ministry and points of contact within the literature of black theology and evangelical writing on the theology and practice of evangelistic ministry. Few scholars writing on the theology and practice of evangelism address implications of black liberation and womanist theologies. In light of the frequent silence, this section will acknowledge specific lessons gained by the field of evangelism from black liberation and womanist theologies. The second section will begin a discussion of the construction of a biblical and theological model for evangelistic ministry that embodies the accountability, lessons learned, and holistic faithfulness demanded by black liberation and womanist theologies.

Points of Coherence

Whether written for academic or ecclesiastical conversation, scholarship on the theology and practice of evangelistic ministry is relatively limited. Writings on evangelistic ministries and church growth have traditionally emphasized the spiritual and eschatological aspects of salvation and atonement over social action. This tendency in wider scholarship to spiritualize soteriology and Christology is observed by black theologians.

> On the other hand, there is the spiritualized Jesus, reconstructed many years later by the Apostle Paul who never knew Jesus and who modified his teachings to conform to the pagan philosophies of the white gentiles. Considering himself an apostle to the gentiles, Paul preached individual salvation and life after death. We, as black Christians suffering oppression in a white man's land, do not need the individualistic and otherworldly doctrines of Paul and the white man. We need to recapture the faith in our power as a *people* and the concept of Nation, which are the foundation of the Old Testament and the prophets, and upon which Jesus built all of his teachings 2,000 years ago.[5]

Inherent to the inconsistencies evident between black liberation and womanist theologies and Euro-American evangelical theology is the lack of attention given to the significance of physical manifestations of salvation in addition to the spiritual in scripture, and the implications of a multi-dimensional soteriology for Christians today. A significant portion of literature within the field of evangelism tends generally to focus on the pragmatics of church growth, employing marketing and other organizational techniques.

This literature, although helpful in applying proven and effective business theories, is most often limited to the context of suburban affluent Euro-American Protestant congregations. In a critique of such literature we might ask: How pervasive is racism in these contexts? To what extent may the kingdom of God be realized in these suburban affluent Euro-American Protestant congregations in light of racism? As Gayraud Wilmore writes:

> We [black theologians] suspect that the conservative evangelical revolution of today frequently masks white supremacy. . . . Black theology has to do with more than the Black Church because it contributes to the enlightenment of white Christians by unmasking the racism and cultural imperialism under the garments of this new evangelical phenomenon. In its best form, therefore, Black theology teaches a theological option for the poor and oppressed that can help all of us to discover a compassionate and holistic pastoral ministry which recognizes the essential coherence between genuine spirituality and liberation politics.[6]

Wilmore's statement points directly to the need for white evangelical theologians to be accountable to black theologians, thus providing the impetus for this chapter. Moreover, a continued discussion of holistic models of ministry and evangelism based in faithful scriptural exegesis and theological reflection needs to take place.

The traditionally polarized situation between verbal proclamation and social action within the field of evangelism has its historical and theological roots in the late nineteenth century, culminating in the early twentieth-century fundamentalist-modernist split within evangelicalism.[7] Although a simplification of the issues, this split can be described as generally representing the separation of verbal proclamation of the gospel from social justice activities.[8] In the latter decades of the twentieth century, literature addressing the theology and practice of evangelism as well as ecumenical international gatherings, such as the World Council of Churches,[9] began to reflect a reconvergence of this polarization. Influences enabling this reconvergence of verbal proclamation with social action and greater attention to holistic evangelism include the growing number of third-world churches and the significance of liberation theology in ecumenical conversations.

An interesting dynamic emerges in that those invested in the verbal proclamation of the gospel, most often Western and especially North Amer-

ican Christians, seem to listen more closely to, and are usually deeply challenged by, third-world arguments from Latin America, Africa, and Asia based
in liberation theology. However, similar themes of liberation, namely black
and womanist theologies, within the North American context are less often
cited by Western scholars addressing the theology and practice of evangelism.[10] This section will explore areas of coherence shared by current scholarship addressing the theology and practice of evangelism, specifically Orlando
Costas and David Bosch,[11] with James Cone's work. Black liberation and
womanist theology's sources of scripture, tradition, and contextualization in
the life and ministry of the church mirror methodologies in the field of evangelism that also rely on the study of biblical and theological models for the
church's practice of evangelistic ministry.

Literature demonstrating the reconvergence of verbal proclamation and
social action provides the best examples of coherence as a result of similar,
although distinct,[12] influences of liberation theology. Among the wide variety of writers on the theology and practice of evangelism, David Bosch and
Orlando Costas are the most clearly influenced by liberation theology, with
Bosch articulating with precision the role of black liberation theology in relation to mission and evangelism. Although others argue for the holistic practice of evangelism grounded in scriptural and theological study, there is a
pressing need for continued consideration of black liberation and womanist
theologies within the field of the theology and practice of evangelism.

David Bosch's seminal text *Transforming Mission: Paradigm Shifts in Theology of Mission,* meticulously critiques the various paradigms within the theology and practice of mission and evangelism. Included in his study is a
treatment of "Mission as Liberation": "The theology of liberation is a multifaceted phenomenon, manifesting itself as black, Hispanic and Amerindian
theologies in the United States, as Latin American theology, as feminist theology, South African black theology, and various analogous theological
movements in other parts of Africa, Asia, and the South Pacific."[13] Bosch
makes the point of including within liberation theology not only perspectives from Latin America but also those based in black theology from the
North American and South African contexts, maintaining the central theme
of "preferential option for the poor." He states: "The practice of racism is a
form of poverty inflicted on people (and, of course, those racially discriminated against are often also materially poor). In this respect, black theology—
as the North American and South African rendition of liberation theology—is
a situational application of the 'preferential option for the poor.'"[14] Parallel to

Cone, Bosch acknowledges the tremendous challenge to the understanding and praxis of ministry and mission arising from liberation and black theologies based on Jesus' ministry with the poor.[15] According to Cone, "How can Christian theology truly speak of the hope of Jesus Christ, unless that hope begins and ends with the liberation of the poor in the social existence in which theology takes shape?"[16]

Additionally, Bosch, with Cone and other liberation theologians, does not exclude God's love for those not oppressed by systemic poverty, but realizes a distinct conversion experience from that of the oppressed: "In their case [the non-poor], however, a different kind of conversion is called for, which would include admitting complicity in the oppression of the poor and a turning from the idols of money, race, and self-interest. This is needed not only because they have been acting unethically, but because they have, through their 'pseudo-innocence' actually denied themselves access to knowledge."[17] Cone also expresses the necessary role of this multifaceted conversion for the privileged oppressors. "The only way people can enhance their vision of the universal is to break out of their cultural and political boxes and encounter another reality. They must be challenged to take seriously another value system."[18]

Bosch's contribution to the field of evangelism is unique as a result of his articulation of black liberation theology as a significant influence for the theology and practice of mission and evangelism. Orlando Costas also presents strong arguments, like Bosch, for the implications of liberation theology from a Latin American perspective upon the theology and practice of evangelism. However, although Costas's biblical and theological models parallel many of Cone's assertions, Costas's Latin American perspective speaks only indirectly to the implications of race for the field of evangelism in North America.

Costas's *Liberating News* expresses the importance of holistic evangelism in the context of the theological model of the trinity. According to Costas, "Evangelization implies living in obedience to God's kingdom in such a way that one becomes a herald of good news and an agent of transformation in any human situation, but particularly in those situations in which there is a threat against life, and injustice and oppression are suffered."[19] Costas considers biblical models of contextual evangelization that locate the communication of the good news from the periphery. "This perspective implies returning the evangelistic ministry to the grassroots of the church and establishing a preferential option for the marginalized of society."[20] Costas's arguments for contextualized evangelization parallel similar statements by Cone. According to Cone, "Christ is not a man for all people; he is a man for oppressed people whose identity is made known in and through their liberation."[21] Cone argues similarly to Costas for the reinterpretation of scripture and theology and therefore the participation in the kingdom of God, although Cone is located specifically within the North American context and includes the perspective of black North American Christians.

> The New Testament message of God's love to man is still embedded in thought-forms totally alien to blacks whose life experiences are unique to themselves. The message is presented to blacks as if they shared the white cultural tradition. We still talk of salvation in white terms, love with a Western perspective, and thus never ask the question, What are the theological implications of God's love for the black man in America?[22]

Both Costas and Cone argue for an appropriate tension between universality and particularity that disallows a misconstruing of universality into a means of oppressive cultural imperialism.

From this brief examination of Bosch's and Costas's work in light of Cone's, several lessons emerge for the theology and practice of evangelism. The importance of biblical exegesis and the realization of the significance of Jesus' ministry with the poor present substantial implications for theology and the practice of evangelism that must reconsider the role of the marginalized in the contemporary Christian church. Implications for reconsidering soteriology also emerge as a result of black liberation and womanist theology. Surprisingly, few studies of the theology and practice of evangelism acknowledge contributions from theological reflection that take seriously issues of race, class, and gender. Carlyle Fielding Stewart also provides significant contributions to the discourse on evangelistic ministry from and to the African American perspective.[23] From a community development perspective, John Perkins also addresses the importance of holistic evangelism in light of issues of race and class.[24] Other scholars such as Mortimer Arias, Ronald Sider, Ben Campbell Johnson, and Donald Moberg present helpful arguments that seem to respond to learning from black and womanist theologies for the holistic embodiments of evangelistic ministries based on scriptural exegesis and theological study.[25] As embodied in womanist theology, issues requiring attention within the field of the theology and practice of evangelism include race, gender, and class.[26] The literature in the field of evangelism is predominantly male and European with few exceptions, although this is steadily changing. Attention to issues of race, class, and gender, particularly multiculturalism, continues to grow, although there remains a need for serious scholarship and attention to black and womanist theologies grounded in scripture and theology for the development of evangelistic ministry.[27]

A Biblical and Theological Evangelistic Model

How do we reconstruct a biblical and theological model for evangelistic ministry that embodies the accountability, lessons learned, and holistic faithfulness demanded by black liberation and womanist theologies? The need for this task of reconstructing an evangelistic model for ministry is apparent throughout Cone's writing and in the scarcity of similar theological reflection that considers the oppressive issues of race, class, and gender in the field of evangelism. According to Cone, "Whatever the exegesis of Scripture and tradition one may advocate, one fact is certain: When a particular interpretation of Scripture benefits people who hold positions of power, it can never be the gospel of Jesus."[28] Cone reminds the Christian community that "theology functions within the Church. Its task is to make sure that the 'church' is the Church. The mission of the Church is to announce and act out the gospel it has received."[29] Cone's statement illumines the holistic nature of the mission of the church, and therefore evangelistic ministry, as both announcement and action of the gospel. This holism is further conceptualized by Cone in light of accountability to the failure of Christians to live out the mission of the church.

> Authentic living according to the Spirit means that one's will becomes God's will, one's actions become God's action. It could be that many will be excluded because their motives were ill founded. And this may mean that God is not necessarily at work in those places where the Word is truly preached and the sacraments are duly administered (as Reformation theologians defined the Church), but where the naked are clothed, the sick are visited, and the hungry are fed.[30]

Cone's critiques clarify the inability of Euro-Americans in North America to embody their Christian faith holistically. "What is strange, though perhaps understandable, is the silence of American theology regarding God's revelation and the oppressed of the land."[31] By truncating and/or spiritualizing scriptural and theological imperatives, much of North American white Protestant evangelicalism seems to have fallen into the systemic sinfulness of racism.

> The sin of American theology is that it has spoken without passion. It has failed miserably in relating its work to the oppressed in society by refusing to confront the structures of this nation with the evils of racism.[32]

> White thought on the Christian view of salvation was largely spiritual and sometimes rational, but usually separated from the concrete struggle of freedom in this world. Black thought was largely eschatological and never abstract, but usually related to their struggle against earthly oppression.[33]

The following brief discussion will explore biblical and theological models for evangelistic ministry arising out of black liberation and womanist theologies that begin to address the complicity of the North American white Protestant evangelical church in sins of racism, classism, and sexism. Pertinent biblical models prevalent in black liberation theology from both the Hebrew scriptures and the New Testament will be discussed, specifically the Exodus narrative and Luke's account of the inaugural address for Jesus' ministry with its jubilary themes. Additional discourse from black liberation theology will inform the theological models for evangelistic ministry based on Jesus' incarnational ministry and participation in the kingdom of God.

Cone repeatedly refers to the significance of the Exodus narrative as a scriptural source for black theology. "Historically, the story began with the Exodus. The Exodus was the decisive event in Israel's history, because through it Yahweh revealed himself as the Savior of an oppressed people."[34] The Exodus and liberation by Yahweh of the people of Israel from slavery in Egypt become the foundation of the covenant invitation. To accept the covenant is not only to live into the freedom granted to Israel but also in obedience to Yahweh. "The covenant not only places upon Israel the responsibility of accepting the absolute sovereignty of Yahweh as defined in the first commandment; it also requires Israel to treat the weak in her midst as Yahweh has treated her."[35] The Hebrew scriptures in general and the Exodus in particular carry significant implications for the mission of the church and evangelistic ministry, as a result of Yahweh's faithfulness to the oppressed. The theme of God's faithfulness to the oppressed continues through the wisdom and prophetic literature and then in the incarnational ministry of Jesus Christ as described in the gospels.

An additional theme of the priority granted to justice for the oppressed in Hebrew scripture is the year of the Lord's favor, or Jubilee, to which Jesus alludes in his inaugural address demonstrated in Luke 4:16-30. The year of Jubilee based on the sabbatical laws of Exodus, specifically Exod. 23:10-14, with their humanitarian motive, combines that humanitarianism with the covenantal obligations of the people of Yahweh to Yahweh and one another. Jesus' ministry continues the jubilary witness to God's partiality for the oppressed, by including the Jubilee year's central themes of liberation and restoration. Although Cone does not specifically discuss the implications of the year of Jubilee for Jesus' ministry and initiation of the kingdom of God with his mention of Luke 4:16-17,[36] the parallel themes of liberation from oppression for the economically poor from Isaiah and the Hebrew scriptures remain prevalent.

> The scandal is that the gospel means liberation, that this liberation comes to the poor, and that it gives them the strength and the courage to break the conditions of servitude. This is what the Incarnation means. God in Christ comes to the weak and the helpless, and becomes one with them, taking their condition of oppression as his own and thus transforming their slave-existence into a liberated existence.[37]

Cone provides a christological reconsideration of scripture and therefore Christian praxis based on the experience of the black community in North America. "Jesus was not an abstract Word of God, but God's Word made flesh who came to set the prisoner free. . . . While white preachers and theologians often defined Jesus Christ as a spiritual Savior, the deliverer of people from sin and guilt, black preachers were unquestionably historical."[38] Cone's reconsideration of Jesus' ministry with the oppressed requires that all those who claim to follow Jesus Christ participate with the oppressed in the struggle for liberation: "According to the New Testament, the kingdom is a historical event. It is what happens to a person when his being is confronted with the reality of God's historical liberation of the oppressed. To see the kingdom is to see a happening, and we are thus placed in a situation of decision—we say either yes or no to the liberation struggle."[39] The decision to participate in the struggle for liberation with the oppressed then constitutes a similar response to that of Israel in covenant with Yahweh following the Exodus. This decision, like adherence to the year of Jubilee, responds to Yahweh's act of liberation in Jesus Christ through acts of liberation with our brothers and sisters in Jubilee forms of shared food, redistribution of capital, and the remission of debts.[40]

In addition to Jesus' ethical emphasis on the physical and economic liberation of the oppressed, the Jubilee was also meant as a metaphorical announcement of the kingdom of God. However, this did not preclude the necessity of participation in the ethical and social implications, but rather incorporated liberation from physical and economic oppression with liberation from sin and death in the context of restored covenantal relationship with God through Jesus Christ. Although Cone stresses historical dimensions of Christology and implications for justice in the contemporary church and society, he does not limit the struggle for justice to history alone. "While God's freedom for the poor is not *less than* the liberation of slaves from bondage (Exodus), yet it is *more than* that historical freedom."[41] Cone avoids a truncated understanding of salvation, thereby maintaining the holistic nature of God's liberating action in Jesus Christ. According to Cone, "Christ's salvation is liberation; there is no liberation without Christ. Both meanings are inherent in the statement that Jesus Christ is the ground of human liberation. Any statement that divorces salvation from liberation or makes human freedom independent of divine freedom must be rejected."[42]

Based on the Exodus narrative and Jesus' inaugural address described in Luke, the theology and practice of evangelistic ministry should demonstrate awareness of the social context of the marginalized and work toward embodying God's liberation from physical, economic, and spiritual bondage. Jesus' ministry with the poor in the context of the kingdom of God witnesses to the significance of social and political justice as well as spiritual and individual salvation. The scriptural models of the Exodus and Jesus' incarnational ministry provide the basis for a more holistic understanding of salvation that challenges the contemporary church to address issues of race, class, and gender that cannot be separated from spiritual wholeness and right relationship with God. Through the power and guidance of the Holy Spirit, Christians of various racial, cultural, economic, and gender perspectives must dialogue and work together to realize the kingdom of God initiated by

Jesus' ministry.[43] Evangelistic ministry that does not take into account this holistic scriptural understanding of Christology, soteriology, and ecclesiology informed by black liberation and womanist theologies truncates the realization of the kingdom of God in the world.

9 | Black Theology and the White Church in the Third Millennium
Like a Thief in the Night

Jim Perkinson

In the spring of 1997, in Union City, New Jersey, an actor named Desi Arnaz Giles received death threats by phone for daring to play Jesus in the Park Theater Performing Arts Center's annual production of the Passion play. His offense? Giles is black. The following weekend he played the devil in a musical in Plainfield with nary a peep in protest. Together these two rather wildly disparate responses to a single person in a succession of roles plot what W. E. B. DuBois once called a "half-named problem" on the horizon of this country, like a coordinate on a map.[1] Or more accurately, they focus vision like the crosshairs of a gun-sight.

In the public sphere in turn-of-the-millennium North America—despite the civil rights movement and affirmative action, despite anti-racist educational initiatives and multicultural political pedagogies—portraying Jesus as black remains a telling litmus test. Juxtaposing dark-skinned humanity and light-bearing divinity is oxymoronic in the culture at large—representing, at best, a peculiar community's peculiar need to affirm itself, or at worst, a terrifying obscenity. On the other hand, combining ebony and numinosity in the key of bedevilment is an old tale, full of woe (and benefits!), leveraging destruction on entire hemispheres and whole continents (and immense wealth for a privileged minority!) over the five-hundred-year progression of this era of history we proudly inhabit as moderns.

Giles-as-Jesus functions as an augury. There is perhaps still no more revealing act of divination in the land of the free and home of the brave than that of linking the hard world of blackness and the holy world of spirit in a single public image. All the demons of night surface howling. In spite of itself, America begins to show.

The Emergence of Black Theology

In 1969, it was the "right on time" genius of James Cone to breathe theological breath into the African bones that littered this country's spiritual (and physical) landscape like a return of the repressed leaping straight out of Ezekiel (Ezekiel 37). Angela Davis and Black Power had certainly put a fist in the air and an Afro in the eye of the camera. And James Brown and the Black Arts Movement had punctuated that epiphany with the unapologetic adjective "Beautiful!" But it was Cone who managed to invoke the most infallible logic of the history. America, from Vespucci on, was the "Land of Biblical Promise" for "Christian" Europe, and its errand-boy "redeemers" thought themselves the closest thing to the second coming that the "new" world would ever witness short of the actuality. Colonial whiteness quickly burned color off the map, buried red in the soil, buried black in the soul, and paraded pallor as the new truth of everything. Lightness was the mode of meaning, the sign of salvation, the transparency of right, the justification of might.[2] All else was a lie, a mode of evil.

And then came Cone, invoking Martin Luther King Jr. and Malcolm X, Marcus Garvey and Harriet Tubman, Henry McNeal Turner and Fannie Lou Hamer, and hosts upon hosts of anonymous elocutors of bright darkness; he gave them all a high-pitched, trenchant purchase on the map of the present. Not just Cone himself spoke, but big-hearted, big-eyed, big-voiced, sharp-tongued, large-minded strugglers with death, and little-educated, little-voiced, heavy-lidded, shy-tongued callers of survival tunes, and leather-handed, lantern-jawed connivers for life, and brokers of root-remedies and sitters of babies fighting for breath, and mamas of families large enough to fill entire phone books, and papas of pickers of entire fields of cotton who still haven't been paid even up to today, and intellectuals and mathematicians and inventors and morticians and hair stylists and novelists and *griot* crooners and blues bawlers and jazz-note rippers of infinity.[3] For various reasons, among many voices, over much time, Cone's take-no-prisoners rhetoric of a black revelation suddenly caught fire in 1969 like a bush in a desert. And it still burns. And many feet have felt the heat. And many more should.

But Cone's importance on the small playing field of public theology today is not simply that he managed to mutter the moan. Indeed, he doesn't mutter, as far as I can tell. But his shout has not been mere bombast nor has it been without back talk. Without moving away from his challenge, he has allowed his own voice to be filled *with* others and to be succeeded, and even exceeded, *by* others.[4] While maintaining the claim that because Jesus was Jewish in first-century Palestine he must be black in twentieth-century North America, Cone has allowed himself to be chastened that Jesus might also be a "she" who is red or yellow or brown, and lower class and lesbian, and even communal and perhaps non-Christian in any obvious sense of the term.[5] At least that seems to be the import of his acknowledgment of "second genera-tion" critiques of his position, which began to emerge with the Theology in the Americas Conference in Detroit in 1975 and have continued in the Ecu-menical Association of Third World Theologians (EATWOT) and numerous other forums ever since. Blackness must be itself unpacked in the cross-hatching of over-determinations specified by the categories of class, gender, ethnicity, sexual orientation, religion, and culture.

And yet blackness remains a lodestone of the question of who God might be in America today. And liberation remains a necessary qualifier for resis-tance to white American accumulation of wealth and power at the expense of so many peoples and life forms around the globe. The black theology of lib-eration is indeed only one particular project of one particular social position in the world of globalizing capital, but its claim to universal significance con-tinues to drill ear holes in a few heads, one of which is my own.[6]

The Intransigence of the White Church

But unfortunately—and fortunately—I am not the white church. The white church would seem to be an as-yet "unmoved mover" before the prophetic bombast of black liberation theology. (Or perhaps it is not unmoved—per-haps we must understand an Aryan Nations–tutored Timothy McVeigh as representing one kind of response to the percolating influences of a black the-ology politics, and Amadou Diallo's killers and their mainstream supporters as another.) But in any case, any generalization about some ideal figment called the "white church" is necessarily a caricature. What is the white church? Or more to the point where is it and what does it serve? Arguably, as a generality, "the" white church is a demographically defined institutional preserve, full of competing discourses and contradictory practices.

Undoubtedly in some of its nooks and crannies, there are some, like myself, who have listened to black liberation theology with a mixture of terror and ecstasy, hearing new depths of humanity sounded out in themselves, finding the mirror suddenly disclosing an alien predator self who must be owned, embraced, repented, disciplined, humbled, and thrown into a lifetime of struggle against itself. Undoubtedly there are some who have come to recognize there is no salvation for whites as "white"—that the fact/fiction of "whiteness" as a form of property, as a claim to status, as a presumption of privilege, as the enshrinement of entitlement, as the climate of a courtroom, as the name of a suburb, as the imposition of a cultural norm, as the posture of a badge bearing a gun, indeed as the sexed and gendered prerogative of dominating power—that that kind of whiteness must be fought against for any light-skinned seekers of the wholeness an olive-skinned Jewish rabbi might offer.[7]

But all appeals to Gallup aside, my experience is that such a churched whiteness is fairly scarce. And *mutatis mutandis,* then, white church response to black liberation theology might best be summed up as "nil." Nihilist engenderments of despair among urban youth of color around the country (like where I have lived in inner-city Detroit for more than fifteen years) has as its unobvious correlate in the gated community of wealth a great huge "nil." Urban ire and suburban ignorance are reciprocal effects of a single system, as indeed are suburban affluence and inner-city effluence. Just check the local bank's ledger or the waste manager's route. And thus black liberation theology has, as one of its primary axes of accountability today, the unmasking of the interdependent linkage between those two disparate and desperate contexts. But the church enclosed in middle-class upward mobility and transnational corporate mentality has never heard of black liberation theology and would not recognize it as either "theological" or "liberative" if it did.

And that is the first and major lesson that such a confrontation would need to occasion. What I take to be the first and major challenge that black theology offers to the country at large is theological notice about an all too physiological war. However small the gestures of resistance, however unorganized and quickly co-opted the counterpoint, "blackness" marks a place in our society where a war is continuing to be waged. It is a war over resources and opportunities, privileges and powers, profits and prisons, genes and genomes.[8] It is as close as the latest stereotype that silently colors my own most recent thought.[9] It is as broad and thorough-going as the entire surface of the planet and who has access to what in any given community. And it is a battlefield where the identity of God is at stake and the practicality of freedom is in question. It is a struggle that continues to accumulate wealth and power and status on the white side of the line of color at the expense of the colored side of the line of whiteness, even as we speak.[10] Yes, blackness itself is a profoundly contested and multiply configured space of identity and meaning on this field of coercion.[11] It is not simply homogeneous. But it does designate one of the few places in which the reality of America can be adequately discerned theologically today. It is not the only one, but it remains a necessary touchstone for every other claim to augur spirit and embody faithfulness.

Among the many dimensions of color present in the country today—in the midst of Chicano brown power, Filipina yellow power, Lakota red power, Chaldean olive power—the colors and features that the dominant culture continues to invest with ideological notions of African-based blackness still mark the point furthest out. Yes, the west coast, the south border, and the warehouse of the unwanted aged called Florida are witnessing the emergence of a new hegemonic other.[12] Yes, even whiteness has its own internal indices of repudiation such as "hillbilly," "trash," "red neck," "blue collar," and "racist."[13] Yes, color is not the only coordinate of concern. But blackness historically anchors the bottom, and today, in dominant culture discourse, it continues to inform the deep meaning of "urban dweller," "drug-seller," "gangbanger," "crime-committer," "welfare cheater," "sidewalk hustler," "thief," "thug," "mugger," "menace," "ex-con," "crack-user," "cop-killer," "copulator," "corn-rowed conniver," "dread-locked gold-digger," "beggar," and "bitch." And thus it also continues to mark the crossroads of consternation in our culture that Spirit, again and again, is forced to occupy as Calvary.

And thus the question remains alive and unanswered in the belly of the white beast: what would it mean for a white man to be saved by a black messiah? And the gender marking and lack of marking are both explicit. The top of the pyramid is still male and macho. The direction from which wholeness is offered is still from below. The center remains an inevitable effect of capitalism that is masked in "white out." The periphery continues to be organized for the eye (by that center) as a pejorative perception of darkness. And white women are played in the middle, as the stakes and the buffer between. Ultimately white male power fantasizes and fears blackness as its sexual *superior*. That is why so much of our history is about symbolic and literal castration of black male bodies and rape of female ones (of all colors, including white). And it is not at all surprising, then, that much of our social stratification—from board room to bedroom to welfare institution to incarceral industry—implements that racialized, patriarchal terror.

In such a context, the messiah could emerge as either "prison-destined man" or "poverty-detained woman." Or vice versa. Or more to the point, as a messianic community of both.[14] And it could comport in almost any shade of opaque. But unquestionably, its most potent apocalyptic appearance in this country still would show itself today as ashe' eyed. Shiny-skinned. Blue-black toned. Mellow boned. Loud-talkin'. Proud walkin'. Chitlin' eatin'. And infamous.

Whether a white church is capable of the kind of conversion such a summons would entail is beyond knowing. But it is not likely—like getting into the kingdom if the price is giving up one's wealth was not likely in Jesus' day (Mark 10:17-31). The real conundrum in the characterization offered above, however, lies in the presumed subjunctive verb mode. Cone's claim is not that this is where God *would* enter our history. Rather, he would claim this is where God now *is*.[15] For all of us. What if that is so?

Indeed—novelty of novelties!—what if salvation actually is all about salvation—that is to say, that there indeed is no wholeness at any level without wholeness at every level? What if, in fact, we *are* interlinked in such a way that the first world *cannot* become healthy without the two-thirds world also becoming healthy? Not as a matter of *pre*scription, but as simple *de*scription? What if the suburb *cannot* quiet its angst without the city finding answer to its anger? (What if, therapy or Prozac to the good, depression and bipolarity are really largely symptoms of the predatory "disconnect" between these communities and real relief possible only through a Jubilee-like intervention freeing financial and social capital for genuinely open circulation?) What if the environment cannot recycle itself into renewal without humanity disciplining itself into reciprocity with its plant brothers and animal sisters in an economy of cycles and seasons? What if white people are in fact dependent upon the quality of their relationship with peoples of color for any claim to a hearing in the court of heaven? (It is surely "court" that is the spiritual destiny of color privilege.) Proud posturing of incarnate whiteness in St. Peter's dock may discover, too late, the head of justice is as unmoved as a dreadlock, and the verdict as hot as a burning spear.

This is the first meaning of black theology for the white church: a gift of anticipation, the taste of judgment ahead of time, before the identity completely sets in, programs the DNA, shouts its sin in red letters dripping black blood, and white people become modern-day Cain trying to leave the scene and discovering it is the very ground they run on that bears witness to what drained from Abel's veins. The white church is a church living largely in denial of a judgment already delivered. If so, white theology must learn the language of a cry being spoken against it[16] in voices that rage to the beat of Puff Daddy or Queen Latifa as well as quietly articulate "Lord, hear our prayer," that may speak Xhosa rather than quarterly earnings, indeed, that chirp and bray and growl and groan as well as wag the tongue of an upright, two-legged creature.

The Insouciance of White Theology

But here, we must nuance the display. White feminist theology—in many quarters—has already begun the hard work of initiation.[17] In early years, it too quickly claimed commonality across the line of color and found itself rebuked. But it has learned, and grown, and sharpened its own tongue. White male theology, on the other hand, has largely played the card of silent rebuff—here and there, voicing a convoluted acquiescence, but rarely taking up the task ready to lose its position or its pay. The juggernaut of the situation can only be jiggered for so long: in a finite universe, justice restored for the oppressed means real loss (and the possibility of a different kind of gain) on the side of the oppressors.

White male theology must learn the lesson of Nicodemus (John 3:1-15). It may come to black theology *incognito,* in the dark of night, wanting to take back to the Sanhedrin a little bit of insight. But it will find itself told that nothing less than rebirth will do—an arduous return back where it came from, back inside its own genealogy, shrinking at every step, back through its history to the womb whence it first emerged, wet and sticky and ugly, there to begin relearning how to crawl. Anything less is mere fiddling and misses the depths of the dis-ease.

And this I take to be the second lesson of the hour: It is not enough for white male theology to learn the meaning of its own unconscious whiteness. It must learn that the very discourse of theology is itself not innocent. Here, black theology has had to confront its own need for exorcism.[18] The demon of disciplinary authority is a second-level principality, not easily augured, exorcised, and sent packing. White supremacy has insinuated itself inside the very text of Christianity, inside the father's voices, inside the *magnum opae* of the entire litany of modern witness, from Descartes to De Man, from Luther to Lacan, from Kant to Kung. When consciousness itself is infected, what is the recourse?

Black theology offers a clue. The issue is not simply the book one reads or teaches. It is as deep as the body one inhabits. Michel Foucault is right, even in his own privileged blindness. The soul is a product of a discipline brought to bear on a skin surface and a posture. Sovereignty has been replaced today by internalized surveillance; the technology of control is not just the whip or baton, but the eye within.[19] Gaining critical perspective is tricky—a matter of thinking new thoughts by becoming a different body. But slave-laboring women and tenant-farming men already knew the trickster remedy two hundred years before.[20] Their bodies were not just property to be deprecated and depreciated.[21] On the sly, in the bush arbor or the clapboard hovel, those bodies became canvases.[22] And their own minds were the brush. The paint was sound and fury, conserved in the tenseness of a muscle, the bob of a head, a gesture thick with resurrection reversals—or with revenge, conserved until the right moment.[23] Entire histories were articulated in small, syncopated shuffle-steps, antiphonal nods, the drawl of a vowel spoken with five meanings in its timbre. Resistance constrained even to the tiniest of cracks in domination's aim at totality is resistance alive and germinating.

But here again, it is largely the women who teach the men—like Delores Williams teaching James Cone that Hagar's un-exodus-like return to the primal family of faith was liberation in the key of survival.[24] But can a theology baptized white and male ever learn even to recognize such sophistication, much less be taught by it? Or has the spike of capitalism's "will to measure" gone too far into the skull bone?

I speak now as one who labors to address other white males about our ongoing (white male) accumulation of fiscal and social indebtedness—1 to 5 trillion dollars for unpaid slave efforts, perhaps 2 trillion more for Jim Crow wage work and industrial extractions, all of which continue to circulate primarily in restricted sectors of privilege in our society.[25] And that is not even trying to calculate the psychological bill for an average of 250 incidents of recognized racist aggressions per black person per year for each lifetime now (and that is only a moderate "middle-class" black estimate).[26] Or the bill for the looming present of a for-profit prison-industrial complex, arresting dark young skin with virtual impunity (when it doesn't kill the arrestee first),[27] integrating itself into our information-age economy as the largest single employer in the country today, sending its stock prices soaring while producing, as its necessary commodity, a criminalized body of cheap, captive labor, to continue the one-sided accumulation.[28]

In this view of our history, whiteness in general and white maleness in particular are living forms of profound social indebtedness. How much do we owe? How can we ever pay up? Can we ever come to repentance and gain genuine self-knowledge under such a burden? But a caution is in order when I address my own community this way. The temptation to rest with guilt here is just that—one more tactic of avoidance that works to white benefit. The task is to own the legitimate message of that emotion—as long as real violation continues, real guilt should and will remain!—and pass through it to action. There is quite enough work to be done in the struggle against racism for white people to be engaged lifelong, alongside of (and accountable to) people of color, initiating resistance to the forces of subordination, defying the odds, facing the anguish, bearing the resulting scars. But the task is not reciprocal. Whiteness does not function in the same way blackness does. The vocation for white people involves a threefold process of ongoing exorcism, initiation, and apostasy.

The Possibility of a White Christian Vocation: Apostasy

Ultimately, the stakes are those of becoming *apostate*—like the early Christians vis-à-vis the Roman pantheon—with respect to the conforming powers that be. The real *sacramentum,* the oath of loyalty for whites, is to become a *militus Christi* for life, struggling spiritually and materially against the tribal god of white supremacy. As such, the task is ongoing, relentless, guerrilla apostasy from that god and the social order it governs. Implied is a recognition that the struggle is about the way a *cultural discourse* functions ideologically and spiritually to carry out and justify a *political economy.* Underclass-fracturing *racialization* serves to implement overclass-solidifying *racism.* Which is to say, the ongoing struggle is over resources, power, and status. For whites, the implication clearly means serious alienation from the white birthright. It entails laboring in the public sphere to unmask the way race is made to function as an arbiter of residential mobility, an organizer of educational opportunity, a prescriptor of promotional possibility, a policer of property and privilege and profit. Inevitably, it means agitating against the enclosure of accumulated wealth in privatized pleasurescapes of gated whiteness and for a different circulation of everything. Pushed to the limit, it could even mean martyrdom. (The apostle Paul, after all, ultimately paid for his championing of the rights of Gentiles to full inclusion in the economy of salvation with his life.) But this overarching characterization of an anti-racist white witness rests on two ongoing conditions of possibility.

The Possibility of a White Christian Vocation: Exorcism

One of the preconditions for such a lifelong vocation to struggle is a necessary *conversatio*—a conversion of life that begins with a spiritual breakout from white supremacy, experienced as a form of *exorcism* that carves down below the brain and consciousness of the problem to its *sedimentation* in the psyche and its *surveillance* in the body. For white males especially, this means undergoing a profound "breakup" of the way power and perception, entitlement and presentiment, are entirely entangled with each other, and (re)discovering other forms of embodiment with which to identify. Exorcism implies an intervention that aims at prying the basic structure of subjectivity loose from its presupposed center to become itself an object of choice—a conscious possibility of either "identification" or "dis-identification." It is a matter of recovering a body from a discourse, not of purifying a person from an influence.

Once we as whites have had the kind of "significant emotional event" indicative of having actually encountered "blackness" at a level deeper than just our eyeballs (often through experiencing ourselves as either the object of black anger or the subject of black humor), two responses generally present themselves. Either we can reconsolidate the safety (for ourselves) and savagery (for others) of white privilege, power, and position, securing our body in the equivalent of a secured enclave (suburb, school, workplace, etc.) whose meanings, methods of ingress and egress, and modes of interaction we control. Or we can embrace the abrasion as an invitation to self-knowledge and allow ourselves to be initiated into the deeper meaning of our own history, as we shall see below. In this latter possibility, we would begin to confront the degree to which white supremacy is a form of cultural habituation naturalized as a patriarchal body. Until we (white males and females both, though differently) understand "in our pelvises" the way the threat of blackness colors our erotic fantasies and constrains our romantic insecurities, we will not yet have gotten to the real roots of racism.

Once confronted at a level that begins to be exorcistic, however, we do not thereby cease to be vulnerable to the influences of the selves we had been before. Racism is not simply an individual affliction but a pervasive environment and an invasive ecology that continually insinuate themselves in spite of personal intention. But such a confrontation does enable us to begin to intuit the depth at which we have been conformed, and to entertain the combination of "agony and ecstasy" required to expand the "field of our embodiment" beyond simply "being white." Confronting white supremacy in oneself, sooner or later, means exploring the possibility of learning to speak in more than just one voice, to express more than just one rhythm, to reiterate more than just one culture. Such an exercise necessarily also means expanding the social field in which such a body moves, of course.

Another way of underscoring the need for this kind of "exorcistic break" is to suggest that race discourse is modernity's own unique form of *witchcraft practice*. It is the colonial creation of white supremacy, which was itself the offspring of Christian supremacy. In the encounter with its "others," Euro-centric Christian arrogance quickly attached its own sense of religio-cultural superiority to its skin surface and began to impose its own religio-cultural meanings of blackness onto subject populations as a justification for eviscerating conquered souls and eating conquered substance ("call a dog mangy and you must kick it; call it meat and you have dinner"). *Imposed blackness* within this scheme became an occulting term that reflexively mystified light skin as a form of political economy entitlement and fetishized dark skin as a "divine/demonic" other, simultaneously Eros and curse. On the other hand, over time the imposed meanings of darkness were wrestled into a tactics of resistance in slave quarters and suffering ghettos. Over centuries, various forms of *expressive blackness* began to emerge as the collective creation of the subjugated until (in the United States) that blackness was publicly asserted in the 1960s Black Power movement as a kind of *counter-shamanism,* soliciting healing through symbolic combat and ritual reversal. And not surprisingly, a third moment of this unequal war of wills has emerged in the phenomenon of *reappropriated blackness.* Here, we find white supremacy's "counter-counter" tactic, skimming cultural creativity off of the surface of subjugated communities to try to remedy its own inner emptiness, but once again losing that (stolen) substance in the destructive impulse to consume (as in the current commodification of rap to sell almost everything). As we shall see, the undoing of white bedevilment does, indeed, lie in the direction of substantive intercourse with "others," but under an entirely different sign from the dollar.

The Possibility of a White Christian Vocation: Initiation

The other precondition for the lifelong engagement against white supremacy is a necessary *transfiguratio*—a discovery of a different kind of power by learning from people of color and women and people of other sexual orientations. This involves *initiation*—baptism—under the hands of a wilderness/wildness figure from the margins like John the Baptist. The world of color is not just to be "understood," but undergone. Understanding something implies just that—standing under it, giving it power over oneself. More graphically for white males, it means learning how to challenge "white supremacist capitalist patriarchy"[29] not just cognitively, not only politically, not simply in terms of a different circulation of resources, but also at the level of its cultural *habitus* and spiritual *incubus.*

White supremacy is one of the preeminent "principalities and powers" of our time. James Cone provocatively began his life's work by suggesting that black *power*—not just black freedom—was the message of Jesus Christ to modern North America.[30] One way of reading that claim is to imagine that behind the veil of everyday appearances, at the level where spiritual forces and cultural climates compete and war with each other, a partial transfiguration was accomplished by black spirituality and black activism. The principality of white supremacy was wrestled into yielding a different kind of potency; a power of oppression was partially tamed and forced to become a power of creativity.

Saying such is not to say black power is simply a refraction of white power—it remains irreducibly unique and nonderivative as a historical force and a collective impetus. But it is to say that "the master's tools have been regularly used against the master's house" with great resourcefulness and prodigious innovation. Neither is this evaluation to be dismissed as romanticization. Black Power as a movement certainly had its excesses and immaturities, its foibles and fallacies (not least of which was its sexism and homophobia). It was obviously quickly "decapitated" (by strategic assassinations of some leaders, imprisonments of others, and co-optations of yet others), marginalized and splintered by the reactions (and partial reforms) of the dominant racist order.[31]

But at the level of spirit, it is suggestive to entertain the idea that, among its other accomplishments, the Black Power movement represents a kind of "spiritual judo" exercised on white power, in which the violent energies of a dominating force were identified, rebuked, raided, and ritually reconfigured into an aggressive and assertive counterpower that has not ceased to have potent effects in the social order.[32] Not least of those effects have been the unmasking of liberal white "color-blindness" as itself demonic and an insistence, in kind, that specific differences between ethno-cultural groups be recognized and valorized. Not only were black people to be embraced as legal, political, and economic equals, but recognized as cultural, spiritual, and social innovators of "otherness." That otherness is not and never has been either equitable with or answerable to whiteness.

And it is just this innovated otherness that represents a paradoxical rebuke and invitation to white people in general and white males in particular. Black power is a resource that white people committed to lifelong anti-racist struggle dare not touch—and dare not *not* touch. It is not enough—it will not be enough over the long haul—for whites (merely!) to work for equality for people of color. The reality of what is—in terms of social mobility, economic wherewithal, cultural norms, and so forth—in our day in fact remains largely an expression of white power. If white people are going to labor for a different kind of world, part of the labor that must be undergone is that of being themselves reconstituted in a different form of power. Empowerment for struggle is crucial. But so is the question of whose power and what kind of power. How anti-racist whites guard against simply one more time reproducing another realization of the power of whiteness—precisely *in* their anti-racist activities—is no mean question. Black power stands out before whiteness as an insoluble conundrum that can also offer irreplaceable reflexivity. White people cannot become black. They can, however, in encounters with others in their spiritual and cultural depths, become more than just white.

The trope here is baptism, or initiation. The issue is not just awareness but experimentation with, and *immersion in* and indeed alteration by, subjugated knowledge.[33] Allowing black embodiments of powerful cultural forms to enter into one's own sensibility, to come up inside of one's own body with all the terror that implies, is necessary for the breakup of white hegemony and habituation.[34] Mystics have sometimes said "it is not possible to perceive in another reality until one has acted in that other reality." At stake here is not just a new cognitive awareness and objectivity about the situation of race, but a new passionate posture and subjectivity founded on a new spiritual interiority.[35] Long-term struggle requires what Bertolt Brecht once called "a long anger." It is a question of allowing a new historical passion to be engendered within oneself that can orient and motivate lifelong combat *because* it taps into currents of vitality that are larger than one's own resolve to remain faithful. As British cultural critic Paul Gilroy has asserted, it is not enough just to be *anti*-racist; there is need to develop more than mere reaction.[36] Expressive black cultures represent a positive and creative articulation of power.[37] The same question emerges with respect to white anti-racist commitment.

What would it take for whites (and especially males) to have formed within themselves the kind of vital ferocity necessary to struggle lifelong against the powers and privileges that whiteness constantly leverages in and around them? The obvious resource is the community that has had no choice about such a struggle. But is it possible for white people to relate to black power in such a way that they are simultaneously warned away from one more gesture of appropriation *and* initiated into their own powers of anti-racist responsibility?

The model here is perhaps analogous to Paul's admonition to the Galatians to submit to a reciprocal and collective gestation process, "until Christ be formed again within them" (Gal. 4:19). Apparently the Christ they thought they had come to know was not the real thing, but a figure and fiction of their own social logic. They had to be "re-incubated" spiritually—forcibly excised from their seductive myth of privilege and pushed back and down into the messy inchoateness of a new birth. They had to learn how to groan again. In the Pauline vision, human groaning opens out into the groan of all of history and time, indeed the very groan and urge of creation itself against bondage, the primal groan of the Spirit over chaos (Rom. 8:12-27; Gen. 1:2). For him, the spirit is a force of creative convulsion, and messianic birth pangs are in evidence everywhere.

What would it take for white "Galatians" today to learn to labor at such a depth? Would it be possible for something like the "agony and ecstasy of Christ inside blackness" to be brought to conception within a white person or community? For white males in particular, "white male pain" is the obvious way into such deeper dimensions of passion incarnate in history. But white male pain is itself a socially produced and mediated sentiment, which feeds on and enforces other forms of socially produced agony (in subjecting women and people of color to its rages and demands, for instance). The problem with much of the men's movement in this country, in focusing on the pain of being male, is that it takes seriously neither pain nor position. Only the top levels of the hierarchy of anguish in our society—only that which is specific to the experience of being a white male—are addressed. And when addressed, solace is quickly sought rather than allowing that pain to become a kind of Dantesque guide to sound out other depths.

In the face of such a failure, baptism is an interesting figure. It invites immersion into the death and resurrection of Christ—but a Christ profoundly incarnate in history. In North American history, that passion, in both of its aspects of agony and overcoming, is nowhere as profound as in black culture. Such is the meaning of Cone's claim that Jesus *must be* black in this country. But baptism then implies that all of us, whites included, are in fact *already* being plunged into blackness as the very condition of our encounter with Christ. To the degree Christ is really being formed in us as North Americans (and not some mythic messiah of our own devising), black pain and power are already at work within us. But are whites capable of letting such a "black passion" live in them, without disingenuously trying to disown their whiteness? Or does white baptism, in fact, only occasion deep interior denial and confusion?

The real task of baptism—its profound initiatory function—is to plunge one into the depths of the world, below words, where experience is not yet colonized entirely by form, to be remade there, in a new form, not controlled by oneself, not beholden to one's own position, not mapped by one's own social programming. It is simultaneously a plunge into the life experience and cultural resistance of those the social order regularly rolls over. As Asian theologian Aloysius Pieris has argued, baptism is double.[38] As exemplified in the life of Jesus, it began in a river and culminated on a hill (Luke 3:15-22; 12:49-53). For him, it was not just a matter of going under the waters and coming up under the dove, but of placing himself *in* the hands of another prophetic leader and of committing himself *to* a social movement already in progress. His immersion designated a lifestyle and exhibited a solidarity. It amounted to a choice about whom he would be willing to die with and what he would die for. Jordan led to Calvary.

But it did so by way of Capernaum. Jesus did not simply study the ethnic and economic and gender wisdom (that is, the black and liberation and feminist theologies) of the peasants and day laborers and bent-over synagogue-goers and uppity sufferers of blood-flows of his day. (Clearly, however, he did deeply imbibe the folk-smarts and arts of resistance of the poor and oppressed he lived among, and regularly offered their actions as examples of faithfulness when instructing his own disciples; see Mark 7:24-30; Luke 9:25-37; 16:1-8; 18:1-8, 9-14.) Rather, he entered into their social circumstance, learned from their cultural experience, and, in challenging their oppressors (his own peer teachers), embraced their political destiny. He allowed his body to be occupied by their energy (the authorities, after all, thought he was "possessed"; Mark 3:20-27; John 8:48). His public discourse was charged with their private anguish (or just how *do* we imagine the emotional tone of his public cursing of the leadership elites? Luke 6:20-26; Matt. 23:13-29). His eloquence was informed with their idiom ("not as the scribes spoke," it says; Mark 1:22). Jesus' admonition to Nicodemus was something he had himself undergone (John 3:1-5). The social immersion he anticipated by way of water he lived out in his flesh, celebrated in his partying, relied on in his politics, and grieved the loss of on the night before the bloodletting (Mark 1:18, 32; 2:31-35; 12:12, 37; Luke 15:1-2; 22:15-16).

Baptism, in this frame, is a plunge not only into the waters of life and death in the abstract, but into the social and existential experience of those around us for whom death is most precipitous and life most precarious. It places the issue of faith on the political and cultural map: it is a matter of allowing one's own experience of embodiment to be accosted by those whose bodies are under assault. It offers wholeness in the key of concreteness. We are drowned in the anguish of the oppressed of our own time and raised in the powers of their particular forms of resistance. Anything less is docetism.[39] If we refuse the social reality, we lose the spiritual efficacy. Until and unless we risk baptism in its most profound political and cultural implications in our own historical setting, we render its eternal possibilities illusory and ourselves impotent. In North America at the millennium, black embodiment of pain and power remains the litmus test of white baptism. Most of us who are pale are hardly even wet yet.

Conclusion

For me, the pivotal issue in white theology's relationship to black and womanist theologies is this latter question of spiritual and emotional empowerment. I regularly drink from those wells not simply as a matter of according them their due hearing. I plunge in rather to rekindle my own outrage and strengthen my own *cour*-rage so that I do not fail to take up my own part in the lifetime of social and spiritual struggle that I believe is the only future worth living for. I grow more and more aware, as the years pass, that the witness to what is indomitable in the human spirit is worldwide, multireligious, polyvocal, many-colored, and ever-surprising. Even as I discern principalities and powers organizing anew in almost unthinkably monstrous modalities today, I also see resistance on the scale of human-sized gestures of joy and defiance proliferating their own arts. NAFTA conspiracy is met with Chiapas determination; Republican attempts to reorganize affirmative action in Houston provoke a coalition reorganization of politics to elect a black mayor. As has ever been the case between domination and its rebuke, it seems to be a race never quite won—or lost.[40]

I personally get knocked down often and depressed readily in my own small sphere of confrontation. But I have learned how to get up, again and again, from very particular friends and very specific communities. They are mostly darker-skinned than I. I take that to be an indication of the other half of the name that this culture still tries to name as "problem."[41] That other name might just be something like "salvation." If we ever got to a point in this world where white people could embrace a black messiah, we could then perhaps finally agree to consign those two fictions about color to the dustbin of history. Until then, my hope will continue to take its orientation from what comes like a thief, cloaked in night.

Part Three

Black Theology and Global Religions

10 Black Theology's Impact on the Ecumenical Association of Third World Theologians

José David Rodríguez

I approach this subject with great apprehension and humility: first, because I am not an expert on the contributions of either James Cone or black theology; second, because my participation in the work of the Ecumenical Association of Third World Theologians (EATWOT)[1] is relatively short, surely not as long nor as significant as that of Cone and other founding members of EATWOT. However, the reason I accepted this task is because black theology in the United States does have a very important contribution for the ministry and theological development of our brothers and sisters of third-world nations, and black theologians, especially James Cone, have helped us become aware of the value and significance of this contribution through their own reflections and writings.[2]

Back in the early 1980s Cone was invited to participate in the Journeys in Faith book series to provide a personal assessment of his experience of faith and life and to focus on those issues central to his theological thinking and witness of faith. As he went about this task, he rendered a powerful testimony of his interest and concern with third-world theologies:

> Besides the black church and community, nothing has made a greater impact upon the development of my theological and political consciousness than the cultures and theologies of Africa, Asia, and Latin America. This influence can be seen in my teaching at Union Seminary, my travels to the Third World, and my theological writings. No longer is Europe generally and Germany in particular the primary place to look for recent creative theological voices. The eruption of the poor in Asia, Africa, and Latin America has created Third World voices in theology that

are radically different from the dominant theologies of Europe and North America. Third World theologians challenge not only the unjust economic and political structures of the world but especially the religious and theological structures that serve as their justification. I believe that no one can do creative theological reflection today without dealing with the impact of those theologians.[3]

Cone's firm persuasion that the gospel is a message of liberation for the world's poor led to his interest in and engagement with the witness of faith and theological contributions of people of other cultures and nations, who shared this conviction on the universal dimension of the gospel: "Because I believe that the gospel is universal and thus intended for all, I have written my story in dialogue with people of other cultures and nations who also regard Jesus Christ as God's definitive and final salvation for humankind."[4]

This dialogue with people of other cultures not only strengthened Cone's foundational belief in the gospel but also expanded it:

From my encounters with the struggles of the Third World poor, existentially and intellectually, my perspective on the gospel has been enlarged and reinforced. The universal dimension of the gospel was revealed in the particularities of poor people throughout the world. . . . Because I firmly believe that the gospel is a message of liberation for the world's poor, I have tried to reflect that theme in my writings about African, Latin, and Asian theologies.[5]

His experience with Christians from Asia, Africa, and Latin America increased his awareness of the common origins of North American ethnic theologies (black, Asian, Hispanic, and Native North American minorities) and third-world theologies.[6] This common ground was found in the effort to develop specific theologies of liberation in direct reaction to the theologies of the first world. "Like Third World peoples in Asia, Africa, Latin America, and the Caribbean, the oppressed peoples of North America do not believe that white oppressors can define for them what the gospel of Jesus is."[7]

Another meaningful consequence of this dialogue was the opportunity to reflect on the weaknesses and limitations of third-world theologies in general.[8] In addition, a mutual and continuous dialogue began to strengthen their intentional effort to affirm and incorporate the experience and culture of the oppressed as a conceptual tool for articulating their own theological perspective.

> But I have been struggling to incorporate the experience and culture of the oppressed into the conceptual tools for articulating black theology. For I contend that our rebellion against Europeans should lead to a second step, namely to an affirmation of our own cultural resources as well as those found among other people who have similar experiences of oppression.[9]

For Cone, there are some important similarities and differences between black and third-world theologies. First, the similarities: He argues that a common ground among these theological perspectives is found in both *their rejection of the dominant theologies of Europe and North America* and *their use of liberation as a focus of their theological concern.* He finds evidence for this claim in two of his earlier works, *Black Theology and Black Power* (1969) and *A Black Theology of Liberation* (1970),[10] and the theological work of third-world theologians belonging to EATWOT. "When one analyses the Final Statements of the five EATWOT conferences to date, the rejection of European theology and an affirmation of liberation are common characteristics."[11]

Cone finds another important commonality between black theology and third-world theologies in their joint effort to *read the Bible from the perspective of the struggles and suffering of the poor for freedom.* This approach has led, among other things, to interpret the passion story as a witness of God's gracious initiative of revealing of self in solidarity with the victimized of the world.

> This is what Third World theologians mean when they say, "God is black," "God is Red," "God is Rice," and other strange ways of speaking when compared with the metaphysical reflections of Europeans. This apparently crude anthropomorphic way of speaking of God is the Third World theologian's way of concretizing Paul's dictum: "To shame the wise, God has chosen what the world counts folly, and to shame what is strong, God has chosen what the world counts weakness. He has chosen things low and contemptible, mere nothings, to overthrow the existing order" (1 Cor. 1:27-28).[12]

A further common emphasis between black theology and third-world theologies is *the affirmation of their own cultural traditions in their theological construction and witness of faith.*

> When black and Third World theologians began to concentrate on distinct black, African, Asian, and Latin theologies, they also realized that their own historical and cultural traditions are far more important for an analysis of the gospel for their struggle of freedom than are the Western traditions that participated in their enslavement.[13]

The affirmation of history and culture in the struggle for the liberation of the oppressed led to an *emphasis on praxis, the need of social analysis (including both race and class analysis), and the endorsement of a type of democratic socialism as an alternative to the present economic social and political order.*[14]

Second, the differences between black and third-world theologies: Cone argues that they can be classified in two broad areas: Those that focus on *sociopolitical liberation* and those that emphasize *cultural liberation.* Some of these differences bring significant distance among these perspectives; others complement and enlarge their particular liberation approach. The dialogue of North American black theologians with African theologians has stressed the first of these emphases,

> The concern of North American black theologians has not been to reduce theology and the gospel to blackness or political liberation. Like our African brothers and sisters, we believe that there is a spiritual ingredient in the gospel that transcends the material conditions of human life. What we reject is the tendency, among some African theologians, to reduce the gospel and theology to a spirituality that has not been carved out of the real-life sufferings of the poor who are engaged in political liberation.[15]

The dialogue with Latin American theologians accentuates the latter emphasis. In the dialogue between black theology and Latin American liberation theology the opposite pole has been stressed. The main question has been: What is the relationship between race and class oppression? Because the Latin Americans are Marxists, they emphasize class oppression, almost to the exclusion of race oppression. In as much as black theologians live in the white racist society of North America, with a heritage of two hundred fifty years of slavery and over a hundred years of white capitalist oppression, it is not likely that they will ignore cultural oppression as imposed by white racism.[16]

The dialogue between North American black theologians and Asian theologians in EATWOT has led to awareness that the differences and similarities between them tend to complement each other.[17] This experience of mutual support has served to improve the dialogue with African and Latin American theologians and a deeper understanding of each other's struggles.[18]

So far I have tried to provide a brief summary of the relationship between black theology and third-world theologies in the context of the work of EATWOT. In so doing I have intentionally selected segments from the works of a North American black theologian to lead us in the exploration of this topic. I now move on to the question, What lessons might EATWOT take from the black theology movement as ushered in under the direction of James Cone?

Cone models in his personal and professional life the gifts of a scholar, the integrity of a leader, and the deep spiritual commitment of a person of faith. As a scholar, he has created the conditions and provided the documentation to listen to the voices of those who, given the color of their skin, have suffered the racism of the white dominant culture but resisted with courage and determination this oppressive predicament. This scholarship has broken new ground and has been so clearly articulated, so thoroughly researched, and so extensive in scope that it affects the lives and witness of people all over the world. His extensive publications and large number of students are evidence of his significant influence. To be sure, it would be impossible to talk about theology or religious thought in the twentieth century without making reference to some of his works.

Cone also models the fairness and integrity of a great leader. His commitment to justice and liberation, learned in his upbringing from courageous and loving parents, has been a staple of his character. His writings show openness to positive criticism, engagement with difficult topics, and honest quest for truth. His relationship with others and stewardship of resources model a deeply rooted respect for the dignity of creation and a willingness to account, and hold others accountable, for personal and public behavior.

Last, but not least, Cone is a living witness of someone who models the deep spiritual commitment of a person of faith. In his case, this deep spiritual commitment emerged and was nurtured in his experience with the black church. This was an experience that provided him the source not only of identity and survival, but also of the sociopolitical struggle for liberation.

> During my childhood, every fight for justice and civil rights was initiated in and led by the church. The leader was usually the minister or some other self-employed black person. Because there were very few black people who were not dependent upon whites for a livelihood, the burden of leadership fell upon the preacher whose salary was paid by his congregation. Seeing so many courageous ministers leading the struggle for justice in the name of the gospel, and also seeing the support of church people, undoubtedly had much to do with why I chose the ministry as my vocation, and also why I chose liberation as the central theme of my perspective in black theology. How could I write about black theology and overlook the theme of liberation in the gospel preached at Macedonia and in black church history?[19]

Black theology's impact on EATWOT is a legacy of wisdom, integrity, and witness of faith, nurturing and leading forward a renewed struggle for liberation in the next millennium. Through faith and maintaining the interest of the majority of the world's people (that is, the poor and the locked out voices), black theology and EATWOT will continue to be important forces in the movement toward justice, peace, and the integrity of all creation.

11 / The Outsider's Role in Socially Engaged Scholarship on African Religion

Linda E. Thomas

African religion, like other world religions, has various expressions and modalities. By saying African *religion* rather than African *religions,* I do not suggest that a singular religion exists for the whole continent of Africa. Rather that African religion with its myriad and multifarious expressions manifests itself as a particular phenomenon in Africa.

A socially engaged scholarship about African religion by an outsider must necessarily begin with the outsider's critical and self-conscious assessment of the presuppositions that she or he brings to the intellectual enterprise. To flesh out my thesis, I first examine the category "outsider." Second, I include the voices that critique those of us who study cultural construction and meaning in cultures other than our own culture of origin. I unpack in an intentional manner the contours of the unequal equation between the knowledge and power of researchers and those of the people who are studied. Finally, I sort through what a critical and self-conscious assessment denotes.

Outsider Defined

Outsiders' epistemological claims gleaned from ethnographic research have become a highly contested terrain for scholarship. For instance, African scholars such as Okot p'Bitek and Ifi Amadiume have negatively critiqued the methods used and interpretations made by Western researchers studying indigenous peoples. They claim that many Western researchers' self-knowledge and unbridled Western perspectives go unchecked in their conclusions based on etic constructs.[1] In a positive vein, anthropological literature is replete with debates about the method for conducting fieldwork and the nature of the relationship between the researcher and those who are the objects of study.[2] Anthropologists writing three decades ago, such as Edward E. Evans-Pritchard, and those writing in the current decade, such as Jean Comaroff, have investigated the religious cosmologies of African peoples.

In order to discuss a socially engaged scholarship about African religion by an outsider, I must define the notion of outsider itself. David Westerlund suggests that "in a sense all scholars are outsiders"[3] unless they believe and participate in the particular religious phenomenon being examined. He argues that scholars of religion who are African tend to be Christian and not necessarily practitioners of African religion. Many African scholars view Christianity as the fulfillment of African religion, and they therefore propagate a theology of continuity in which Christianity forms the apex of the positive attributes of indigenous religions. This perspective presents a problem for Westerlund, and thus he suggests that even a scholar of African descent sometimes functions as an outsider in African religion.

This definition differs from that of Okot p'Bitek. He argues that Western researchers are outsiders because they possess an inherent template that assumes European culture and lifeways to be superior to African culture and lifeways. P'Bitek offers the following critique regarding the imposition of such a Western hegemonic cultural template on ethnographic research: "Western scholarship sees the world as divided into two types of human society: one, their own, civilized, great, developed; the other, the non-western peoples, uncivilized, simple, undeveloped. One is modern, the other tribal."[4] Westerlund underscores a notion of outsider in contrast to the self-understanding of the indigenous community under study. For p'Bitek, the question of insider/outsider is not primarily a question of believer and nonbeliever. For him, an outsider in the study of African religion imposes cultural and political sensibilities privileging the superiority of a Western way of life.

A representative group from African Independent Churches (AICs) in South Africa concurs with this negative characteristic in the definition of outsider. This committee published a report titled *Speaking for Ourselves*. In it we find the following comment on Western research on AICs:

> It is not surprising that we do not recognize ourselves in their writings. We find them seriously misleading and often far from the truth. They are full of misunderstandings, misconceptions and falsehood. In trying to understand us outsiders suffer serious handicaps. They have their own frame of reference: the assump-

tions of anthropology or sociology or a Western theology. We find ourselves judged in terms of these norms.[5]

For me, the concept "outsider" has at least four aspects. First, the outsider does not belong to the indigenous culture. Specifically, the outsider does not share the mother tongue of the indigenous communities that are the subject of study. Similarly, and in agreement with Westerlund, the outsider does not believe in the indigenous religion of his or her informants. In this instance, I highlight language and religion as two dimensions of culture.

Second, an outsider, especially from the West, carries along a Western template that categorizes and organizes data from the field according to the norms of Western scholarship and a Western way of life.

The third and fourth dimensions of my definition arise from longitudinal fieldwork that commenced in 1991 in South Africa, where I examined (a) the special oppression experienced by black South Africans who are members of St. John's Apostolic Faith Mission Church located in Guguletu, an African township in Cape Town; (b) the testimonies they gave about issues that affected their lives; and (c) healing rituals they performed four times daily as a source of restoration.[6] St. John's, like many AICs, brings together a community of people whose cosmology arises from the synthesis of precolonial African religion and Protestant Christianity.[7] I conducted research for this study from June 1991 through January 1992, July and August 1992, and July and August 1994 and 1996. While participating in church services, being a part of the daily activities of several families, and conducting in-depth interviews, I sought to understand the ways that members singularly and collectively designed adaptive systems of support to oppose degrading social conditions that were the result of race discrimination and an economic scheme that created conditions of perpetual poverty for many black South Africans. With this experience as background, I claim that an outsider is one whose class status distinguishes him or her from the informants' community. Finally, the outsider's country of origin may differ from that of the subjects of study.

Conversation with Members of St. John's: Issues Related to Influx Control

In 1991 the membership of St. John's[8] consisted of forty-eight people. Sixteen of the eighteen members[9] (fourteen women and four men) interviewed migrated to the Cape Peninsula from the Eastern Cape between 1942 and 1991. One person was born in Cape Town, and another was born in the Northern Cape Province. Four women talked explicitly about being arrested for not having passes; one of the four was arrested three times. All four were not defended for their infraction of the law, and all were kept in jail overnight in Langa upon their arrest.

Mama Myira Zotwana,[10] who was apprehended two weeks after she came to Cape Town in 1952, told me about what happened when she was arrested:[11]

> I was called by my brother to come to Cape Town to take a look for a job at St. Monica's Home, but we were not given a permit to stay in the Cape. They gave me about two weeks. The next time I went to the office to ask for some more days, they arrested me, saying I ought to have gone back to the Transkei. They put me in the office there by Langa, to sleep there that night. My sister-in-law came to Langa to fetch me the following day. She had to pay for me.
>
> I didn't go back to Transkei. I was staying in the home of my aunt and uncle. After that they [the officials] didn't meet me on the way going up and down. I did stay in Cape Town. I never had a job. Then I just got a husband and stayed here in the location.

When I asked Mama Zotwana why she was arrested, she responded: "It was because we were not to come into the Cape. The Cape was for the Coloureds. That was the only reason they told us." Mama Zotwana's story duplicates the experience of others who came to the Western Cape looking for work and attempted to escape the harsh life of the rural areas. When people arrived in the city, however, there were many challenges.

Several topics emerged as informants told me their life histories during structured interviews.[12] Since these interviews were conducted in June 1991, immediately following the abolition of the Population Registration Act and the Group Areas Act, the effects that Apartheid had upon the lives of informants and their families were discussed. Those discussions, which are outlined below,[13] included issues about work, violence, and education as they related to Apartheid. Six informants made explicit comments about Apartheid. One man who had worked in the mines was extremely articulate about the ways Apartheid affected his life. Women commented about Apartheid's restrictions (for example, segregated trains, marriage) and their relation to education and violence. Some informants talked about whether the repeal of Apartheid legislation would bring authentic change to their lives. We turn now to comments that informants made about Apartheid and related issues.

Discourse about Apartheid

Nozipo, fifty-one, who was employed as a "tea girl" at a hotel in Bellville, said the following about Apartheid:

> It is still very difficult to talk about Apartheid, because there are so many things that don't encourage us,[14] that don't give us hope. Apartheid is slowly, slowly going away. But still you can see it's difficult to die. It doesn't die. It still exists.
>
> As for me, what I can explain is that I don't see any changes at the moment. There are places where they don't allow us to enter; even our wages are not the same with Coloured people. I don't want to say anything about it.[15]

While it was difficult for Nozipo to talk about Apartheid or the lingering effects of the Cape Coloured Preference Policies and what she perceived to be inconsistent wage earnings between Coloured and blacks, she found her voice and spoke about these issues. The cardinal point is that she did not feel encouraged and articulated that one of the effects of Apartheid is not to feel encouraged, which is a quality-of-life issue. She admitted that things were changing but the ramifications of Apartheid were still present.

Voices that Critique Outsiders

In 1970 Kenyan anthropologist and historian Okot p'Bitek wrote a blistering critique of Western anthropologists who study African religion. He suggested that Westerners "hellenize" African religion by forcing it to be viewed through lenses frayed with colonial presuppositions. He challenged African scholars to "expose and destroy all false ideas about African peoples and culture that have been perpetuated by western scholarship" and to present African institutions in a true and truthful light.[16]

Nigerian anthropologist Ifi Amadiume likewise critiqued Western scholars who misrepresent African people. Addressing Western feminist scholars, she went further than p'Bitek and asked, "Why the interest in us? Why do you want to study African women?"[17] Launching her own study of gender and status roles in Ibo society, Amadiume made a distinctive contribution. She used indigenous categories to examine, analyze, and interpret Ibo society. By using internal categories rather than imposing Western constructs, she presented a set of conclusions that differ from the findings of previous researchers. In *Male Daughters, Female Husbands: Gender and Sex in an African Society,* Amadiume claimed that persons acquire gender identity separately from biological sexual identity. Moreover, in Ibo society, she argued, gender construction is malleable and to a large extent more determinative of the political status of Ibo women than sexual identity.

African scholars such as p'Bitek and Amadiume and other indigenous scholars such as Chandra Talpade Mohanty, George Tinker, and Edward Said posit explicitly that Western approaches often oversimplify complex realities and obscure the truth about insiders' lifeways. They do so by using categories and primary units of analysis and interpretation external to the culture studied. As this applies to African religion, it means that some Western scholars ignore the fact that religion may not even be a category within the language and meaning system of those being studied. It means that some intellectuals fail to deal with the problem of cultural translation. Scholars must ask intentionally how researchers can work effectively when meaning systems differ. Moreover, some scholars may not consider the impact of multiple and overlapping systemic jeopardies such as racism, sexism, ethnic bias, classism, and imperialism. Finally, scholars may ignore the effect that colonial and state governments have had on institutions that affect the everyday life of indigenous citizens.

Thomas Blakely, Walter van Beek, and Dennis Thomson respond to these critiques in their volume *Religion in Africa: Experience and Expression.* They distinguish themselves from Peter Berger and Robert Towler, who use methodological atheism to study religion.[18] Blakely, van Beek, and Thomson examine religion as a cultural system. They consider African religious experience and expression within particular cultural and empirical contexts. They call their approach "methodological agnosticism," which includes a "just do not know" approach to the empirical study of religion. Moreover, they stress that a focus on religious experience and expression demands an involvement with historical processes that shape the context in which Africans live.[19] Finally, these authors argue that translation and comparison present fundamental methodological problems in studying African religion. How does one explain "cultural meaning from one cultural system into a different cultural system"?[20] The task of interpretation challenges researchers, especially when the explanatory theory and cognitive reasoning[21] systems differ significantly. Thus, categorical comparison among differing cultures poses difficulty and often obscures meaning. In other words, we need alternative methods in order to compare differing religious meaning systems more effectively.

My experience of being an outsider whose social location is an African American woman from the United States makes it necessary for me to reflect a little on my own background. There is not a simple way to describe myself. I am a womanist anthropologist, which means I deal with issues of race, gender, class, sexual orientation, ecology, and postcolonial studies in a manner that addresses the experience of those who have been and are marginalized by systems of power. Having experienced race and gender oppression in the United States means that I approach my work with a template of experience-based knowledge as well as cognitive knowledge about systemic power on micro- and macro-levels. My interest in AICs in South Africa has always been based on my interest in learning the ways that people of African descent preserve themselves in macro- and micro-systems that attempt to shut down their life force.

Critical and Self-Conscious Assessment by Outsiders

The social context and inherited cultural values and paradigms of the researcher affect the outcomes of our research. I suggest that the outsider must engage in a critical and self-conscious assessment of her- or himself. Edward Said, in his groundbreaking text *Orientalism,* presents a helpful explanation; he employs the theoretical insights from Italian communist intellectual Antonio Gramsci.

> In the *Prison Notebooks* Gramsci says: "The starting point of critical elaboration is the consciousness of what one really is, and is 'knowing thyself' as a product of the historical process to date, which has deposited in you an infinity of traces, without leaving an inventory. . . . Therefore it is imperative at the outset to compile such an inventory."[22]

I argue that "knowing thyself" specifically demands an unpacking of the "inventory" of the outsider. Inventory here denotes awareness of one's "circumstances of life."[23] The scholar must announce his or her epistemology, position in society, and relationship to a particular socioeconomic class.[24] In other words, the scholar must locate her- or himself socially, economically, philosophically, and positionally as an agent of a particular historical point of view arising from the circumstances in which she or he has lived and by which she or he is influenced.

In addition to locating ourselves, the outsider needs to hear insiders' voices and let them be heard in the published texts. Karen McCarthy Brown builds on this new method of ethnography. She calls on social science scholars to locate the indigenous voices of our ethnographic research and enable them to speak for themselves. Brown summarizes this point explicitly: "The people who are being studied should be allowed to speak for themselves whenever possible, for they are the only true experts on themselves."[25] This new method of ethnography or postmodern anthropology responds to the critique from insiders who argue that outsiders wield a great deal of independent cultural and political power in the research process itself. We must provide some space for listening and amplifying the words, interpretations, and stories of the informants from the field as an effort to release this interpretive stranglehold on the part of the outsider.

The very method of scholarship has to undergo a change. Standard ethnographic data collection generates a one-way perspective. The anthropologist goes to the field, records primary information via observation, filters this experience through his or her own interpretive lenses, and finally publishes a report. In contrast, I call for a dialogical methodological paradigm in which the researcher submits her- or himself to an ongoing conversation with the informants. In fact, the informants no longer remain informants but become actual interlocutors. In this method, the investigator not only gathers data but shares of himself or herself in speech and action. At this juncture my approach falls within the tradition developed by such scholars as Paul Rabinow and Jean-Paul Dumont.[26] Restated, the informant moves away from being an object of study for the expert, unilateral voice of the ethnographer and becomes a subject in conversation. Thus, instead of having ethnographer as subject studying informant as object, we have two subjects in dialogue. Paul Rabinow concludes a similar methodological shift from his fieldwork in Morocco.

> Fieldwork, then, is a process of intersubjective construction of liminal modes of communication. Intersubjective means literally more than one subject, but being situated neither quite here nor

quite there, the subjects involved do not share a common set of assumptions, experiences, or traditions. Their construction is a public process.[27]

Conclusion

This chapter has presented a complex approach for the outsider who wishes to undertake socially engaged research. *Socially engaged,* in my sense of the term, means a profound process of reflexivity on the part of the outsider. Researchers must be aware of themselves and the critical dynamics of power positionality, historical traditions, social locatedness, and symbols that affect their relationship with informants. Researchers need to take more risk by confessing their limits as outsiders and listen genuinely to others' cultures and epistemology. In sum, postmodern anthropology requires a conversation not an examination. The researcher and the researched engage in a dialogue between two subjects. Through an intersubjective exchange the indigenous community helps create a more representative portrayal, interpretation, and understanding of the complex and nuanced indigenous cultural matrix.

12 / Black Theology and Ecumenism

Iva E. Carruthers

The Burning Bush

The evolving corpus and legacy of the works of James H. Cone are seminal and central to late-twentieth- and twenty-first-century ecumenism within both the African American religious context and the larger Christian church. In the halls of academia, within the walls of the black church, and at the table of ecumenical discourse, the man and message of James Cone has been like a burning bush—for some reflecting the light of God, for others a smoldering thorn of discomfort that will not die out.

There are three lenses through which to capture Cone as the burning bush. The first lens situates him on the continuum of African American scholars and theologians who experienced and attempted ecumenical strategies of theologizing, praxis, and organizing against oppression of a slavocracy and its consequences. The second lens takes a snapshot of Cone's personhood and how his spirit, intellectual prowess and focus, and physical stamina ignited and fueled black ecumenical expression—both as an individual on a mission and within the context of an organizational framework. The third lens is a wide angle on Cone's audience, challenging us to hear that prophetic voice that continues to propel the theological paradigmatic shift into issues of the twenty-first-century reality, connecting racism to the degradation of the earth.

Language consideration is a primary imperative of ecumenical and cross-cultural dialogue. In the Christian tradition, *ecumenical* is tied to the Greek concept of *oikoumene,* referring to the "whole household of the inhabited earth." It is also related to the household instruments of economics and ecology. Thus, we see it expands to not just the Christian world, but also the entire world, most of which is not Christian, and to the earth as an inherited gift evidencing natural laws. This definition is fine and serves to clarify who is at the table and provide some pointers as to what might be menu items.

However, an additional meaning of *ecumenical*, which affirms African American faith tradition, is expressed by the Yoruba concept of *Orita*, meaning, "where the ways come together."[1] The theological usefulness of this construct, as an extension of the traditional meaning of *ecumenical*, is of extreme importance in understanding the particularity of the African experience and people of African ancestry. *Orita* captures the significance of interconnectedness and purpose between the secular and sacred in the black religious cosmos. *Orita* is where the ways come together in God-encounters and divine context to champion the cause of African people's liberation within and outside Christian experience. *Orita* is where dialogical space is expected and affirms the African view of ontology, ethics, and politics as methodologically and practically inseparable. *Orita* is where the power of the intellectual meets the pain of the people in the spirit of the divine—unleashing a profound burst of seismic energy and potentiality.

Ecumenism and *Orita* in the Struggle for Liberation

Black religious experience in the United States cannot be extricated from the struggle for liberation, literally and spiritually, nor can the struggle for liberation be extricated from black religious experience. Thus the spirit of *Orita* surely was present in the holds of the slave ships as millions of Africans tried to make ontological sense of their new reality as an ecumenical moment across ethnic community, language, gender, and age differences. The imperative of liberation in the context of God-talk was central to the black sacred cosmos. And ecumenical organizing and evangelization were thus wedded to various schemes of nineteenth- and twentieth-century liberation, emigration, reparation, and recolonization affecting the United States, Canada, Mexico, South America, the Caribbean, and West and South Africa. Thus, as we consider the concept of *ecumenism/Orita* in the context of black theology, we find an ecumenism that respects and welcomes differences, which include communitarian and integrated scholarship and worship; ancestral presence; God's care invoked and evidenced by herbal baths, dance, drums, trees, and rivers; and a praise and worship style that has natural vitality. These are all "a word, a memory of God."[2] Thus, Cone's voice is borne out of a long legacy in which the faith in and power of God were appropriated in multiple ways to protect and empower communities of exile as they struggled for understanding and liberation.

The religious and ecumenical sparks of three of the best-known U.S. slave revolts and their leaders occurred within the historical backdrop of the Haitian revolution, where the first slavocracy was successfully overthrown by slaves: in 1800 in Richmond, Virginia, Gabriel Prosser; in 1822 in South Carolina, a Methodist, Denmark Vesey; and in 1831 in Southampton, Virginia, a Baptist, Nat Turner. These men were very religious, articulating and appropriating theological themes to organize the revolts.

In 1829 Robert Alexander Young issued the Ethiopian Manifesto, "Defense of the Blackman's Rights in the Scale of Universal Freedom," evoking a black messiah. That same year, David Walker, a faithful member of a Boston Methodist church, issued the *Appeal to the Coloured Citizens of the World,* a call to arms.

In 1843 Henry Highland Garnet, a Presbyterian minister, issued his call to slaves: "let your motto be resistance. . . . Trust in the Living God." His childhood friend, Alexander Crummell, was an Episcopalian who had been refused admission to the leading Episcopal seminary, General Theological Seminary. In 1875 Garnet issued his noted declaration that blacks had a divine obligation to fight off oppression and demand liberation.[3]

Martin R. Delaney issued his *Condition, Elevation, Emigration and Destiny of the Colored People of the U.S.,* copublished by Frederick Douglass. He and Douglass shared the sentiment that "I would rather be a heathen freeman than a Christian slave."[4] Delaney would travel throughout the Caribbean and Africa with an Episcopal bishop, James Theodore Holly.

Rev. Samuel E. Cornish edited the *Freedom's Journal* with John Russwurm.[5] Ex-slave Baptist minister Rufus Perry spoke of the ancient Egyptian, Libyan, and Ethiopian presence in the Bible a century before Cain Hope Felder's *Troubling Biblical Waters.*[6]

Edward W. Blyden, born in 1832 in St. Thomas, was a Presbyterian. He was a world lecturer and interdisciplinary scholar on Christianity and Islam. He was fluent in several languages and became president of Liberia College. For some, he might be considered the father of pan-African theology.

The National Negro Convention Movement, begun in 1830, was initially dominated by Richard Allen, founder of the African Methodist Episcopal (AME) Church. The Niagara Movement birthed the NAACP (National Association for the Advancement of Colored People) in 1919. Both were secular extensions of the black church.

Bishop Henry McNeal Turner of the AME Church was editor and contributor to the *Voice of Mission, Christian Recorder,* and *Crisis* magazines. His insistent voice, heard from the pew to the first World Parliament of Religion, declared "God is a Negro" in 1898. He established the AME Church in Africa and was an early proponent of pan-African theology and politics.

Within the constraints of their times, despite the triple jeopardy of race, sex, and class, black women such as Jarena Lee, Sojourner Truth, Harriet Tubman, Eliza Turner (a bishop's wife who was thrown off an Atlanta bus one hundred years before Rosa Parks), Fannie Helen Burroughs, and Fannie Lou Hamer were religious thinkers and political activists.

And many are quick to forget that the so-called Negro national anthem written in 1906 by J. Rosamond and James Weldon Johnson, "Lift Every Voice and Sing," was a hymn and a prayer.

Called and Set Apart

In the midst of the struggles of the civil rights and Black Power movements, on July 31, 1966, the National Committee of Black Churchmen (NCBC), spirited by the known and unknown sisters of the movement, brought *Orita* to center stage with the issuance of a manifesto in the *New York Times*. Congressman Adam Clayton Powell (who was also a minister), Martin Luther King Jr., Charles Spivey of the National Council of Churches, Wyatt Tee Walker, and Elijah Muhammed were just a few of the people brought forth by the spirit of *Orita* during this period.

It is within the ancestral historical lineage of these religious thinkers and political activists that the burning bush and prophetic voice of James H. Cone would propel ecumenical discourse, black and white. His voice would create space, even if it did nothing else. As such, Cone's voice was to become a metanoic nerve energy that empowered individual and organizational praxis toward a systematic and irrevocable approach to theological reflection and action. Cone was a burning bush not to be consumed but to transform.

In 1968 Albert Cleage, a United Church of Christ minister, published *The Black Messiah*. In 1969 James H. Cone published *Black Theology and Black Power*. When NCBC met at Interdenominational Theological Center (ITC) on June 13, 1969, they looked specifically to Cone to shape their foundational consensus document.[7] From that moment on, there was no turning back the influence Cone would have upon the leadership and ecumenical organizations active on the threshing floor of theologizing and human social justice activities, including people of all hues, political persuasions, genders, sexual persuasions, and classes.

Because it is so critical not to romanticize leaders or isolate them from the work of those they represent or influence, Cone's ecumenical contributions are best seen as interwoven in the meaning and life of organizations, specifically the Black Theology Project.

Cone's *A Black Theology of Liberation* was published in 1970. In 1971 he attended the NCBC's meeting in Dar es Salaam, Tanzania. There he met African theologians. The conference theme was Black Identity and Solidarity and the Role of the Church as a Medium for Social Change. In its wake, in 1974, C. L. R. James convened the Sixth Pan African Congress in Dar es Salaam, after several years of international regional meetings.

In 1971 Gustavo Gutiérrez's *A Theology of Liberation* was published, and in 1973 both it and Cone's *Black Theology of Liberation* were translated. In May 1973, the World Council of Churches met in Geneva. Cone was present and said this was his first real encounter with Marxist thought.[8] Cone's ideas had brought forth new fruit to nourish the world of the diaspora, Africa and Asia.

By 1974 Allan Boesak was already referencing Cone's work to provide a theological foundation for anti-apartheid activity in South Africa.[9] In 1975 Desmond Tutu would also embrace the quest for common cause in black theology and African theology, noting, "Westerners usually call for an ecumenical, a universal theology which they often identify with their brand of theologizing. . . . Theology is a human activity possessing the limitations and the particularities of those who are theologizing."[10]

Cone was at the forefront of dialogue and exchange between a black theology of liberation and the multifaceted forms of Asian theologies. At the invitation of the Korean church in Japan, he presented at the 1975 conference "The Church Struggling for the Liberation of the People."

Within the Americas, the 1973 Geneva conference had set the stage for exploring the commonality of interests between the black and Latin American conferees. But this potentiality of mutual solidarity was short lived when in 1975 Sergio Torres, a Latin American theologian, convened a conference in Detroit to introduce Latin American theology to white American theologians. This was largely done without including those representing the black theological and church community.

At the Detroit meeting, some thirty black delegates were present among some two hundred delegates. Insulted by the presumptions and domination of white theologians, Cone led a caucus protest that resulted in the restructuring of the conference agenda and theology in America. Affinity projects were formed, including the Black Theology Project, the Hispanic Project, the Asian American Project, and the Indigenous Project.[11] That moment sparked the birth of a particular organizational force, the Black Theology Project (BTP) of Theology in the Americas, an organization born out of the ecumenical/*Orita* dynamic. The BTP's subsequent importance to ecumenism/*Orita* within and outside the black church is noteworthy. In *For My People,* Cone wrote: "The milestone marking the return of black theology to the black church was the Black Theology Project Conference in Atlanta, August, 1977."[12]

Cone's seminal reflections and evolving work armed and spawned the intersection of black activists in the ecumenical movement, particularly the BTP. In its earliest mission statement, BTP articulated a commitment to self-definition, praxis, inclusivity, and international community. The project defined itself as "an ecumenical African American Christian group devoted to the discovery, development and promotion of historic and contemporary black religious thought and action. . . . We are a people spread across the world . . . struggling daily to bring justice and equality to all people everywhere."[13] The idea was to create theological clusters as reflection/action groups throughout the black church and the country.

In October 1977 Cone participated in the Encounter of Theologians in Mexico City, where a "new mutuality of acceptance to oppressed allies" was lifted up.[14] In December 1977 he and Gayraud Wilmore, another BTP founder, joined others at the Ecumenical Association of Third World Theologians in Accra, Ghana. In 1979 Cone went to Sri Lanka to the Asian Theological conference where he met with seventy-five delegates from eleven Asian countries.[15]

By now, Cone and BTP had created a community of religious scholars, thinkers, and activists whose reach was revolutionary and global. This was evidenced by the strong vision statement put forth in 1977 at its first major conference in Atlanta at ITC:

> We have come in quest of authentic liberation for ourselves and our people. We have come seeking God's will for our people in a time of crisis . . . by the power of the Holy Spirit. We speak from the perspective we call black theology: black because our enslaved foreparents appropriated the Christian Gospel and articulated its relevance to our freedom struggle. . . . Theology because our people perception of human life and history begins with God, who works in the person of Jesus Christ for liberation. That church must be one with and inseparable from our brothers and sisters around the world who fight for liberation in a variety of ways, including armed struggle.

It was at this conference that Cone delivered his historic address "Black The-ology and the Black Church: Where Do We Go from Here?" Cone called for "new concepts and new methods" for systematic race conscious sociopolitical global analysis, including shedding American capitalism and its role in global oppression. The conference resolution was a "Message to the Black Church and Community." Wilmore calls this the beginning point of the third stage of black theology (NCBC the first; the Society for Study of Black Religion and the Academy the second). Here the *ecumenism/Orita* spanned the con-tinuum from Catholics to radical Marxists, to pan-Africanists; from black denominations to blacks within mainline denominations; from theologians to street people. The tentacles of James H. Cone and the leadership of the Black Theology Project had indeed achieved its global vision.

In the Eye of the Storm

In 1984 BTP co-sponsored the fourth annual Inter Ethnic Indigenous Dia-logue, where a resolution was passed to establish official ties with the Caribbean Conference of Churches and the All African Conference of Churches.

In 1985 Yvonne Delk, BTP founding member, was appointed as commis-sioner to the Program to Combat Racism of the World Council of Churches. In May 1986 BTP was officially represented at the National Council of Churches conference in Nanjing, China. A letter of gratitude for BTP indi-cated that several million Christians were supportive of what BTP stands for and the lectures of Dr. Cone; within three days after Nanjing, eighty-six statements were translated and distributed across China. In 1988 BTP accepted an invitation for ecumenical dialogue with Brazil's National Com-missions to Combat Racism against Negro and Indian, led by Rev. Anatonia de Sant'Ana.

During this same period BTP was granted delegate status to the All African Council of Churches, participated in a dialogue in the Philippines, and was involved in a dialogue on racism in Europe sponsored by the British Council of Churches. BTP was officially consulted by the National Council of Catholic Bishops on its stance against apartheid and was the host to the Christian Dalit Movement of India, largely composed of the untouchable caste, with which it engaged in dialogue and to which it offered resources.

In 1992 BTP cosponsored and participated in an All Africans of the Americas Conference in Havana, Cuba, where theologians, pastors, and laity met from the United States, Brazil, South Africa, and all over South and

Latin America, commemorating and studying the life and work of Martin Luther King Jr. The focus was specifically on the struggle for justice and liberation in the Americas, and fourteen members of BTP participated, including Jeremiah Wright, Jualyne Dodson, Thelma Adair, Calvin Butts, Gayraud Wilmore, and James Cone. Jesse Jackson brought Fidel Castro to the Martin Luther King commemorative worship service, reflecting the first time in twenty-five years that Fidel Castro had crossed the threshold of an evangelical church.

Cone was one of the first theologians to acknowledge his early failure to address the pervasiveness of sexual oppression in the church in general and the black church in particular. And BTP was one of the first organizations to affirm the need to address sexism within the black church tradition. At BTP's very first convocation, "Black Feminism, Black Women, and the Church" and "Changing Ideas of Family Life and Sexuality" were workshop topics.

Jacquelyn Grant, one of the first generation of Cone's students, became a BTP director. She audaciously and respectfully challenged a black theology "that continued to treat Black women as if they were invisible creatures who are on the outside looking into the Black experience, the Black Church and the Black theological enterprise. . . . It is only when Black women and men share jointly the leadership . . . that Black Theology can become a theology of divine liberation."[16] Commenting on the role of black women in BTP, Wilmore said: "Black women have given us our most effective inspired leadership. The great new phenomenon of Black religion in the US is the ascendancy of Black women—not just in church affairs, but in theological work and in ministerial and administrative roles."

The reach of black theology of liberation and womanist theology nurtured ongoing tension and creative ecumenical dialogue with feminist theologies, stirring a discourse on the globalization of women and perspectives of theology as related to patriarchy, power, and racism.

Too often the visions and voices of people, from a perspective of organizational and communal strength, are muzzled or overshadowed by the focus on the accomplishments of a few or the oblique unconsciousness and forgetfulness of the work of a whole. And yet the whole is always greater than the sum of its parts. This understanding is especially critical in the context of a people whose survival against oppression at so many levels is wedded to the capacity of each generation to take up the mantle of liberation.

Through the metanoic and synergistic *Orita* the work of Cone and the BTP singularly and collectively transformed the religious landscape from the academy to the pulpit to the pew. When *Black Theology and Black Power* was written, and when BTP was founded, few black academics had a voice, much less a program, from which efforts to articulate and create systematic theologies from a black, African, and/or pan-African perspective existed. Little attention had been given to the intentional convergence of black theologians, ministry, and laity in the context of praxis and church leadership. The womanist center at ITC was nowhere on the radar screen.

What many take for granted in the early twenty-first century is in large part the result of what the BTP members did the last thirty years of the twentieth century, leveraging their spheres of influence. Such influence is epitomized by the successful struggle to have issued the National Council of Churches' document calling for the transformation of seminaries, schools of theology, and religion with the inclusion of racially and ethnically diverse people as directors, trustees, faculty members, professors, and administrators.

The national board of the BTP was an ecumenism/*Orita* of disciples committed to social justice and black liberation theology. The legacy of BTP's national board, including James Cone, was shaped by some of the most influential, tenacious, uncompromising models of black liberation theology and praxis ever seeking to align the Word of God with the work of the people.

The members of BTP did not always agree on the means, but they shared core values. The membership list is long and includes representatives from black churches that seek to model and replicate the ideas that flowed from the energy of Cone and organizational efforts like those of BTP. They include pastoral leaders such as Jeremiah A. Wright, Calvin Butts, Wyatt Tee Walker, James Forbes, and Carolyn Knight. They include national church leaders such as the late Charles Spivey, Yvonne Delk, and Tyrone Pitts. They include academic leaders such as Cone, Jacquelyn Grant, Dwight Hopkins, Robert Franklin, Jamie Phelps, and Cain Hope Felder. Cornel West served as one of BTP's executive directors. Thus, students and mentors met with a spirit of transformation and action.

Demonstrating interdependent ecumenical influences, paralleling Cone's work, and shaping black liberation theology and praxis was the way in which Cain Hope Felder's *Troubling Biblical Waters* became a catalyst for dialogue among black theologians, black (and white) biblical scholars, and black church communities.[17] The multifaceted dialogue affirmed that the Bible was not the only legitimate source for theologizing.

As its last executive director, I am a witness that the BTP was the significant watering hole, repository, and clearinghouse of ecumenical and sociopolitical religious activity among men and women whose souls resonated with black liberation theology. Its rich and dynamic history of academic debate, struggle for intellectual space, and organizational independence represents a little told, if not unknown, story of who all nurtured, shaped, strengthened and disseminated black liberation theology and how and where it happened. Like a mother who gives birth to her children and sees their good works, so the BTP was the womb that incubated the dialogue and ultimate praxis of liberation theology in the context of what it means to be of African ancestry and Christian. Its history points to a center, where Cone's ideas were in the eye of the storm, and Wilmore was in the swirl of the wind with watchful eye and quick pen, attempting to capture the moment and take advantage of the opportunity.

The River Still Flows—the Bush Still Burns

As we entered the twenty-first century, Cone would say of Wilmore, "I dedicate *Risks of Faith* to you because you are my friend and colleague in the black theology movement, who was never afraid to take risks for black people. And for the communities of color throughout the world, for whom risks of faith are a daily reality." As one of BTP's most insightful and honest critics, Wilmore said, "BTP was where black theologians using the term broadly, are in communication with other ethnic groups and where a vital collegiality and contact is seriously pursued with Christians in the third world."[18]

Black theology of liberation is a permanent revolutionary force in the world order despite aspects of its unfulfilled mission. Cone and others have dared not only to direct the path but to stay on course in the spirit of *Orita*, confronting the reality that the demands of the twenty-first century may be even greater than before. Certainly, the stakes are higher. In a very real sense, the more things changed, the more they stayed the same.

The intersection of racism, sexism, classism, economics, and black liberation theology is critical to understanding Cone's challenge to the twenty-first-century ecumenical community. "Liberation is not a process limited to black-white relations in the United States: it is also something to be applied to the relations between rich and poor nations."[19] Many continue to engage in theological dialogue and tension with the ideas and personhood of the burning bush, James H. Cone.

Dwight Hopkins, a second-generation Cone scholar and currently Professor of Theology at the University of Chicago School of Divinity, distinguishes between black theology within African American religious studies and black theology of liberation. The former is grounded in reformism; the latter requires a structural analysis of power and is targeted to the least in society. "Constructive black theology of liberation must acknowledge and take into account the presence of power alongside, behind and below the monopoly capitalist political economy in America."[20]

Cone would add: "Liberation knows no color bar. The very nature of the gospel is universalism, that is, liberation that embraces the whole of humanity."[21] And so, the critique is ongoing and knows no boundaries.

Dennis Wiley, another one of Cone's second-generation students and now a pastor of a historic black church in Washington, D.C., has synthesized the twenty-first-century challenge for the black church: "Black theology is a tool that can empower the Black Church, and the Black Church is a vehicle that can liberate the African American community. . . . The Black Church must once again become one with the poor and one with the community."[22]

Jeremiah Wright, a preeminent pastor and scholar and Cone's peer, posits a corrective stance of Cone's earlier views on the black church and black theology. He argues that an underground theology, grounded in African tradition, fed the current of resistance to psychological and spiritual assent to oppression. Not abandoning but strengthening that underground theology is a necessity and challenge for the twenty-first-century black church.[23]

Cain Hope Felder, Professor of New Testament Language and Literature at Howard School of Divinity, cautions that basic biblical historiography still claims primacy as an agenda item of black theology of liberation.

> Despite all the evidence that indicates a manifest Black biblical presence, Eurocentric church officials and scholars have tended to deny or otherwise overlook or minimize the fact that Black people are in any significant way part of the Bible itself. . . .
>
> Many in the 1990s may think of a Black Jesus as an oddity or scandalous distortion of historical facts. Perhaps, the claim is acceptable when limited to theological metaphors of Black theologians like James H. Cone or Allan Boesak, but hardly. . . . The whole ridiculous point of creating the geographical designation called the Middle East . . . was an effort to avoid talking about Africa! It was a sign of academic racism that thoroughly sought to de-Africanize the sacred story of the Bible along with the whole

sweep of Western civilization. Palestine has always been exactly where it is today, namely, in Northeast Africa. It is a sad commentary on modern civilization that some human beings must vilify other cultures and people in order to create a mythology to feel good about themselves.[24]

Reflecting on the significance of black theology over the past thirty years for black Catholics, Sister Jamie Phelps, also a BTP founder, said the question in the Catholic church and elsewhere was race then. It is still race, and "a few highly publicized 'black stars' in politics, sports, literature, science and the corporate world" do not negate the racist problematic.[25] Cone agrees and calls for a radical race critique that is presently absent in "all these new theological constructs."[26] "The challenge for black theology in the twenty-first century is to develop an enduring race critique that is so comprehensively woven into Christian understanding that no one will be able to forget the horrible crimes of white supremacy in the modern world."[27] He continues to challenge the white church and academy to confront the sin of racism and all its tentacles. "If we could get a significant number of white theologians to study racism as seriously as they investigate the historical Jesus and other academic topics, they might discover how deep the cancer of racism is embedded not only in the society but also in the narrow way in which the discipline of theology is understood."[28]

He challenges the black church and black liberation theology to be more at home and trusting of one another and with womanist theology. Liberation theologies and African theologies must find their common prophetic voice to address and redress centuries of oppression. And black liberation theology must continue to find its voice and create new possibilities with those committed to the particularity of feminist, Asian, and Latin American theologies, taking head-on issues of sexism, classism, colorism, homophobia, and religious and ethnic cleansing.

According to Cone, now that humanity has reached the possibility of extinction, a critique of this ethos of entitlement and abuse, domination and inequitable distribution of the earth's resources is warranted.[29] We all must seek to accept responsibility as inheritors of the earth, ever seeking to a moral ethic in the age of the genome and technocracy.

> Every sphere of human existence is determined by ecology. It is not just an elitist or a white middle class issue. . . . The survival of the earth, therefore, is a moral issue for everybody. If we do not

save the earth from destructive human behavior, no one will survive. . . . What is absent from much of the talk about the environment in First World countries is a truly radical critique of the culture most responsible for the ecological crisis. . . . I have a deep suspicion about the theological and ethical values of white culture and religion. For five centuries whites have acted as if they owned the world's resources and have forced people of color to accept their scientific and ethical values.[30]

And thus, Cone has uncovered the liabilities of a society, clothed as a democracy but essentially evolving as a social technocracy, undergirded by advanced computer technology, and now with concentrated and automated knowledge systems of the human biological genome.

Finally and emphatically, out of the particularity of the triple jeopardy of black women, womanist theology might be called the soul of black theology of liberation. As Emilie Townes says, "never content to merely react to the situation, [womanist theology] seeks to change the situation."[31]

When radical and alternative ways of thinking about something moves from outside the circle of that which is normative to inside the circle of reasonable discourse, the possibility of a major paradigm shift has been created. In geology, parallel phenomenon shifts are seismic energy and can cause an earthquake. Space is being made.

These paradigm shifts change how the intellectual elite of a society or community thinks about a problem. These shifts can serve to unearth that latent and stilled nerve force in the minds and souls of individuals into a new reawakening of who they are and what they must do. Eventually the paradigm shifts permeate the vision and indwell in the subconscious and consciousness of a people, their self-identity and aspirations.

If all this is true, we can conclude that an unparalleled contribution to the seismic shift in theology was incubated during the past thirty years. Because of the BTP and James Cone, the master teacher and mentor, those who came and those who come to the *ecumenism/Orita* table are better off, and the world is a bit smaller. In understanding the particularity of our selves, regardless of our social location, we come to better appreciate the particularity of others and are better able to find a basis for bringing about a universality of human experience in the context of social justice.

Through Cone's witness and work, the dynamic nature of the ecumenical movement in the context of black liberation theology is revealed. By his example and prodding, an ongoing vitality adds to the imaginations of new theologians, seminarians, and scholars, who may envision a new human science and theology of praxis that of necessity forges *Orita,* "where the ways come together."

Today, some may say, "Dr. Cone, well done"; others may say, "Look at what we have wrought." And he might reply, "You knew I was a snake when you took me in." Whatever the case, all must say that at the close of the twentieth century and the opening of the twenty-first century, ready or not, implicitly or explicitly, ecumenical and cross-cultural theologizing and praxis have to factor in the prophetic voice of James Cone.

"There is a river," and the power of Cone's contribution to the ecumenical community is like the dynamism and ebb flow of the river: theologizing in the context of a changing reality, always acting on a hope and faith for a "not yet" in the "already." There is an urgent need for black theology to continue to respond to its reinvention and reiteration in the dynamism of globalization and pluralization.[32] Cone's legacy is a burning bush, inflaming courage, change, conviction, and commitment.

Thank you, Burning Bush, James Hal Cone.

13 / American Indian Religious Traditions, Colonialism, Resistance, and Liberation

George E. Tinker

That the People May Live!

Self-mutilation. Self-torture. These were the judgments expressed by appalled missionaries and U.S. government officials. And the ceremony is indeed demanding and even brutal in ways. Months of preparation and days of hard physical labor culminate in four days of dry fasting (no food, no liquids); dancing from dawn to dusk under a one-hundred degree sun in a confined sacred center; and finally offering the flesh of one's chest to be skewered and tied to a tree until dancing tears the skin. Few people in their right mind would willingly choose to engage in such a religious act of self-abuse.

And yet, as the dancers leave the center at the end of the fourth day, tears of sadness roll down one dancer's cheeks and drip onto the wounds from the day before. The impending separation from the center, from the tree that has given its life even as the dancers sacrificed themselves, generates this bitter-sweet melancholy, and the dancer finds himself mumbling a prayer of commitment promising to return the following summer.

They come to dance for a great variety of reasons. Actually each Indian person has his (or increasingly her) own discrete reasons that may or may not be shared with others. Yet, in actuality, there is only one reason to dance this ceremony: "That the people may live!" Anyone who does not understand this simple fact should stay home or at least stay out of the center, perhaps remaining under the arbor where learning can take place and where one can support those in the center. There is too much at stake. The well-being of the whole community depends on the hard spiritual work of a few who have made the commitment on behalf of the whole.

Beginning in the 1880s, in the interests of the doctrine of Manifest Destiny, it became U.S. government policy to outlaw specific American Indian ceremonies that were deemed dangerous impediments to the twin projects of civilizing Indian peoples and systematically relieving them of their land holdings. U.S. churches contributed significantly to this cause of colonial expansion by providing on-site policing services (missionaries) to ferret out secret performances of ceremonies, disrupt them, and destroy religious artifacts that were seized in the process. While these missionaries had no official sanction to perform such civil police services, they were never restrained by civil authorities but rather appear to have been greatly appreciated in their vigilante activities.

The ceremonies quite often continued in one fashion or another in spite of attempts to end their observance. The ceremonies were performed in hidden locations, often in abbreviated form and transformed in other ways to make concealment and continuation possible. One particular category of Lakota ceremony became a night-time ceremony that is, even now, typically conducted in complete darkness, a remnant of the earlier necessity for concealment. The perseverance of these ceremonial forms and of Indian cultures in general in the face of such intense repression and oppression is itself a testament to the tenacity of Indian peoples and their ongoing commitment to resistance and struggle. Needless to say, the combined efforts of church and state to rid North America of pagan Indian ceremonial life never quite succeeded.

With the intensification of the modern indigenous movement of resistance, beginning in the 1960s and reaching an apex in the emergence of the American Indian Movement after 1968,[1] a renewed pride in Indian identity began to erupt and along with it a renewed interest in the ancient ceremonial life of the peoples. What had been hidden or practiced by only a few in remote locations for so long suddenly began to claim a place in the public consciousness of Indian communities in one nation after another, with Lakota ceremonial practice taking center stage among both urban Indians and New Age whites. What had been revived as a tourist attraction at Pine Ridge in the sixties was brought back into the open as a legitimate ceremony with stricter and more traditional observance on the Pine Ridge and Rosebud Reservations during the seventies at Porcupine and Kyle, Ironwood Hilltop and Crow Dog's Paradise. With this spiritual renaissance, Indian identity was rekindled with a new pride, becoming more and more intimately connected to the Indian political resistance of the day. This renaissance of Indian traditional ceremonial life has continued unabated until today and shows little sign of ebbing soon. It speaks to the persistent and enduring attachment of Indian people to their traditional cultures and structuring of society. Yet there is also a cost to pay related to the complex and always lingering effects that European and Euro-American colonization has had and continues to have on the well-being of Indian communities. This chapter will look at the non-Indian appropriation of Indian ceremonial life as a means of unraveling some of the complexity.

Commitment and Vicarious Suffering

All Indian ceremonies contain some aspect of commitment—both to the ceremony itself, that is, to the spiritual presence that empowers a particular ceremony, and to the community in the context of which the ceremony is performed.[2] Many ceremonies also contain some aspect of vicarious suffering. While the purpose of the suffering is usually expressed in terms of some benefit for the community as a whole, its intensity can be of considerable magnitude for the individual. The strong sense of "doing" is part of what makes these ceremonies so appealing to American Indians as oppressed peoples living in these late stages of colonization and conquest.[3] In the midst of political and social hopelessness marked by extreme poverty and continued pressures from the systemic power structure, which pushes Indian peoples today toward a standard of compliance with the terms of colonization, these ceremonies provide hope. It is in the commitment and the carrying out of these ceremonies that many Indian people achieve some sense of doing something concrete about the community's ongoing sense of injustice, degradation, alienation, and all the dysfunctionality that emerges from successive generations of colonial imposition. In the suffering we experience in these ceremonies, there is hope for the people. Our pain is short by comparison to the pain of the community. We choose it for the sake of the people.

Vicarious suffering of the individual on behalf of the community is also part of the ritual drama typical of the Purification Ceremony, or Sweat Lodge, as it is colloquially known. In this ceremony the heat can be so intense for so long that the participants must encourage each other to "remember" why they are there, to concentrate on their prayers and not to focus on their own pain. Some Euro-Americans have asked over the years whether this ceremony is not similar to a sauna. While I have never *prayed* in a sauna, and therefore find the question somewhat bewildering, I can attest that the Purification Ceremony is typically a couple of hours longer than the ten-minute sauna stay recommended by physicians and certainly much hotter. The lodge itself is a symbolic microcosm of the earth. Our suffering is the substance of our prayer and is willingly endured for the sake of the earth and all of our relatives who live on it. Our prayer is especially for the community in which we thrive.

Likewise, the Rite of Vigil requires a commitment to a period of rigorous fasting—abstaining from both food and water—while bivouacked on a hillside far from the center of the community, confined in a small ceremonially marked area, perhaps a body length and a half in length and width. The duration of the ceremony varies from a single day and night, perhaps for an adolescent completing his first Rite of Vigil, to a more typical four-day period in the modern context. In ancient times there are stories told of people completing six-day ceremonies with regularity and even up to ten and eleven days, far in excess of what modern medical science would allow as possible without the replenishing of body fluids. While I have made a conscious choice *not* to provide an "instruction manual" for Indian ceremonial life and therefore do not intend to discuss the technical aspects of the spiritual experiences associated with these ceremonies, it should be apparent enough that the spiritual commitment needed to complete such a regimen far exceeds the physical requirements. While there is always a personal benefit from completing this ceremony, and even personal accretions of spiritual power, these benefits are always experienced as intended to help the individual in the person's commitment to the well-being of the whole. Quite typically in the Lakota context, for instance, the community will greet the individual upon completion of the ceremony not with an exclamation of "congratulations" but rather with a simple handshake and the words "thank you"—thank you, because the community has benefited from the person's successful completion of the commitment.

While variations of both of these ceremonies are common to a great many Indian nations in North America, the Sun Dance is a more regional ceremony native to the Great Plains and Great Basin, north and west into Canada and south into the prairies west of the Mississippi River. Again, one commits to this ceremony on behalf of the community whole, even when each participant has personal reasons for having initiated the commitment. The ceremony involves a pledge to personal deprivation (no food and no water) and the physical effort of sustained dancing over a three- or four-day period, depending on the particular national tradition,[4] through the heat of mid-summer days, and sometimes with dancing even extending through the

night. In the Lakota tradition the vicarious nature of the ceremony is cap-
tured in a common acclamation: "That the people may live!" The ceremony
is sometimes referred to as an annual world renewal ceremony and can be
described as maintaining the balance and harmony of life. Thus, whatever
the personal reasons for an individual commitment to complete the ceremony, the greater good of community well-being is always most prominently
at stake.

Colonialism, Neo-colonialism, and Resistance

These ceremonies are three of the most common practiced today by a variety
of Indian peoples but by no means the only ones. They have also become
common in urban multitribal Indian communities. They have become symbolic of our continuing cultural resistance to the colonizer at religious, social,
and political levels. While the ceremonies have important aspects of spiritual
power associated with them, they also have a distinct political and social
power related to the cohesion of the community and its focus on resistance
and liberation.

Countless Indians on virtually every U.S. reservation have been with-
drawing from the Christian churches into which they were missionized and
are making their return to these sorts of traditional ceremonies. The incon-
gruity of maintaining Indian self-pride and self-conscious identity as Indian
communities while participating in a religion imposed on us by our colonizers finally began to resist the inroads made by several generations of missionary imposition on our Indian communities. Many younger Indian clergy and
some of the congregations they serve have moved to reshape the Christianity
they have embraced through a reinterpretation of the European and Euro-
American theological and faith categories in language and material forms
that better reflect our Indian identity. Yet for the majority this shift is inadequate and still leaves the colonized with a religious tradition that belongs to
and derives from the colonizer. In the unhealthy and dysfunctional colonized
world that we Indian people inhabit in North America today, it seems that
the healthiest persons are those who have engaged in full-voiced resistance to
continuing colonization and have found a return to traditional ceremonial
life as a significant part of this resistance. Thus, the boldest of the younger
Indian clergy have hearkened to the call of these traditionalists and can be
found participating in the traditional ceremonies, praying in ways that an
earlier generation of missionaries would have criticized as devil worship.

Indian Religious Traditions as Commodity in a Mass Consumption Society

The young man had wandered in early to the site of an urban Indian community religious ceremony. The ceremonial leader met the man cordially. Because of the colonial phenomenon of "mixed blood," it is often not possible to ascertain by sight whether a person is Indian, so the leader asked the man whether he was Indian and what tribe he might be. The young man's honest reply was, "No, I am just a white man who is a pipe carrier." Just as easily and genuinely, the leader responded by asking, "Oh! Who do you carry a pipe for?" Possessing an Indian community religious symbol but living a polar-opposite existence in a non-Indian world, the young white man had no answer to the question but, rather, had to ask the meaning of the question. In reality, he knew who he carried this pipe for; he carried it for himself and for his own spiritual empowerment. Someone had sold this young man a pipe and a bill of goods to go with it.

Colonization and the processes of forcing assimilation are not yet done with Indian peoples. Even as we seek new ways to embrace ourselves as Indian communities, the colonizer has found new ways to impede Indian healing and to steal away what is left of Indian identity, cultural values, and traditional lifeways. The newest threat to Indian well-being actually builds on the impoverishment that has been established by five centuries of invasion and conquest, yet it involves a seeming affirmation of Indian cultures. Perversely, however, it includes an inculcation with a robust strain of the mass consumption virus. The appeal of easy cash accumulation for individuals who are accustomed to poverty is sometimes too great to refuse.

Over the past three decades Euro-American entrepreneurs have discovered that Indian culture has a dramatic appeal to those New Age aficionados whose sense of spiritual poverty has whetted their appetites for the exotic and reduced their economic wealth proportionately. First Carlos Castañeda and then Lynn V. Andrews found that even wholly fabricated but exotically romanticized tales of Indian mysteries could gain them both academic credibility and wealth at the same time.[5] While Thomas Mails's subject in *Frank Fools Crow: Wisdom and Power,* unlike Andrews's or Castañeda's protagonists, was an actual human being, Mails's subject had conveniently died at the time of publication, making validation of his writing equally impossible.[6] The writings of all three belong to a particular genre of modern gnostic fantasy.

These parodies of Indian spiritual traditions have spawned countless copycats, some of whom have gained credibility by spending a short time in actual Indian ceremonies indulging their fantasies. Recently, the Florida American Indian Movement reports that a white woman calling herself "Bear" (a catchy, Indian-sounding name), having danced in a Lakota Sun Dance ceremony, has established herself in the "how-to" workshop business and drawn 250 people at $1,500 per person to a recent event. The susceptible are quickly separated from their wallets in return for some illusion of spiritual well-being, but Indian people are left the poorer as misperceptions and falsified interpretations of our world are sold for profit. Thus, Indian cultural traditions, those particularly that are identified as spiritual or religious traditions, have emerged as commodities of trade in the Great American Supermarket of Spirituality.

With this discovery of Indian spirituality as a growth industry, many Indian people with a little knowledge, that is, significantly more knowledge than Castañeda or Andrews, began to move into the marketplace as well. While Andrews and Castañeda made up fantasies that sounded Indian but were actually fabricated lies, the Indian purveyors of spirituality are also engaged in selling a lie. In their case, the lie is decorated with enough genuine Indian forms and structures that the purchasers are led to believe that they are indeed buying the genuine item. Yet, there remains a significant and substantial set of differences between Euro-American New Age belief structures and those of Indian peoples. For the purposes of this chapter, I would like to describe a single but definitive distinction between the two.

New Age Individualism and Indian Community: A Colonial Clash of Values

Beginning already with Aristotle (in the fourth century B.C.E.), but accelerated by the next generation of Hellenistic philosophers (Stoics, Epicureans, Skeptics) from 300 B.C.E. on, Mediterranean and, hence, European thinking took a decided turn toward the emergence of the individual. With the conquest of Alexander the Great, Aristotle's pupil, Europe began to experience the steady decline of the importance of community as the city-state was supplanted by empire followed by empire, and Greek philosophy shifted subtly away from Aristotle's search for the "good" toward the Hellenistic search for the wise individual. Both religion (the "mystery religions") and philosophy in the three centuries leading up to the emergence of Christianity became increasingly concerned with the salvation of or the behavior of the individual, a trajectory that led directly to the emergence of the Cartesian self more than a millennium and a half later (and *the ludic postmodern American selfish self* at the end of the second millennium C.E.).

It should be of little surprise, then, to discover in New Age aficionados a spiritual focus on the self and the engagement of spiritual experience for the sake of personal self-enhancement or the accrual of personal spiritual power. Whether this is good or ill is beyond the purview of this chapter. I only intend to emphasize that this modus operandi is diametrically opposed to ceremonial intentionality in any American Indian traditional cultural context.

When New Age aficionados invade Indian ceremonies, then, they represent another sort of colonizing virus that threatens the health of the communities into which they have invited themselves or to which they have finagled an invitation from Indian people unaccustomed to saying no and too weak from generations of colonization to change that cultural habit of hospitality even when their own survival might depend on it. Many of these spiritual seekers are genuinely well-intentioned and seriously seeking for something more substantial than the spiritual experiences of the churches into which they were born and raised. Typically, they see themselves as sharing a world-view with Indian people: a concern for environmental issues, an openness to the universe as an expression of pervasive divinity, a sense of the interrelationship of all things and especially all people, and a sense of the immanence and accessibility of spiritual power. All these may be thought of as laudable, yet they are not yet Indian; indeed, the New Age seeker may find her- or himself as the distinct opposite of what Indian religious traditions represent. Namely, the New Ager is a prime example of the Western, European, Euro-American cultural value of individualism in its starkest naïveté.[7]

The viral aspect of this introduction is that the individualist belief inserted into an Indian community by the New Age adherent can very quickly affect especially the younger generation of that indigenous community. This is a common experience in urban Indian communities where there may not be immediate access to traditional teaching elders. Thus, we have a generation of young people who are learning, or mis-learning, how to be Indian from non-Indian individualists. New Agers, to this extent, are finally much more effective in destroying Indian cultural values than several generations of missionaries and government functionaries, especially in this late period of (neo)colonialism.

Christianizing the Language of Ceremonial Traditions

As the Euro-American virus of individualism infects Indian traditional communities, the final conquest of the colonizer is most apparent in the changes that occur in the ways Indian people themselves talk about their ceremonies. This shift to individualism, marked by the participation in a ceremony so that the individual might gain personal power, is what I refer to as the Christianizing of Indian religious traditions. It represents a serious colonization of the American Indian mind, one that may or may not be immediately recognizable by the person whose mind is so affected. The gospel of this Christianizing process is not Jesus but the Euro-American/Christian cultural value of individualism. The result of this Christianizing process is to further erode the Indian value of community and to bring us one step closer to the modern globalization of culture around Western values. The surface structures of our ceremonies may continue to look Indian, but the deep structure of meaning that undergirds the ceremony is slowly changing.

Most critically, the infestation of individualism that comes with the New Age invasion of Indian ceremonies means that there is a subtle degeneration in language. It spreads the virus even among the teaching elders and spiritual leaders of a community as they struggle to translate their culture and the meaning of their ceremonies into language that can be accessed (and often accessed for money) by those who come out of a radically different set of cultural behaviors and values. As I have already noted, it is very difficult for Indian people to say no. This is especially true when the white supplicant comes to an Indian ceremonial context with greater economic resources than either the spiritual leader or local Indian people in general. Even without engaging in the active marketing and selling of ceremonies, the spiritual leader may find him or herself the recipient of some financial benefit. However small that benefit may be, it has a great impact in an environment of poverty. Yet with the appearance of the first of these Euro-American supplicants the degradation of language about the ceremony already begins as the spiritual elder changes the language of explanation in order to accommodate an outsider with money.

I am not arguing that these traditional spiritual leaders intend to change the meaning of the ceremony. Rather, I believe that their language about the ceremony changes gradually over time as each elder struggles to communicate with the outsider, to translate from one culture into another. It seems to be a natural colonizing process that the colonized shift their language in order to accommodate the understanding of the colonizer. Yet I should clarify here that this "natural" process is really an unnatural process of oppression and conquest that has inherently logical and devastating effects on both the colonized and colonizer. So it becomes a natural response on the part of the oppressed to accommodate power! As a result, the traditional elder may make small shifts in her or his language, so small that they may be imperceptible even to the speaker. Yet slowly, the meaning of the ceremony is Christianized toward the Western, Christian valorization of the individual. Eventually, even the young people from the elder's own community pick up this new language, not knowing that it is new or that it represents a concession to the dearth of understanding on the part of colonizer participants, and the virus of individualism has suddenly gained a firmer foothold. Suddenly, it seems, the ceremony is engaged in order to enhance one's personal spiritual well-being or power rather than the well-being of the community.

The net result is a tragic loss for both Indian peoples and for Euro-Americans. For the former, a way of life is changed forever. The latter have paid out bundles of dollars in return for the purchase of an illusion of Indianness, for a spiritual experience that they can wear with pride but that has little meaning in terms of what is actually claimed for it. For American Indian communities there is a loss of culture and erosion of the value system that has given indigenous traditions the strength to resist the full power of colonization until now. For Euro-Americans and Europeans, the addiction to power and dominance is enhanced as they respond to the illusive surface structure of Indian ceremonies and colonize them into a new religious resource for the colonizer, a resource clothed with the appearance of righteousness—much as statutory rape can be clothed with the claim of consent.

What we are experiencing in the Indian world is the globalization of ourselves as a commodity and the concomitant transformation of our cultures toward an emerging world culture marked by market symbols of global consumption, like the McDonald's, Nike, Pizza Hut, and Sony billboards in every major third-world city. Perhaps technology can provide for a new spirituality that will prove satisfying to our "Star Trek" descendants. Unfortunately, there may be no alternative as the globalized, Christianized indigenous religions of the world lose their antiquity and the cultural value base upon which they have always been predicated.

Native American Generosity and Spiritual Scalp Collecting

At a deeply philosophical level, then, the question must be raised: Can and should non–Native Americans participate in the ceremonial spirituality of Native American peoples? This question seems ever-present these days in my classroom, in discussion at lectures, and in the mail that arrives on my desk daily. For the most part, the question is articulated by people whose sincerity I do not question. They voice, at least, a great respect for the ceremonies but also a deep-felt need for their individual participation: in pipe ceremonies,

Sweat Lodge purification rites, Sun Dances, and a variety of other events. Many of these non-natives have come to see Native American ceremonial spirituality as somehow essential to their own well-being.

For their part, Native Americans have responded in a variety of ways across a spectrum of possibilities. Many, especially Lakota practitioners, have welcomed non–Native American participation and have seen their spirituality as a human universal. They have become virtual missionaries developing converts and followers in places as far removed from their own lands as Oregon and Germany. Some have made the teaching of native spirituality a for-profit industry servicing a spiritually starved Euro-American clientele. While they inevitably alienate themselves from their own people, the financial rewards become especially lucrative in places like Malibu, Marin County, Boulder, Aspen, or Germany. There continue to be significant communities of people, however, who resist either these missionary or these economic impetuses and continue to see their ceremonial life as a community event closed to outsiders.[8]

Since opinion seems so divided among Native American practitioners themselves, a corollary question becomes even more important. Namely, who are the appropriate spokespeople for giving an authoritative answer to the first question? Non-natives who have participated in native ceremonies invariably announce that they were, in fact, invited by Indian people themselves to participate. The invitation, in a sense, becomes their passport into the spiritual world of Indian peoples. The actuality is that hospitality is one of the most important virtues in every Indian community. This makes it most difficult for Indian people to say no, even when it means the invasion of ceremonial privacy, and often even when we do mean no. Non-Indians seem, correspondingly, to have difficulty in not taking advantage of Indian peoples in any context, even taking advantage of extreme generosity. It can be argued that Euro-American people are culturally good at taking what they want or think they need but have great difficulty in receiving any gift, especially if understanding the boundaries of the gift is implicit in the giving. Euro-Americans are best at imposing on others rather than offering their own gifts. Somehow, it is never quite clear that there are some things that we do not want to share.

Even in those cases, however, where a non-Indian has a clear invitation from an Indian participant, the question must be raised whether the Indian person has the right to extend the invitation. In any Euro-American context, of course, the invitation of one individual to another individual can be taken at face value as a valid and authentic invitation that the other person may accept or refuse merely on the basis of personal preference. The complicating factor in the American Indian ceremonial context is the community. Since the ceremony is a community event and all participants affect the entire community and its ceremony, who does have the right to invite a non-member into the community intimacy and privacy of ceremony? While this complexity should be a warning to all of us in the Indian community in terms of our sense of generosity, it should also be taken seriously by our Euro-American relatives. Any non-Indian who is so invited needs to question seriously within himself or herself whether the invitation is even remotely valid and genuine—even if it comes from a higher-status elder or leader.

Generosity: A Dysfunctional Virtue

I have already begun to suggest that the enduring results of colonialism have left Indian people fighting with chronic levels of dysfunctionality, which may lead to inappropriate invitations to intimacy, much like many other abuse survivors in our modern world of violence. Indeed, we find quite often that the very values our cultures have always lived can become a part of this dysfunctionality when they are lived too uncritically in our modern relationship with our colonizer. That is to say, even virtues can ultimately prove to have a dysfunctional potential, especially in our contemporary world of colonial power and transition. The Indian valorizing of the virtue of generosity, as we have already begun to see, is one example.

The missionaries who intended to civilize American Indian peoples found much to criticize in Indian cultures. The propensity of many Indian cultures for a family to periodically give away all or much of its accumulated wealth consistently came under missionary attack as diabolical. Since the church has always intended that peoples' generosity extend primarily to itself, one can sense how a people's generosity toward one another may have presented a significant threat to the church. Be that as it may, generosity is counted as one of the cardinal virtues by nearly all Indian peoples.

In my own tribe, traditional leadership on the council of "little old ones," the $No^nho^nzhi^nga$, was contingent upon proving oneself with regard to this virtue. For instance, a candidate for appointment to the council will have given away all that his (and occasionally her) family has on at least three occasions.[9] Along with bravery, intelligence, and community morality, generosity helped to define those who were paradigmatic for the whole community. The open generosity of Indian peoples in New England upon the first arrival of English colonizers is well known. Without the agricultural skill and generosity of the original inhabitants of the land, the colonists would have certainly perished during their first winters in North America.[10] To this day, to admire something in another's possession quite often means receiving it as a gift. Such an ethic proved to be foreign and alienating to the missionaries, even as it proved useful in building solid community existence and alliances within and among Indian nations.

While the virtue of generosity as different Native American peoples practice it can be touted as something superior to the values of civilization imposed on Indian peoples by the Europeans, it has also become susceptible to abuse, misappropriated by our white relatives and misdirected by Indian peoples themselves. The inability of Indian people to say no, for instance, to the white, New Age invasion of Indian spirituality leaves our communities extremely vulnerable. The ethic of generosity dictates that we share what we have with all those who come our way. Food is always shared with a guest who happens to drop by, and it is only natural that what we treasure most highly, our spirituality, can also be so easily and generously offered to others. What we are dealing with today is a *spiritual* giveaway in which Indian generosity has been pressed to an extreme of dysfunctionality. Moreover, as we seem to invite more and more white relatives to join us in our traditional ceremonial life, the very ceremonies that give us life are being changed before our eyes, even though we do not usually recognize the change.

The modern Indian context of conquest and colonization has resulted in significant levels of emotional and mental health dysfunctionality, from chronic, community-wide levels of depression, to widespread alcoholism; high rates of teen suicides; serious alienation from the Euro-American culture of work and achievement; and an ongoing mental colonization. One result of this process is a pervasive co-dependency with our colonizer,[11] resulting in what I would characterize as a serious addiction to the color white. There is a constant need for approval of white institutions (especially government and church), white authority figures, and white friends. Thus, when Euro-Americans clamor for acceptance into our ceremonies, all too often we are flattered and feel a sense of affirmation for our culture and our religious traditions instead of being wary, guarded, suspicious, and distrusting.

The co-dependent need for approval on the part of the abused person is a common theme in contemporary mental health analysis. In the same way, Indian people, struggling with our own history of abuse under the paternalistic abuse of colonialism, seem to have some underlying need for white approval. Indian churches clamor for the approval of white bishops; Indian national government figures clamor for the approval of Washington, D.C., and its array of senators and congresspersons; Indian national community agency employees all clamor to meet the approval of the U.S. government's BIA (Bureau of Indian Affairs) or Indian Health Service bureaucracies. Always, we are susceptible to the well-meaning, liberal do-gooders who want so much to help us and tell us what is best for Indian peoples. White greed compounds this Indian dysfunctionality in the rape of our natural resources, in extraction contracts that are entirely too favorable to the multinational conglomerates that enrich themselves almost at will on many reservations.[12] Likewise, the New Age aficionados move into our world with words of affirmation about the spiritual treasures of Indian peoples and then proceed to steal those treasures just as they stole the land a generation or two earlier.

Many kind-hearted Indian persons respond in this co-dependent relationship out of a felt need to help our white relatives find their way spiritually. Yet it seems that there is an even stronger felt need to garner the approval and affirmation of these same spiritually impoverished white friends.

A useful summary of the issues might be generated by posing afresh the question, Is the sharing of Indian ceremonial life helpful to either Indian or non-Indian people? The following attempts to index briefly my response to this question:

1. It contributes to the colonialist project of destroying Indian culture, Indian ceremonies, and Indian communities in unintentional ways.

2. Cross-cultural differences make it very difficult for non-Indians to internalize Indian cultural values and behavioral habits and make it almost invariably a necessity for Indian structures to remodel themselves around non-Indian structures.

3. As a result, the Euro-American participant usually only has a surface structure participation in the ceremony. There is a deep structure significance, of course, for both Indian and non-Indian participants, but the significance is quite different in each case. The sense of personal spiritual self-enhancement that is so central to Euro-American New Age participants means that they only experience the illusion of Indianness and the illusion of spiritual power. The result is not at all real, or, to the extent that the experience is real, it is no longer in any way Indian.

4. Along with the communalist/individualist cultural difference comes another significant difference regularly overlooked by New Age wannabes.

Namely, American Indian national communities are what is often referred to as modal social organizations, as opposed to sodal social organizations. That is to say, having an Indian nationality and hence participation in the ceremonial spirituality of the community are not voluntary acts like joining a church. Rather, the concept of modality signifies that membership in the community is a birthright. This means that New Agers who invite themselves into Indian ceremonies enjoy a privilege that we Indian people do not and cannot. New Age Euro-Americans are able to choose their tribe of presumed affiliation from among a wide range of choices, whereas Indian people are stuck, so to speak, with the tribe of their birth. For New Agers, choosing Indian spirituality and choosing a particular Indian community whose spirituality they will imitate is much like choosing a church denomination or congregation. That, of course, is the history of voluntary organization in the United States, dating especially from the eighteenth century. Indian people choose neither tribe nor clan. We are what we are by birth. Indeed, it is the advent of Euro-American voluntarism (the invention of denominations and denominational choices) that has proven so fracturing of Indian community. New Age invasion of Indian ceremonies portends a radical continuation of that fracturing process for Indian communities.

5. In many cultures, spiritual knowledge is not the universal right of all citizens in the national community; there is a division of labor according to clans and societies. In many cultures different clans or societies have particular responsibilities for parts of a national ceremony. The success of the ceremony then depends on the appropriate participation of each clan and society in the nation, performing its discrete role in the ceremonial whole. Not only does the whole community depend on each subgroup to do its part, but the knowledge associated with each part belongs to the particular clan or society that is responsible for performing it. Other clans, other family members, other neighbors may indeed have no right even to claim any part of that knowledge. The Hopi spokesperson Talayesva, for instance, declines to comment on such knowledge when pressed by Leo Simmons, the anthropologist, on exactly such a basis.[13] The sentiment expressed as "I have a right to know!" is an inherently white and Euro-American valorization of the individual, whether anthropology/scientific scholar or New Age aficionado. "I have a right to know" is countered by the communitarian interest in the good of the whole. Pressing the individual's presumed right-to-know can violate the good of the whole, especially when that right-to-know is pressed by someone outside of the community itself.

6. White involvement in Indian ceremonies eventually is harmful to our white relatives because it reinforces the inbred sense of white privilege that is the heritage of every Euro-American person in North America, just as male privilege is the heritage of every male. One can hear the appeal to white privilege in the seemingly neutral claim of many of our white relatives: "Spirituality does not belong to anyone." Yet the neutrality dissolves as one understands the white claim on Indian spirituality and either the replication of our ceremonies or the direct participation in them. "You must share" is a second claim, one that holds us to a dysfunctional valorization of our own cultural value of hospitality. Yet it needs to be emphasized that we hurt our white relatives and friends when we naively invite them into our private, community ceremonial life. We are only encouraging the final act of colonization and conquest. In an amazing but convenient turnaround, our ceremonies are no longer castigated as demonic, savage, and uncivilized; instead, with Indian land and natural resources already stolen, our ceremonies have become the new prize possession of the colonizer and their theft the ultimate act of postmodern colonialism. It is a new version of the colonizer indulgence in colonial exoticism, a fetishization of Indian people and Indian traditions.[14] This becomes a primary reason for arguing that the inclusion of white folk in the community intimacy of our ceremonies is not healthy for those white relatives, especially if they really do want to make a difference in the world and find creative ways to do things differently.

14 Ecology as Experience in African Indigenous Religions

Edward P. Antonio

It is often claimed that Africans and other indigenous peoples are very close to nature. This theory, together with the idea that Africans have a holistic view of the world in which everything (human as well as natural) is organically interconnected, has led some scholars to the view that in the ecological wasteland that modern society is fast becoming, the recovery of a meaningful and more balanced form of life requires a repristination of African traditional values. On the face of it this might suggest the existence of an ecological discourse embedded in both African worldviews and African lifestyles. Yet no one, as far as I know, has done any meaningful research to show either the existence of such a discourse or, indeed, to examine the ecological implications of the claim that Africans are close to nature.

Here I will look at some elements of African worldviews within which is implicit a theology of nature and ask what, if anything, this theology has to say about the preservation of the natural environment. Second, I shall suggest that closeness to nature in itself is no guarantee of an ecologically sensitive practice. In other words, I shall contend that African theologies of nature do not yield a ready-made ecological discourse, which, by our sheer exposure to it, will pull us back from the precipice of ecological disaster by compelling us into environmentally friendly patterns of behavior. Third, and seemingly paradoxically, I shall also argue that the "raw materials" of African theologies of nature offer, within the context of a hermeneutical reconstruction, rich resources for minting or developing useful ways of thinking about nature and how best to move away from our present exploitative attitudes toward it to friendlier ones.

Notice that I speak of theologies of nature rather than of natural theologies. This is because I wish to distinguish, on the one hand, those patterns of thought that emerged in medieval Europe and sought to explain natural phenomena as partly an expression of God's general revelation and partly a distinct realm somehow opposed to the divine or the sacred, and, on the other, African understandings of nature as sublime and therefore as a repository of sacred tokens or signs of the presence of divinity throughout the cosmos. To understand the ways in which Africans experience nature I shall begin with an account of their beliefs about both nature and God or the divine.

The idea of starting with a description of African views regarding natural phenomena arises somewhat indirectly from two important considerations, both of which seem to be central to how environmentalists have been putting forward a case for a balanced approach to ecosystems. The first consideration is contained in Lynn White's essay "The Historical Roots of Our Ecological Crisis," first published in 1967,[1] in which he blamed Christian theologies of creation for the manner in which they came to shape a dominating mentality toward nature in Western thought. White saw this mentality as the root of the ecological crisis. Clearly an implicit premise of White's criticism is that worldviews matter not only in that they mold behavior but also in that they do so in ways that carry material outcomes for the world around us. Since White published his paper, the search for a sound eco-ethic has overtly or otherwise taken it for granted that how we think about the world, what we claim about what gives our relation to it meaning, determines or at least shapes the nature of that relationship.

The second consideration that explains why I start with a description of African worldviews as they pertain to nature derives from the importance given to the notion of the indigenous in postcolonial and postmodern discourses. Both these discourses have taught us that formerly subjugated knowledge and the marginalized moral economies of indigenous peoples are not simply phenomena of exotic interest, or phenomena whose interest is simply predicated upon their symbolic or material value for the communities concerned and thus to be tolerated in the name of some form of liberal egalitarian sentiment. They also have, besides their own intrinsic worth, something to teach us about how we ought to conduct ourselves in the face of the continuing denudation of nature and the loss of humane values in order to recover a balanced sense of our place in the universe.

Much of this has no doubt involved highly romanticized and in some instances even caricatured images of the indigenous. But, again, what is important for the purposes of this chapter is the suggestion that if our worldviews are letting us down, we need to find alternative ones. The idea is that in order to effect the sort of changes in our activities that will result in the healing of the earth, we need to change how and what we think about our relationship to it. The recommendation, then, is that we ought to look to Africa for the appropriate lessons.

If, from the range of indigenous systems of belief found in the world, we should settle on any one as offering suitable models for bringing into being the necessary changes in our thought patterns, what justification would we give for our choice? The question of justification is an important one because it is directly related to what it is we believe the indigenous has to offer that cannot be found in the hitherto dominant worldviews.

Students of African religions appear to be unanimous that African cosmologies divide the spirit world into nature spirits on the one hand and human or ancestral spirits on the other. The category of nature spirits itself falls into two other subcategories: earth spirits and sky spirits. This division represents a complex understanding of the structure of the universe and the interrelationships among different parts of nature as well as between nature and human beings.

Here we shall be concerned with nature spirits, particularly those associated with the earth. Belief in nature spirits is, of course, not universal in Africa. According to the literature the highest concentration of spirit beings is found in West Africa. What is interesting about virtually all earth spirits is the manner in which their individual identities are articulated in terms of some dimension of nature. Each spirit performs a number of functions in the domain of nature over which it presides. Let us take as an example: the water spirits. Water is life; upon it depends the fertility of the land and the purification of the body, the soul, and the general well-being of the community. Water in rivers, lakes, and seas also sustains fish and other creatures that provide food for humans. Belief in water spirits represents a community's recognition of the importance of water as both a social and a spiritual resource. The functions of water spirits are in this regard fourfold. First, they act as representatives of the nature of water itself in much the same way that in modern science hydrogen and oxygen represent it. Second, water spirits symbolize the material benefits of water, such as fertility, good health, and purity. In turn, water itself symbolizes the spirit as a life-sustaining force. Third, they act as the moral guardians of rivers, lakes, and seas such that no community can abuse these resources without incurring their wrath. Fourth, the spirits serve as explanatory elements for the origins, necessity, and uses of water.

Water spirits are, of course, not the only earth spirits, nor do they exhaust the function of such spirits. To be sure, every aspect of what in modern terms we would call the ecosystem has a spirit or divinity assigned to it for its protection. Thus trees, mountains, rocks, animals, reptiles, the cosmic elements, and so forth are integrated into different cosmologies through the agency of spirit beings.

These cosmologies lay down the rules governing how humans ought to relate both to the spirits and to the different aspects of the environment over which these beings have jurisdiction. On this account, then, the entire structure of the universe is given a spiritual valorization. The question here is whether this spiritual value is of any ecological significance. Those who have urged us to turn to indigenous thought because of its alleged proximity to nature believe this spiritual value does have ecological significance. But I wish to contest that view by showing that it is mistaken in a number of respects. The ecological significance of nature spirits in African traditional religions cannot simply be deduced from the mere existence of such spirits or from what is believed about them outside of the context of the uses to which Africans in traditional communities put nature. Such a conclusion ignores the fundamental ways in which perceptions of natural phenomena and their uses are doubly constituted by, on the one hand, nature itself and, on the other, cultural processes. The latter are, at certain crucial levels, carriers of efforts to understand and contain nature. But the way in which nature shapes our perceptions of it is already itself a product of cultural interpretation.

The notion that the positing of spirits as nature-entities or of nature as a set of spirit-entities automatically implies a balanced ecology involves an attempt to derive culture from nature. Ecology, at least as both a study of the ecosystems and an existential practice oriented toward the health and maintenance of such systems, does not derive from the simplicity of nature or, indeed, from anyone's being close to nature, but rather from human relationships thereto. In other words, ecology is a product of our (problematical) interaction with the ecosystem. Thus the determination of the spiritual valorization of nature in African traditional religions depends on how Africans have traditionally interacted with it. The sense of this argument depends, in fact, on what is meant by the environment, which, to be sure, is not simply a geographical locality under the control of designated spirits. It is also a space of production in relation to which people seek to realize a range of productive, symbolic, and ritual intentions. As David Cooper has put it, a true environment is one in which people have an *intentional* relationship to the world around them.[2] It is a field of significance. The tilling of land, the tending of animals, hunting, fishing, the gathering of wild fruit and other roots for food and medicinal purposes constitute the basic elements of such a field of significance. How these different activities hang together, that is, the significance they carry, points to three things: (1) the structure of the world, (2) the understanding of the world as the realm of utility, and (3) how relationships (among people and between people and the world) are defined.

Here I shall deal only with the first two. The first of these has an explanatory value. It is here that the role of nature spirits is of fundamental importance. For they offer the metaphysical key that unlocks the realm of utility, and thus they link the human need for survival to the necessity of production. Because without this necessity nature would appear entropic and unable to satisfy human needs. The presence of nature spirits in the physical world not only guarantees the latter's orderliness but also connects its origins to God (since the spirits are God's agents) and thus serves to explain the nature and purpose of the world. But since African religions are predominantly this-worldly we can take it that their understanding of the nature and purpose of things is equally this-worldly.

That is why the realm of utility is so vital. The basic elements that constitute the environment as a field of meaning or significance, which I referred to earlier, thus define the world as both the locale of the satisfaction of human needs within the context of productive activity and a discursive domain of regulations that expresses the demands of the spirits about how nature shall be treated in the process of production. The connection between production and the demands of the spirits is best seen in ritual and symbolic activity. In many communities agricultural or hunting projects are in most cases preceded by the performance of ritual in which the help of the spirits and through them of God is invoked. Or, again, we can observe how sacrifice and offerings are used to obtain the assistance of these spirits in times of natural crises—drought, failure in hunting, or when some sacred aspect of nature has been violated. The undertaking of these symbolic activities has the effect of partly transforming the elements of production on which the meaning of the environment depends from being purely physical into being both moral and spiritual: moral insofar as every act of production must follow a prescribed path and must avoid transgressing the relevant taboos, and spiritual because due recognition must be given to the spirit(s) overseeing the physical space in which production is taking place.

My emphasis on production as the means by which Africans seek to configure a field of significance, an environment, is intended to draw attention to their highly utilitarian attitude toward nature. This is quite in keeping with the anthropocentric character of African religions on which many scholars have remarked. And I use *utilitarian* here to designate the ideas (1) that a person's behavior must be such that it is always directed toward the greatest happiness for the greatest number of people in the community and (2) that the path to such happiness involves, among other things, the instrumentalization of nature. By this, I do not mean that the anthropocentrism of African religions tends toward the domination or mastery of nature as is the case in certain forms of anthropocentric thought in the West. Rather, the instrumentalization of nature connotes the idea of use or of nature understood (however implicitly) as a means to an end. What occludes a dominating attitude toward nature is precisely the symbolic transformations that occur in production upon the recall, through ritual, of the lordship of nature spirits over the physical world.

Now all this might seem to suggest a happy coincidence of forces, human and spiritual, all tending toward a balanced natural environment, a situation in which the human realm is kept close to nature by a network of needs and moral requirements—such as the need to satisfy the spirits through offerings and sacrifice (and what must be offered or sacrificed are gifts of nature), the need for meaning, the need for material well-being, and so on. In other words, it would seem from the foregoing that African religions offer a cosmology that involves an inherent respect for nature that, given the importance of the utility of the physical world, is rooted in daily experience. It would also appear that because of the role of nature spirits, such experience configures the natural environment as a field of spiritual significance.

At first sight all this seems to conform to the arguments of some environmentalists that indigenous cosmologies provide alternative models for rethinking the human place in the world. But is this really so? I think not. To begin with, the relationship between nature spirits and the physical world over which they exercise dominion is highly ambiguous. There is no evidence that the prescriptions they lay down regarding how humans ought to deal with nature are ecologically intended. These prescriptions are better understood in terms of the explanatory function of spirit entities as guarantors of cosmic order in a certain part of the universe. This claim is not unlike that made by Jürgen Moltmann in his discussion of the role of the Spirit in the Christian doctrine of creation, in which he distinguishes between the cosmic and the reconciling/redeeming modes of its operations.[3]

Moreover, the order the nature spirits sustain is primarily cosmic rather than ecological or moral. The point here is not that cosmic order does not presuppose a morally or ecologically balanced structure of things. Rather, the notion of cosmic order has no relevance here since the idea of a cosmic ecology or a cosmic morality is logically incoherent. We simply cannot morally imagine what such an ecology would be like. In the case of nature spirits, we are dealing with a limited domain of immediate experience, and we can imagine what responding appropriately to their prescriptions would be like. But insofar as this implies that such responses are of any ecological value, it begs the question under discussion here of the relevant senses in which nature spirits are disposed toward the physical world. I am contending that the relevant sense is primarily cosmic and not environmental.

The relationship between the spirits and humans is also ambiguous. There is no evidence that while operating purposefully in the realm of utility and availing themselves of its materials, humans consciously or otherwise assume responsibility for the protection of nature. This is in fact not their role but that of spirits. For humans to do otherwise would be a form of hubris fraught with dire consequences for both humans and their use of nature. Indeed, in these cases nature itself can be used by supernatural entities to visit such consequences on a whole community.

Insofar as humans obey the spirits to be respectful toward nature—admittedly, almost always—the expression of their obedience is equally ambiguous. For it is not the case that the whole of nature is inhabited by spirits but only certain designated parts of it. Sacred mountains, trees, rocks, and rivers are good examples. But these sites normally involve only a small part of the totality of any given natural environment. The greater part of that totality is thus excluded. In other words, by choosing to inhabit only certain sites within nature and urging respect toward those sites, the spirits sanction a highly selective and discriminatory respect. This of course reflects the effect of hierarchy in African cosmologies. If the function of nature spirits is understood ecologically rather than cosmically, as I have suggested, then the fact that they institute such a discriminatory principle of respect would point to a bad ecology, one that would be incapable of coping with the whole question of the protection of biodiversity or natural variety. This is not to suggest that Africans do not respect those parts of nature that they are not specifically enjoined to revere by the spirits. But the sources of whatever respect is accorded other parts of nature than those considered sacred must be sought elsewhere than in the supposed role of nature spirits.

There is, however, an objection here that it will be well to dispose of right away. Some may claim that my account overlooks the fact that Africans do not normally distinguish between the sacred and the profane and that there-fore the reverence extended to sacred aspects of nature is easily transferable to the rest of nature. Regrettably, it is not a fact that Africans do not distinguish between holy and unholy spaces. One can marshal a host of empirical exam-ples to dispose of this romantic myth. I do not have the space to do that here. I shall mention only one, perhaps extreme, example. While it is taboo to defecate on a holy site, one can do so anywhere else in the bush. What is this, if not a pragmatic distinction between the sacred and the profane? Again, the very idea that only certain spaces enjoy a qualitatively different kind of rev-erence is enough to demolish the notion of an undifferentiated and undiffer-entiating religious consciousness. By implication this means that the ecological significance of African religions does not lie, if indeed it lies any-where, in such a closed space.

What then are we to make of the claim that because Africans are close to nature their experiences and cosmologies yield patterns of thought and prac-tice that it would be desirable to follow if we are to avert ecological disaster? This claim is problematic in a number of respects. The problems it causes are partly philosophical and partly ideological. Philosophically this claim is based on two related premises, both of which are untenable. The first is that closeness to nature implies ecological sensitivity. The second is, granting for the moment the first premise, that the nature of the environmental problem (assuming there was one) that necessitated the ecological sensitivity posited in the first premise was in some significant sense similar to our problems today and that the solutions applied to it can, allowing relevant adjustments, also be applied now.

Regarding the first premise, closeness to nature in itself implies no ethic of responsibility that is ecologically applicable. Animals, including humans, are a part of nature and live in close proximity to other parts of it. But, except in the case of humans, we cannot imagine what it would be like for a beaver or a zebra to protect the environment in a morally significant sense. They may protect their own environment in response to certain evolutionary urges. But this would not be because there is a *perceived* ecological problem threatening the species. Instead, the "problem" is anticipated in the evolutionary process and the necessary mechanisms to forestall its realization are built into it. A noncarnivorous animal is not motivated by the desire to protect species diversity; it is simply not biologically suited to eating other animals.

Similarly, when Africans avoid killing their respective totems (animals serving as emblems of lineage identity) for meat or using certain plants for

food, this is not because they are trying to preserve nature, thereby expressing their proximity to it; it is because they are following certain social rules.
Of course the social rules may require respect for nature, but that is not their
primary aim. Indeed, it is possible to argue that in most cases such respect is
largely functional in its intention to serve the social and moral ends of maintaining the communal bond; whatever ecological benefits accrue from this do
so only derivatively.

According to the second premise, attending sympathetically to a people's
style of kinship with nature is supposed to facilitate the task of recovering a
redemptive ecological memory to be used as a basis for redressing current
environmental problems. This presupposes that there is some match or fit
between the ecological contexts of traditional and modern societies. But such
a view is, needless to say, false. In other words, the nature and scale of the
environmental problem in traditional societies is in no significant way comparable to the problem today. Quite apart from the obvious fact of enormous
historical, economic, and cultural divergences, there is, first, the problem
that the ecological crisis today is the result of a highly complex technological
culture linked to the politics of an expansionist capitalism underwritten by
the ideology of progress. I do not intend to repeat here what is now a familiar story—that this progress has essentially meant plundering the earth in
search of surplus value. This is a culture whose technologies have permitted
human beings for the first time in history to produces gases that have globally poisoned the rain forests, the oceans, the content of the air we breathe,
and even the skies.

Moreover, it is not just nature that has been endangered by capitalism's
Faustian quest for profits; human life itself is now lived under the constant
threat of annihilation by weapons of mass destruction. But our ecological
perplexities are not fully explained by simply blaming them on technology as
if the latter is inherently evil. Behind the technology and the political institutions that license its production and use stand invasive religious and secular ideologies whose global reach has been as extensive as the ecological
destruction they have sanctioned.

On the basis of this reality it can be suggested that the lack of fit between
traditional and modern experiences of environmental crises is best understood
not simply as a problem about what Western civilization has done to nature
but also as a problem of what it has done to other cultures in its encounter
with them. In some ways modernity's destructive impact on nature has been
paralleled only by its negative impact on non-Western cultures. Environmen-

tal history is full of examples of how whole cultures were sidelined and condemned in the name of progress and, not without irony, also in the name of
an ecological science that promised better protection of nature than the
indigenous practices.[4] Yet it was precisely this ecological science that was in
many instances responsible (for example, through the global phenomenon of
the creation of national parks[5]) for problems of soil erosion and siltation
caused by massive relocations of indigenous populations into arid reserves.

We can draw three conclusions from this situation. First, the environmental problem today is different—in terms of size and impact—from anything that has ever been experienced in human history. And this question of
size and impact is as much a natural as a cultural problem. Here lies another
irony: a worldview given over to the ontological difference between culture
and nature produces historical experiences in which both are destroyed in
terms of what are supposed to be their mutual interests.

Second, since the content of the environmental problem is primarily
defined by human interaction with nature, that is, by the extent to which cultural attitudes shape what nature is and how it is to be utilized and managed,
it is important to locate the claim that certain groups of people are close to
nature in the context of how definitions of nature and culture are in fact created. It would also be necessary to determine just what this claim means. In
a short essay it is obviously impossible to make either one of these moves in
an adequate fashion. Thus we can only hint that future research on how the
claim that Africans are intimate with nature has been applied will have to
take seriously not only the socially constructed character of the claim itself
but also its ideological status.

The connections between these two are made evident in the fluctuating
attitudes of whites to Africans' relationship with nature. Historically, the
record shows that, at its best, colonial ecology sometimes classified indigenous people as part of nature in the colonized lands, to be included with the
fauna and flora of those lands in the national parks that were being set up all
over Africa. These parks were established both as a way of preserving the
"pristine beauty" of the natural environment and a way of entertaining the
aesthetic gaze of commercial tourism. At its worst, colonial ecology not only
derided indigenous agricultural practices and customary attitudes to nature
but also sought to drive Africans out of nature by forcibly relocating them
into reserved lands not fit even for animal habitation. Here was clear denial
that Africans were close to nature in any aesthetically, morally, or ecologically
meaningful way.

In other words, the alleged kinship of Africans to nature emerges from this as a socially constructed and politically contested idea in which contradictory romantic notions about the environment are at work. The basis of this was of course that will to power that has dominated so much of Western thought since the sixteenth century. The colonial context provided an ideal setting for the exercise of this will to power both on other cultures and on nature. I am suggesting here that ideas of nature are not always, if ever, politically innocent and that the claim that Africans are close to nature occurs in a historical context in which it cannot be exempted from the ideological ambiguities that have underpinned its uses in the past.

In making the observation that colonial ecology embodied a socially constructed view of nature, I do not wish to suggest that indigenous pictures of the environment were themselves the result of natural processes, that is, that they were not socially constructed or were somehow directly derived from nature itself. Rather, I wish to emphasize that the politics of colonial ecology were defined in confrontation with a different understanding of nature that incorporated or was indeed predicated upon certain cosmological considerations (for example, the role of spirits in nature), whose relevance to the protection of the environment lay precisely in the contribution they made to the socially constructed character of indigenous views of nature.

This emphasis on the social dimensions of indigenous ecologies is meant not just to indicate the distance between nature and culture, which is always socially inscribed in the construction of both and in the dialectical relationship between them, but also to suggest that this distance is itself an important part of how the interaction of members of traditional communities (no less than that of other humans) with their environment is ceaselessly traversed by a certain refusal to be close to nature. For not only is nature the realm of utility and production, as I discussed above, it is also the embodiment of the sublime, the marker of the outer periphery of the beginnings of transcendence, the place where humans, ancestors, and gods enter into precarious fellowship with one another and where that fellowship is regulated in terms of the coexistence of the distance and proximity of nature and culture.

The idea that indigenous peoples are close to nature is not politically innocent. It is linked to various romantic notions of nature in European thought, of translating the very different worldviews within which traditional ecologies developed and functioned into ways of thinking and modes of practice that would make them relevant or applicable to the global culture of late capitalism. Although the appeal to the language of kinship with nature is meant to hint at the possibility of just such a translation, it is in fact the need for kinship that points to the lack of fit or congruence between traditional and modern experiences of ecological disaster.

To approach African ideas about the environment in terms of the connection between production and utility is to recognize that relations between humans and nature are discursively organized within the domain of a social rather than a natural ecology.

15 A Theological Reflection on the Korean People's *Han* and *Hanpuri*

Yvonne Lee

Context

It is a difficult struggle to search for the God who is different from the hegemonies of the "official" religious and theological traditions. Within this context, I attempt to construct a liberative Christian theology based on the concepts of *han* and *hanpuri*. Though some may respond sarcastically to such an attempt, I must pursue what I need to in order to free myself from any colonial mind-set before my God. To me, a Christian God as the creator, the sustainer, and the liberator basically means a God of *hanpuri* for the *han*-ridden Koreans.

I would assert that Koreans are the people of *han* whether they would agree with it or not. This *han* lives, breathes, and abides in Koreans, as the shadows of our unconscious lives that we do not always recognize. *Han* also transmits from generation to generation, both downward and upward. Since *han* is a spiritual entity, it moves freely, without being bounded by a linear historical time frame. For instance, my paternal grandmother shares my *han* of being a Christian who suffers a "confused" cultural, ancestral, national, and religious identity. Thus she willingly journeys with me in my soul-search. On the other hand, she also speaks of her *han* to my soul either through my shaman informant, Kim Keum-wha, or in my dreams. So, I have come to carry my grandmother's shadow of *han* that was lived and endured by my grandmother, an outcast[1] shaman woman in the rigidly hierarchical Confucian society of Korea.

With this explanation, there emerges a series of questions related to my grandmother's *han*. Why did my grandmother become a shaman? Why did shamans become outcasts? What did the Confucian heavenly orders of the rulers of Korean society do to my grandmother, and why? What did the Buddha of my Buddhist convert father do to her, and why? What did my Protestant Christian God do to my grandmother? What "evil" things did the shamanic gods and my shaman grandmother do to the Confucian heavenly rulers of Korea, her Buddhist son, or her Christian granddaughter? How can I be a liberated and liberating Christian without answers to these questions? Upon searching for the answers, I am inclined to believe that *han* and *hanpuri* might be the key generators for the liberation of Korean people, who include myself, my grandmother, and my family. I write this chapter based on this hunch and the ceaseless quest for the pluralistic religious justice and liberation.

Han and *Hanpuri* as Key to a Liberation Theology

The term *han* is a complicated word. It cannot be described in a simple language frame. *Han* is the complexity of mind and spirituality of Korean people. It develops either from their ontologically ill-starred or socially unattractive living situations. Thereby, understanding the concept of *han* in a fuller sense requires a painstaking endeavor to understand the life context that produces *han*. In other words, one must grasp the meaning of *han* that is evoked, caused, lived, and endured by the particular life context of Korean society.

Following this line of logic, Korean minjung[2] theologians have attempted to grasp the sociobiographical picture of the *han*-producing Korean life context in doing a liberation theology designed for the *han*-ridden Korean people. Thus minjung theology has incorporated the social aspect of *han* into its field and begun to explore the concept of *han* in this scope. Suh NamDong, a pioneer minjung theologian, describes *han* as "the suppressed, amassed and condensed experience of oppression caused by mischief or misfortune so that it forms a kind of 'lump' in one's spirit."[3] Hyun Hyunghak, another first-generation minjung theologian, underscores the aspect of *han* as feelings. To him *han* is "a sense of unresolved resentment against injustice suffered, a sense of helplessness because of the overwhelming odds against us, a feeling of total abandonment, a feeling of acute pain of sorrow in one's guts and bowel making the whole body writhe and wiggle, and an obstinate urge to take 'revenge' and to right the wrong all these constitute."[4] Chung Hyun Kyung, a feminist second-generation minjung theologian, adds a broader scope: "This feeling of Han comes from the sinful interconnections of classism, racism, sexism, colonialism, neo-colonialism, and cultural imperialism which Korean people experience everyday."[5] To Rita Nakashima Brock and Susan Brooks Thistlethwaite, two leading American feminist theologians, *han* refers to "the stored grief of frustration and resentment, the bitterness of suffering endured without relief."[6]

I think of *han* as the Korean people's "root experiences" or "collective consciousness."[7] *Han* is a cluster of feelings and energy that springs from a deep and painful recognition about one's tragic life situation in an unjust social system. Thoughtful and carefully organized attention is required in order for *han* to be constructively resolved. Otherwise it will continuously grow and eventually explode out of control. The damage from such an explosion is profound. Killing, madness, and other tragic violence occur and harm both the *han*-ridden victims and others. Suh Namdong suggests the "fourfold *han*" of the Korean people:[8]

1. *Han* of all Koreans who have suffered numerous foreign invasions throughout Korean history.
2. *Han* of minjung who suffer the tyranny of internal rulers.
3. *Han* of Korean women under Confucianism's strict imposition of cultural, social, and legal rules.
4. *Han* of the outcasts, or Korean minjung outside the social rank. They had a social status below the commoner minjung, such as hereditary slaves, butchers, prostitutes, shamans, and some Buddhist monks of both sexes.

Given Suh's point of view, we know why all Koreans are considered *han*-ridden. Any Korean fits one or more of the fourfold categories of *han*. The intensity and the depth of the *han* of the Korean minjung women are greater because of the double-bound nature based on gender and class. Likewise, the *han* becomes triple-bound for outcast Korean minjung women, such as shaman women, female slaves, prostitutes, and female family members of a hereditary butcher. It is also this reason why Koreans, especially those minjung women, need liberation (resolution) from their *han*-ridden life situations.

How have Koreans dealt with their *han*? There have been basically two ways of *hanpuri* ("resolution of *han*"): one that is constructive; the other, destructive. Also, the term *hanpuri* has its root both in the secular and in the Korean shamanic religious tradition. *Hanpuri* simply means a release of *han* when used in the secular sense. This secular *hanpuri* can be constructive if directed carefully through thorough meditation or counseling. Nonetheless, Korea's political, social, and cultural history has been filled with those destructively utilizing *hanpuri*. *Han*-ridden royal families, nobles, and elite, and some *han*-ridden heroes and heroines of the base rank or the outcasts, have shaped Korean history with destructive *hanpuri*.

On the other hand, *hanpuri* can be constructive when it is used properly in a religious form. The Korean people's experience of *han* and their need for *hanpuri* have been the backbone of the theological beliefs and practices of many Korean minjung women—both shamans and believers of all the foreign religions in Korea, especially Protestant Christians. Some have been remarkably transformative and liberating in doing their *hanpuri*. Others, as the majority of minjung women, have fallen into traps where their *hanpuri* were misconducted.

In the Korean shamanic tradition, *hanpuri* takes a ritual form called *kut*. This *kut* gives many *han*-ridden clients "the voiceless ghosts to speak out their stories of Han," as Chung Hyun Kyung explains.[9] *Kut* has been considered a powerful means of resolving *han* for many Koreans. It is perhaps because *hanpuri kut* offers a sacred public space and time sanctioned and justified by the supernatural. In *kut* the shamans possessed by the supernatural acknowledge and name the *han* of their clients. They also authorize and direct their resolution during their ecstasy. Brock and Thistlethwaite define *hanpuri* as follows:

> The release of *han* begins, in the women's shaman rituals of Korean culture, through the moment when the spirits pour out their grief and anger through the voice of the shaman, who has gained the power to contain their presence. . . . In the safe space created by rituals led by women, the speaking of *han* commands listening and solidarity. The speaking and listening must then lead to changing the unjust situation. This ritual act is *han-pu-ri,* "the opportunity for collective repentance, group therapy and collective healing for the ghosts and their communities in Korean society."[10]

It is not only the result of the *hanpuri kut* that is liberating. The process of *hanpuri* in *kut* is also liberating to the *han*-ridden minjung women and the *han*-ridden shaman woman performers of *kut*. With the authority, space, time, and freedom sanctified and granted to them in the name of *kut*, the *han*-ridden shamans resolve their *han*. And oftentimes they do it through rebellion against the power, values, and norms of the *han*-causing Korean

Confucian cultural and social structure. The shamans know that it is the society defined and manipulated by the upper-class male rulers that has been the cause of their in-depth *han*. It is the *han* of being less than a full human, an "inferior" woman, a lowly minjung, an outcast shaman, and a Korean minjung shaman woman who has been a vulnerable object of social, cultural, and religious oppression.

Still, how do they actually rebel against their *han*-causing social system? As many of my videotapes collected during my field research in 1994–96 show, they do it by acting "abnormally" in the public setting of *hanpuri kut*. They prepare lavish food dishes, both ancient and modern. These are the foods they cannot afford to buy or eat in their day-to-day lives. Moreover, they wear the costly costumes of the Confucian officials, or of the aristocrats that they would not be allowed to wear otherwise. They use loud music that society says virtuous women should not be associated with. They gather together in a public gathering that is normally for males only. And these repressed women make the ritual setting extremely emotional and highly spiritual by talking loudly, singing, drinking, and dancing. Normally, no virtuous women in a strictly Confucian community, even in contemporary times, would be expected to act so "inappropriately."

In this ground-breaking way, those shaman women and others in *kut* have caused their opponents to scream in outrage. What an amazing freedom, what a great pleasure, and what a powerful protest it is! Their rebellion and resistance demonstrated through their ritualistic processes are indeed powerful. For in *kut* even male high officials must bow down to shaman women who speak the divine words. No wonder those noble and righteous Confucian men or upper-middle class Korean Christian women become more troubled and get angrier and more hysterically oppressive against shamanic believers. Sadly, they do not know that their troublesome anger belies their substantial loss to Korean shamanism in the competition among religions.

Furthermore, those despised and "evil" Korean minjung shaman women, as the lowliest of all the lowly groups of people,[11] even claim divine power and authority through divination and extraordinary performances. They heal the sick, prophesy deeply concealed family secrets or fate, and ride and dance on double-edged straw-cutting blades without suffering injuries. People become awestruck by their accurate divination and other supernatural revelations given to them. People are surprised when they recognize that those amazing performers are merely "lowly shaman women." They watch the shaman women rejoicing through each step of the *hanpuri kut* procedures. People acknowledge how the shaman performers are courageous, careful, and faithful in taking their divine gifts. They know that in *kut* shaman women resolve not only the *han* of their clients but also their own *han*. This is the way in which the clients and the performers of Korean shamanism dynamically liberate themselves from their *han*—both through the process and by the successful results of the *hanpuri kut*. Who can be spiritually more powerful and effective in resisting the *han*-causing structures than these Korean shaman women?

The *Han*-Ridden History of Korean Shamanism

Shamanism cries out for the respectful social status and the religious legitimacy that it used to have. Here, one wonders how Korean shamanism has become a religion of *han*. Originally, Korean people were believers in Korean shamanism. Under official leadership and authority, such as that of the kingly priests or the priestly kings,[12] Korean shamanism was a proud indigenous national religion. It was observed in unity and harmony by all the Koreans: kings, aristocrats and commoners, males and females, the old and the young. Traced back to the ancient period, Yi Nung-wha's *Chosun Musok-ko* depicts well the details of the history of Korean shamanism. According to him, the monarchs of the ancient Korean states were called "shaman" *(Chachaung),* which originated from the name of the heavenly prince (Hwanung).[13] And Hwanung was the father of the founder (Tangun, or "shaman king") of Kochosun, the first ancient Korean state[14] before the separation of political leadership from religion.

However, this royal, political, and priestly position of Korean shamanism has been lost over time. In contemporary Korean society, it has become as low as one can imagine, since it has been treated as a superstitious or evil custom practiced by lowly outcasts. Korean shamanism became *han*-ridden as the colonial religions (such as Chinese Buddhism, Neo-Confucianism, and Protestant Christianity) came to occupy the original status and position of Korean shamanism. Once shamanism lost its high religious, social, and political status, its believers were also relegated to a lowly status.

Meanwhile, the Neo-Confucian culture became powerful and dominated the lives of Korean people, first with the ruling nobility and later with the commoners and the outcasts. It grew until it became the iron-concrete political, social, cultural, academic, moral, and religious system in Korea. The strong political, economic, and military supports from China, as the colonizer of Korea, ensured the steel-like grip of this colonial culture. After the demise of the imperial power of China in the late nineteenth century, the

United States and its Protestant Christianity took over the high standing long held by China in Korea.[15] In short, the survival of foreign religions and the demise of the indigenous religion largely depended on the colonial power of the endorsing country of a foreign religion. Chinese Buddhism and Confucianism survived and prospered in Korea under the toadyism widely demonstrated by the Korean rulers, who called China their "Big Brother." Confidently and submissively, these rulers believed in the overall superiority of the colonizer. One observes this fact in the extraordinary amount of elegant writings in Chinese penned by procolonial Korean elites.[16]

When the United States took over China's place in the minds of Korean people in the twentieth century, conservative Protestant Christianity transmitted by the American missionaries functioned as the frontier agent of American neo-colonialism. Along with America's anti-Communist involvement in the war in Korea (1950–53), followed by the division of Korea, the United States' new role as "big brother" fascinated many Koreans. They witnessed that America was mightier and greater than their former big brother, China. Also, American Protestant Christianity augmented its power in Korea because of the already existing hierarchical and imperial system. Brock and Thistlethwaite correctly observe that because of their similar patriarchal characteristics, Confucianism and Christianity in Korea went hand in hand.[17] They also note that the two religions are similar in sharing the hierarchical and prejudicial nature of colonialism that has economically, religiously, and culturally marginalized Korean shamanism believers.[18]

This history reveals why the minjung believers and performers of Korean shamanism have been *han*-ridden and have needed *hanpuri*, the resolution from *han*. Shamanic concepts of *han* and *hanpuri* have been a powerful key to the liberation of such *han*-ridden Korean minjung, including Korean shaman women. *Hanpuri* can be an equally powerful liberative device for the psychologically tormented Korean Christian minjung. They need to be free from the anguish driven by their own oppression that compulsively represses their unconscious shamanic shadow of *han* and *hanpuri* inherent in them.

This is a serious challenge, given the colonized minds of too many Koreans. For instance, traditional Korean Protestant Christians have great difficulties in believing that a shamanic concept such as *han* or *hanpuri* would ever be salvific for anyone, including the believers of Korean shamanism. The trouble is that, in their colonized minds, they cannot have doubts about the hegemony and universality of conservative Protestant Christian traditions. The same holds true for their monopolized doctrine of blessings and salvation, in that they believe in no other salvation except the one through Christianity. Ironically, they do not see that any religion that does not free its believers from such arbitrary and fear-evoking doctrine cannot be salvific by virtue of its violent and oppressive nature. So there has grown a great chasm between the indigenous believers and the Protestant Christian believers in Korea. This incompatible gap has partly been what makes the birth of a liberation theology based on *han* and *hanpuri* extremely difficult regardless of the compelling need. This is the nature of the colonialism in Korea.

Han and *Hanpuri* as Manifested in the Princess Bari Myth

With this complex overview of the challenges and possibilities of *han* and *hanpuri*, I now want to explore the theological issues and dynamics entailed in both concepts for Korean minjung women. It seems to me that the life story of Princess Bari best depicts the theological dynamics. Princess Bari was a charismatic shaman woman portrayed in a myth that prevailed during the late ninth century. Though we do not know the period of its origins, usually it takes two to three generations for a myth to be prevalent.

The Princess Bari (meaning "the deserted") was born the seventh daughter of King Ogu, who had no sons. She became a target of the king's anger and was abandoned on Mt. South (Namsan). She was raised by a poor elderly woman. Meanwhile her royal parents became critically ill. They needed to take the immortal medicine water from the *suhbang sehgeh* ("the netherworld of the dead"), which was very far away. The road to it was rough. The six princesses of the king refused when they were asked to go on the journey to get the immortal water. However, the deserted Princess Bari volunteered to do so in order to save the lives of her parents. The journey to the *suhbang sehgeh* was extremely difficult. It caused her to fulfill many unbearable and impossible tasks, signifying the severity of the dead world. However, she was able to complete all the difficult tasks and finally obtained the medicine water from the *suhbang sehgeh*. Arriving back home, she revived her parents, who had been long dead, with the immortal water she had drawn from the netherworld. In appreciating for this life-reviving act, the king offered Princess Bari half the nation. But Princess Bari refused to take his offer. Instead, she asked for his permission to become the first shaman of the nation. She wanted to be a powerful healer of the wounded, as she was once wounded.[19]

Unlike Princess Bari, portrayed as the first shaman in this myth, according to the Tangun myth the original ancestor of Korean shamans was a male. The first written version of the Tangun myth was found in an ancient Chinese history book called *Wei Shu,* written circa 386–534 C.E. Unlike Princess Bari, who was socially deserted and religiously degraded, Tangun held the highest political, social, cultural, and religious status during his reign (2333–108 B.C.E.), both as first shaman and the national founder. He was the grandson of the celestial god ("Heavenly King," Hwanin), born to Hwanwung (the son of the Heavenly King) and the earthly Bear Mother goddess.

Thus, comparing the Princess Bari myth with the Tangun myth about the origin of Korean shamans, we see several significant factors. First, the originator of shamanism changed from a male national founder to an abandoned princess. Second, the Princess Bari myth changed the nature of shamans from the priestly ruler to the charismatic wounded healer. Third, the Tangun myth endows Tangun with divine power, authority, and legitimacy by virtue of his incarnate god nature, while the charismatic healing, life-giving power of the abandoned princess was achieved only through voluntary suffering and a compassionate, triumphant death. Unlike Tangun's naturally given supernatural power, which empowered him to rule and serve, the shamanic charismatic power was fought for. In other words, the *han*-ridden, abandoned shaman women attain supernatural power only through their willful passion and enduring compassion. It is important to note that Princess Bari's supernatural power was used for the service of *hanpuri,* not for ruling like Tangun.

Thus, the origin of the shaman and the nature of shamanic power portrayed in the Princess Bari myth signify the intensity of the *han*-ridden life situation of the Korean minjung shaman women during the ninth century and later and their determined struggles for *hanpuri.* They also indicate significant change in the political, social, cultural, and religious structures of Korean society around the ninth century, toward the end of the Silla dynasty.

While Chinese Buddhism and Neo-Confucianism prospered as the dominating political ideologies in Korea, Korean shamanism entered a deep crisis. The ruling men and the minjung women changed their religious position: the former became part of the Chinese Buddhist leadership competing among the powerful, the latter became the new leadership of Korean shamanism seeking to sustain the powerless.[20] While Korean men tended to move toward the politically and religiously powerful, the politically powerless minjung women tended toward the indigenous religion that was available to them.

Picking up the role of the abandoned indigenous religion in this context, the shaman minjung women strove to overcome the social, cultural, and religious turmoil in Korea by reviving the sacrality, identity, and power of their religion. With the limited means of communication in premodern Korean society and the illiterate situations of the Korean minjung women,[21] perhaps the creation and revising of myths through oral transmission were one of the most readily available and effective means for making theological, spiritual, or religious appeals to the minds and souls of the people. The birth of Princess Bari might have been created by the believers of shamanism in this context. Korean shamanism needed an urgent recovery in order to function as a healing and life-giving religion. The new and charismatic way of *hanpuri* as introduced in the Princess Bari myth seems to be a powerful indication of struggle for the survival and thriving of shamanism as an indigenous religion over against the oppressive nature of colonial religions.[22]

Here I will underscore two liberative aspects of *han* and *hanpuri* that the Princess Bari myth seems to convey as a solution for the minjung shaman believers. First, it portrays the *han* of a young woman suffering for her low social status as a daughter despite the parents' high social and political status. It reminds us of a young black slave girl being taken away from her mother, father, brothers and sisters, friends, and home and being sold to another slave master of an unknown place. But Princess Bari overcomes this sexual discrimination by observing a theology of *han* and *hanpuri* that forgives, reconciles, and even loves the very ones who deserted her. This act of overcoming the pain of abandonment could have been a sign of Korean minjung women's assimilation into the cultural and social pressure imposed by Buddhist and Confucian leaders. Nonetheless, I am inclined to believe that it was rather a sign of the mystical power and energy produced by the Korean minjung shaman women's theology of *han* and *hanpuri*. Through the charismatic power that the wounded heroine embodied, based on *han* and *hanpuri*, suffering Korean minjung shaman women found hope for the revival of their dwindling religion and moved toward its powerful enactment. Also, it was the only way for the minjung shaman women to survive in a hostile society.

Second, it speaks to the *han* of a poor minjung woman under various forms of unbearable suffering. Here again, Princess Bari, our mythic heroine of liberation, overcomes such hardship by practicing a theology of *han* and *hanpuri* that sustains her own life and that affirms, heals, and renews the life of others. Kim Keum-wha, the shaman informant for my field research in Korea, attests to this extraordinary power of *han* and *hanpuri* in her daily practices. Her passion for her own *hanpuri* and compassion for others' *han* interweave and manifest ecstatically in her supernatural experiences. Suffering has been a similar fate for every single Korean minjung shaman woman, even in today's Korea. This is why Kim Keum-wha cannot live even a day without constantly generating her passion for *hanpuri* and compassion for the *han*-ridden others in her daily life.

It is now clear that the myth portrays Princess Bari as a *han*-ridden outcast, Korean minjung shaman woman. It is also clear that her shamanic *hanpuri* was life-giving, life-sustaining, and thereby salvific and liberative. However, it seems important to me for us to pause at this point and ask some questions. What would have happened to Korean shamanism if the mythic Princess Bari had pursued her *hanpuri* based on an oppressive theology that rules, exploits, ousts, and destroys innocent people at the social margins? Would the daily refreshed passion and the constantly recommitted compassion still be in that theology as the essential generating power and energy of *han* and *hanpuri*? Would there be any liberative and healing substances or signs left in Korean shamanism by now if it had taken a power-oriented theology? Would the conservative Korean Christians still despise the shamanic theology of *han* and *hanpuri* if it had become "official" and bureaucratized and had turned against the liberation of the *han*-ridden minjung? Truly, no liberation theology shall claim to be liberative for *han*-ridden Korean minjung women unless it understands, embraces, and frees their *han* from 1,700 years of religious and cultural oppression and offers an appropriate form of *hanpuri*. To free themselves from a colonized theological, cultural, and psychological mind-set, Christians or Confucians will need the courage to embrace this powerful concept of liberation, namely, *han* and *hanpuri,* that has been bred by the Korean shamanic culture.

16 / A Black American Perspective on Interfaith Dialogue

Dwight N. Hopkins

One of the pressing challenges of black theology in the new millennium is to increase the interfaith dialogue on a global scale, beginning with various expressions of liberation theologies throughout the world. The only international network of liberation theologians is the Ecumenical Association of Third World Theologians (EATWOT).

The origin of the concept for an international dialogue among liberation theologians in Africa, Asia, and Latin America came in 1974 from Abbe Oscar K. Bimwenyi, a Roman Catholic student from Zaire studying theology in Louvain, Belgium. As a result of his vision and the preparatory committees composed of representatives from Africa, Asia, and Latin America, the organizing conference that gave rise to the Ecumenical Dialogue of Third World Theologians (later Dialogue was changed to Association) took place in Dar es Salaam, Tanzania, in August 1976. Since that time, EATWOT has held different continental and intercontinental dialogues with the specific focus on Africa, Asia, Latin America, and the Pacific Islands. And it has taken up the theological significance of race, indigenous peoples, and third-world women.

Why We Must Engage in Interfaith Dialogue

Interfaith dialogue is an urgent call for the present and future for all of us concerned about the future of the world community. I think this is so for at least three important reasons. First, the overwhelming majority of the earth's people are of faiths other than Christian. Likewise, the overwhelming majority of the earth's people are poor and oppressed. If Christianity is based on a faith that takes seriously the full humanity of the poor, then we are faced with the challenge of recognizing one undeniable fact: the majority of the world is non-Christian and poor. Gustavo Gutiérrez writes: "The interlocutors of liberation theology are the nonpersons, the humans who are not considered human by the dominant social order—the poor, the exploited classes, the marginalized races, all the despised cultures."[1]

Asia is the most populous region of the globe. Aloysius Pieris from Sri Lanka has stated that the characteristic feature of Asia is its vast poverty and its multifaceted religions. The impact of colonialism and imperialism from the West contributed significantly to the underdevelopment of Asia. Though the West did "export" its culture, it has not been able to use its Christianity to penetrate or replace the indigenous religions of Asia. Christianity is a minority religion. The great religions and cultures of Asia have stood the test of time, existing before the creation of Christianity and possibly outlasting Christianity. We cannot be in Asia and avoid seeing and feeling the presence of a different view toward nature, music, poetry, human interactions, rituals, history, and so forth. Buddhism, Taoism, Hinduism, Shintoism, Shamanism, Confucianism, Islam, and other faith traditions flow through the veins and are part of the hustle and bustle of most of Asia.

In Africa, Islam and African indigenous religions and cultures are all concrete and strong realities for the peoples there. Though Christianity has become a permanent feature of this continent more so than in Asia, the Christianity of the West still has not replaced or erased other faith traditions. In fact, many of the peoples of Africa who are in the rural areas or in communities outside of the urban areas still practice their indigenous religions and cultures. And even where Christianity has "converted" people, many of these people have combined Christianity with their indigenous religions or, in times of crisis, rely on the indigenous belief systems and cultural practices. In other words, Africa's own indigenous cultures and worldview remain a force even today.

In Latin America, it seems that Christianity has become the dominant religion, with Roman Catholicism making the first beachhead and Protestantism being a relatively latecomer. At the same time in some areas, indigenous cultures and people still have their own faiths. In other areas, descendants of Africa have developed unique faiths. And even some of the folk religions have combined indigenous religions with Christianity, particularly with Roman Catholicism.

In the United States, Christianity is still without question the dominant form of religious activity. Though white mainline denominations are suffering from a slow membership growth, Christianity is remarkably vibrant. This is so especially in churches for minorities—people of color, or third-world communities within the first-world superpower. We see this reality in the growth of third-world Christian communities. We also see this in the growth of so-called Word churches or transdenominational church growth. Christianity has a monopoly. But, nevertheless, the fastest-growing religion in America is Islam. And some of the great Asian religions and expressions of African indigenous religions are slowly appearing.

The second reason for the importance of interfaith dialogue in EATWOT is the need to take the work and words of Jesus seriously. One of the most quoted biblical passages in EATWOT books is Luke 4:18-19:

> The Spirit of the Lord is upon me,
> because he has anointed me
> to bring good news to the poor.
> He has sent me to proclaim release
> to the captives
> and recovery of sight to the blind,
> to let the oppressed go free,
> to proclaim the year of the Lord's favor.

This statement by Jesus is seen as the core of the gospel message. To believe in Jesus is to walk the way of Jesus. In the world today, which people are lame or blind, in jails, suffering from physical abuse, unemployed and underemployed, lonely and unloved? These are victims from all faiths. If we are to follow the way of Jesus and be with the poor because that is where Jesus resides, then we are not bound by church doctrines or institutional restriction. In fact, to be with Jesus will mean, in many cases, not ever being in a Christian institution or context.

Furthermore, this divine revelation that dwells among the poor in their struggle for full humanity is not only contained in the way of Jesus. If God is the spirit of freedom for the least in society, then this spirit has to be active as an event and process of struggle even where the name of Jesus is not known. We cannot confine our experience of God within human-made doctrines or beliefs. Again, Gutiérrez instructs us: "Liberation theology categorizes people not as believers or unbelievers but as oppressors or oppressed."[2] In fact, to use church tradition or a narrow biblical interpretation to say that God is only or exclusively where Jesus is present is to reduce God's power for, love of, and presence with those who hurt the most in the world. God continues to unfold a new common wealth of a life of abundance against the reign of evil and mammon wherever it shows its ugly face. Among the cries of all the marginalized peoples, God reveals God's self in all faiths around the globe. To deny this is to possibly participate in a new form of imperialism—a Christocentric imperialism against the majority of the other faiths on earth. As Aloysius Pieris correctly claims:

> The vast majority of God's poor perceive their ultimate concern and symbolize their struggle for liberation in the idiom of non-Christian religions and cultures. Therefore, a theology that does not speak to or speak through this non-Christian peoplehood is an esoteric luxury of a Christian minority. Hence, we need a theology of religions that will expand the existing boundaries of orthodoxy as we enter into the liberative streams of other religions and cultures.[3]

Finally, interfaith dialogue is crucial because the international economy of monopoly capitalism, the destruction of indigenous cultures, racial discrimination against darker skin peoples around the world, the oppression of women, and the attack on the earth's ecology are global processes that do not limit themselves to the Christian community. When American monopoly capitalist corporations seek cheap labor in Asia, particularly among Asian women, these companies are not concerned about whether the workers are Buddhist or Christian. The bottom line is taking their labor power in order to make profit. When American monopoly capitalist corporations pursue investments in Nigerian oil, it does not concern them if the workers there are Muslim, indigenous religious practitioners, or Christians. Finance capital can own both a textile factory in Indonesia comprised of Buddhist women while simultaneously owning an oil refinery in Africa comprised of Islamic workers. In other words, global capital has already begun the process of interfaith interactions among many of the poor of this earth. But it is a dialogical process where healthy faith conversations are too often subservient to the needs of profit and the accumulation of more profit and capital.

How to Carry Out Interfaith Dialogue

In an interfaith dialogue, it is important to take indigenous cultures seriously. Many peoples of the third world do not have a word for religion because faith is not a separate sphere (unlike the European Enlightenment's definition of religion). Faith is part of the culture; it is part of their everyday behavior. It is lived out daily in their relation to the air, fire, rain, flowers, mountains, water, food, animals, the living-dead ancestors, the unborn, and other family relations. So dialogue begins by recognizing not institutional organization, church tradition, or doctrines, but by seeing people and their physical bodies, where they are and how they live out their faith in their total commonplace being. Even among many poor Christians, they are often following certain doctrines and performing different rituals that look like Christianity, but, in fact, they are mixing pre-Christian religious and cultural belief systems and practices with Christianity. Simply to think that poor Christians are only Christians because of the Sunday church services and the various celebrations on the Christian calendar is to miss the rest of their way of life from Monday through Saturday. Esau Tuza from the Solomon Islands comments on the persistence and mixing of indigenous religions alongside and with Christianity:

> Our worship based on ancestral belief is not dead. Our ancestors are very much alive and thriving. They make their way to the church buildings via the grave and the cross. We pay them traditional respect through reverence and prayer. They follow us from the church buildings to the world where we live and witness with the rest of God's people, knit together in love and service. Only Christian colonialists, who seek to find God in Western garb, will not be able to see this truth. Despite this, of course, we consciously or unconsciously live side by side with our ancestors.[4]

Thus we must see and hear and feel faith as a total way of life for the poor.

Because most of the world's poor speak their faith (both in societies that do not rely primarily on written texts and in those that do), interfaith dialogue has to be sensitive to the language of oppressed people.

> Asia is diversified into at least seven major linguistic zones, the highest that any continent can boast of. There is, first of all, the Semitic zone concentrated in the western margin of Asia. The Ural-Atlantic group is spread all over Asiatic Russia and northwest Asia. The Indo-Iranian stock and Dravidian ethnic groupings have their cultural habitat in southern Asia. The Sino-Tibetan region, by far the largest, extends from Central Asia to the Far

East. The Malayo-Polynesian wing opens out to the southeast. Last but not least is the unparalleled Japanese, forming a self-contained linguistic unit in the northeastern tip of Asia.[5]

Language is not merely a medium or method of expressing beliefs, like some type of tool that is neutral and does not play a decisive role in the process and creation of faith. Language is key to understanding and experiencing the ways people believe and live with their God of hope, survival, and liberation. Multiple languages, therefore, are important to know. EATWOT and other institutions concerned about the realignment of power relations need to carry out interfaith dialogue in other languages in addition to those brought by colonizers and missionaries to the third world.

Moreover, we need to find a way to hear the indigenous languages of people when we dialogue about different faiths. Language is part of the culture of a people. And culture is the context of faith. Language gives us a feel for how people live their lives. It helps us understand the different shades of meaning that they experience regularly with God. Language speaks to the role of men and women in a society of believers. For example, in some indigenous cultures and in some African communities, there is no separate pronoun for female and male. This is radically different from the patriarchal language of English, which not only distinguishes between male and female but consistently refers to God as "he," implying that females are made in the image of a male God. This is not just a question of semantics or sentence construction. It speaks more importantly to who has power in society and whether or not it is equally distributed among people in a culture. Moreover, to speak the language that expresses the different faiths of different peoples is to be involved in the rhythm of those communities. Some languages are spoken very fast with diverse accents; others are spoken more slowly. Both are dynamics that express the ways of life of various people. And these ways of life are integrally linked to how and what people believe.

To share with different faiths, we will have to see, hear, and listen to different cultural expressions of these faiths. Many peoples have their own legends and folktales as a major way of keeping together the group's identity, dreams, tradition, morals, and connections to the divine. Some tales or dreams speak of liberation by using a small animal or animals who outsmart bigger animals. Others have tales about heroic figures who are bigger than life, part human and part supernatural. Legends and folktales give people inspiration, perspective on the immediate and present problems they face, and hope that there is a force greater than they are and that it has preceded them and will be there after they have departed from this world.

In other words, people find hope, energy, and determination in their own indigenous stories. Poetry—its content as well as its form—also expresses faith. Similarly, songs are basic to all societies of believers and are extremely significant in interfaith dialogue. Plays and skits speak about what different people believe in, too. And finally, within culture, most peoples have developed a certain wisdom of the folk that is not learned through books but accumulates over long periods of time from the trials and errors of daily life. It is the wisdom learned through frequent life experiences. These are the unrefined expressions of faith so widespread in the faith of the people that to them it is simply common sense or simply the way life is. Faith in cultural expressions is, then, crucial.

Interfaith dialogue will also be helped when we pay attention to how people carry out their ordinary lives of survival. How are different faiths affected by how people produce and reproduce their lives? In rural areas without running water, how does the routine ritual of taking buckets to the river or to a common water faucet affect the faith of those who do this regularly? How does it influence the times of day that they worship? Does this give them a different perspective on nature, human purpose, and the divine? And how might they envision all of these interacting? Why are certain animals considered sacred? Is it because of particular traditions, because of the scarcity of these animals in the society, or because these animals symbolize something else like sacrifices? For instance, the South African theologian Gabriel M. Setiloane claims the following about the relation between humans and animals as seen in African indigenous religions' creation stories: "Humans emerge out of the hole in the group *together:* men, women, children with their animals. This stresses the uniqueness and right-to-be of every group and species. Even animals have a God-given right-to-be, and must, therefore, not be exterminated."[6]

What do the relationships among crops, agricultural seasons, and rain and thunder tell us about people's faith? Is it possible for a healthy interfaith dialogue to occur if we are not aware of how God or other expressions of the divine reveal themselves through rain and thunder and the success of planting and harvest? If people's experience of that which is greater than themselves is linked closely with whether or not their communities eat or drink, then the presence of the divine with the poor has to be seen in how they grow and harvest their crops for survival. Manuel M. Marzal has observed the

Indian culture of the Quechua in southern Peru. He finds that despite modernization their precolonial culture remains very much intact in the following ways:

> cultivation of the soil and raising cattle as the basic economic activities; vertical control of the ground to safeguard its use by the various ecological levels; reciprocity as a fundamental norm for coexistence in this environment; kinship and the compadre system as the basis of social organisation; dualistic criteria in the conceptualisation of social life; use of the Quechua language as the basic means of communication; communion with nature through the deification of the earth and the hills that mark the boundaries of the dwelling place of each community; celebration of the patron saint's day as the most important religious rite, which carries with it certain implications about the distribution of the communal power and wealth.[7]

The emotional makeup of diverse communities is also important. How do people deal with grief, pain, and death? When babies or children die, how do the community and its faith respond? Do the people ask questions of God, other spirits, or ancestors? Does the faith community become weaker in its relation to the divine? What ways do they hold themselves together and what answers do they provide for or receive from their God? What does their faith tell them about the fate of the child or baby who is dead and what do they believe about the people whose child is now gone? Not only does understanding tragedy and grief help us in the interfaith dialogue, but knowing how people celebrate aids the dialogue. What is valuable in a community that causes a people to celebrate and be thankful? Is it the birth of a child or of a male child, the successful obtaining of food, a wedding that brings together different families, the rite of passage of girls and boys into womanhood and manhood, or an annual ritual of remembering an elder who has passed away? Similarly laughter, how people laugh, why they laugh, and what causes them to laugh can help in finding out more about the faith of others.

In the same way, dance plays an important role in sharing faith. The movement and gestures of the body tell a story of what are the life and death concerns of a community. For instance, when a visitor to the Kpelle people of Liberia was initiated into the experiences of this indigenous culture, she learned how music is integrally part of the culture as a spiritual experience.

Reporting on her initiating process, she concluded the following:

> A quality performance, said a number of Kpelle people, depends upon the aid of the supernatural. Really good singers, dancers, or instrumentalists could not operate at such a level unaided. Normal human performance was simply much more ordinary. As I apprenticed myself to learn to play the koning, a triangular frame zither, I learned firsthand about this. At my third lesson when I was still playing rather crudely, Bena, my tutor and an expert koning player, said, "You need to know about the spirit. As soon as you start playing fine, it will not be you who is playing but the thing behind you [spirit]." And so I learned concretely of the supernatural part in all excellent music.[8]

Here music defines the identity of the community in relation to their connection to divine spirit. The releasing of the self and the body to the instructions and presence of the spirit was the means of becoming fully oneself.

In addition, social relations of power within societies will determine different ways of believing. Who has power and decision-making privileges? Who owns the wealth and the major sectors of the economy? Who has the final say or the main voice about how the goods and services are distributed? Who interprets how the community relates to the resources provided by nature? Who determines what in nature is sacred and who can touch these sacred objects? How does the authority of the sacred person get passed down from generation to generation? Are things shared in common or are there specific roles for certain people or parts of society? Are these roles fixed and why are they fixed? Is there any mobility in a community, and who is the mobility for and not for? How power is allocated among people in a society needs to be made explicit in interfaith dialogue.

Furthermore, in the interfaith dialogue, we need to be aware of the different impact race and dark and light skin have on a community of believers. If dark skin is equated with evil or not in the interest of the community, this will affect both the lighter skin people as well as the darker skin people regarding what they believe in. Usually it says something about the color of the divinity or representatives of the divinity that people worship.

For over fifty thousand years, black people have been in the southwest Pacific—Australia and the surrounding islands of Papua, New Guinea, Tasmania, Solomon Islands, Vanuatu, New Caledonia, and Fiji. Despite the

European missionary success in introducing Christianity, indigenous and pre-colonial black culture and black faith still persist. In his call for a better understanding of "black humanity," Aruru Matiabe (from Papua) writes:

> The religious beliefs and ceremonies of blacks in their natural state imbued life with profound meaning and did allow for true communion with the divine. White Christians could have found much there that was valuable had they looked before so many of them denounced it as totally wrong. Every person is a creature of God, and this God does not belong only to whites. Blacks have a spirit just as whites do; skin color does not matter because, not only are we members of the same species biologically speaking, but also we have the same Spirit within us. . . . It was thus wrong-headed for whites to have expected blacks to renounce their past . . . and completely accept the ways and the god of the European.[9]

Color not only speaks directly to which god is present, but also helps to determine the psychology of different races or shades of color among people. It raises the question of a hierarchy of worth. This can translate into who is thought to be the most worthy of receiving the resources and privileges that God has provided for that community.

Related to race is caste, which also determines discrimination. A clear example are the Dalit, the Black Untouchables, of India. The ruling group in India, a minority population known as the Hindu Brahmin, has established a hierarchy in social relations in which the Dalit suffer not only because of their dark color, but also because they are either at the bottom or outside of the caste system. The Hindu Brahmin ideology sees the Dalit as pollution, according to V. T. Rajshekar:

> Every Hindu believes that to observe caste and untouchability is his dharma—meaning his religious duty. But Hinduism is more than a religious system. It is also an economic system. In slavery, the master at any rate had the responsibility to feed, clothe and house the slave and keep him in good condition lest the market value of the slave should decrease. But in the system of untouchability, the Hindu take no responsibility for the maintenance of the Untouchable. As an economic system, it permits exploitation without obligation.[10]

Rajshekar continues by claiming that "the Indian Black Untouchable not only cannot enter the house of a Hindu, but even his very sight or shadow is prohibited by the dictates of the Hindu religion."

The issue of gender is closely connected to the different issues surrounding race and, likewise, must be taken seriously in all interfaith dialogues. Oftentimes, men occupy positions of authority, control, and ownership in society, the family, and their relationship to women. In the rituals of faith, men frequently function as the official representatives of the divine. This gives them the privilege to have an authority to represent, speak for, be closer to, be an interpreter of, or even embody the divine purpose within the community of faith. In other faith communities that rely on a written sacred text, men are able to interpret the mysteries of these texts if women are not recognized equally as keepers of the text. This can give males access to the major source of power—that is, the power to speak for God, other divine spirits, the ancestors, or nature.

Land, as a key part of nature, will have to be at the center of dialogue with indigenous communities of faith. This is true because theologically their religions hold earth in high regard and because politically they are fighting capitalist governments and corporations who have stolen indigenous peoples' land. Rosario Battung confirmed this fact for the indigenous of Asia:

> Land remains central to our indigenous people's quest for wholeness of life. In their continuing struggle for ancestral domain vis-à-vis the government's development schemes, they have maintained a deep reverence for nature. Nature involves not only land and resources but the very life and culture of indigenous people. To take away the land would mean their death, for land is not commodity but home.[11]

Whether it is considering earth as mother or believing in precolonial stories depicting humanity and animals emerging from a hole in the ground, indigenous peoples position the land at the center of their cultures and faith. The earth is sacred.

Dialoguing around what is spirituality is also crucial in interfaith conversations. From a liberation perspective, spirituality is not relying on accumulating material things and not seeking profit as our goal in life. Spirituality is the integration of the emotional, physical, and intellectual, and it is the communal sharing of all the resources God has given humanity. Spirituality is both an interior process of coming closer to liberation and an exterior process of struggling for liberation. Regarding the interior, this means being free from harmful desires and negative thoughts about oneself, others, and nature.

For example, the Tseltal, an indigenous Indian people of Mexico, say the following about lack of internal harmony: "Of a person who is indecisive, worried or two-faced they say *cheb yo'tan*—two hearts; of a suspicious or distrustful person *ma'spisiluk yo'tan*—one who does not act with his or her whole heart; of a jealous person *ti'ti 'o'tantayel*—a biting heart."[12] Wholeness on the inside defines liberation as freedom from personal addictions, including addictions to material accumulation and profit. The interior freedom, in addition, allows us to achieve an internal feeling of peace, power, and love of one's self so that one's mind, soul, and body can focus on serving the poor in the process of liberation.

The exterior spirituality means to make a conscious decision to be with the economically poor and oppressed in their movement for liberation. Divine spirit is embodied, incarnated, and represented by the plight and success of the least in society as they struggle to survive and reach their full humanity.

In fact, it is the spirit of liberation that is the common basis for an interfaith dialogue whose purpose is liberation. When we meet other faiths, how is the spirituality of liberation manifested in them? How do the poor and the least in a society struggle to reach their full potential; that is to say, what is their movement to become fully what they have been created to be? At the same time as they reach their full humanity, how are they growing in such a way that full humanity helps nature to be healthy? Anne Pattel-Gray, an Australian Aboriginal, gives one answer when she writes: "Our spirituality begins from the day we are born, and continues in how we live, how we care for our brothers and sisters, how we deal with our extended family, and how we care for God's creation. It is all balanced and cannot be divided."[13] A liberation spirituality as the norm in interfaith dialogue means that the oppressed have internal peace, justice, and freedom, and this is expressed in the external social relations with their families, communities, and nature. This liberation will be obvious in the new status of women and darker skin people, the communal ownership of all resources, strong connections to the elderly and children, and the renewed well-being of nature.

Part Four

Black Theology and a Persevering Faith

17 | Living Stones in the Household of God

M. Shawn Copeland

> Come to him, a living stone, though rejected by mortals yet chosen and precious in God's sight, and like living stones, let yourselves be built into a spiritual house, to be a holy priesthood, to offer spiritual sacrifices acceptable to God through Jesus Christ. (1 Peter 2:4-5)

This passage is from an epistle of inconclusive date and uncertain authorship. Tradition attributes this letter to the apostle Peter and dates it in the early 60s C.E.—more than nineteen hundred years ago. At the same time, many biblical scholars consider the language and style of the letter to be too polished, too sophisticated to have been written by a mere fisherman from Galilee with only rudimentary, if any, education. Scholars admit the possibility that Peter may have dictated the substance of the letter to Silvanus who, in turn, shaped and polished the Greek.

The letter is addressed to communities of Gentile Christians living in the northern and eastern part of Asia Minor, what we know today as Turkey. Although the letter indicates no official state oppression of Christians, about half of its contents is devoted to concern for those under persecution. Indeed, many of the members of these communities are socially, politically, and existentially vulnerable to persecution—slaves, wives of nonbelieving and/or abusive husbands. The new believers, men and women, face harassment from their family and relatives, friends and neighbors. The author of this letter calls these followers of the Way "aliens and exiles" (2:11)—terms that indicate their precarious condition in a hostile cultural milieu; they have found a home in Christian community.

This letter reaches out to those "exiles . . . who have been chosen and destined by God the Father and sanctified by the Spirit to be obedient to Jesus

Christ and to be sprinkled with his blood" (1:2). Because this new faith has called them to break with the social fabric of their community, these men and women endure exclusion and rejection. Their nonbelieving family and relatives, friends and neighbors simply cannot understand why these sober and sensible shopkeepers, bakers, weavers, housewives, and teachers have joined this strange new religion; why their slaves and wives have such confidence and hope. So, in fear and disgust, the nonbelievers ridicule them and their faith: "Whoever heard of worshipping some man who was crucified?" "He must have been a criminal, that's what the Romans did to criminals thirty years ago, and that's what they do today!" "What's all this talk about him rising from the dead? Don't nobody come back!" Thus, the nonbelievers taunt, even physically abuse their friends and neighbors simply because these ordinary people, so very much like them, believe in Jesus of Nazareth. Peter's letter reminds the new Christians of the dignity, the greatness of their vocation, and exhorts them to stand firm in the faith even as they endure suffering and abuse.

> In this you rejoice, even if now for a little while you have had to suffer various trials, so that the genuineness of your faith—being more precious than gold that, though perishable, is tested by fire—may be found to result in praise and glory and honor when Jesus Christ is revealed. (1:6-7)

Moreover, this message holds out a model to believers: "As he who called you is holy, be holy yourselves in all your conduct; for it is written, 'You shall be holy, for I am holy.' . . . Rid yourselves . . . of all malice, and all guile, insincerity, envy, and all slander'" (1:15-16; 2:1). As Jesus suffered, as countless other Christians suffer for the sake of his name, so too these exiles are to make of their suffering an offering. Thus, the new believers do not face alienation and oppression, suffering and evil alone: they have been brought into "an inheritance that is imperishable, undefiled, and unfading"; they are "protected by the power of God" (1:5). Just as God chose Jesus to be the cornerstone of the new temple (2:6-7), so Christians are to be a "chosen race" (2:9), "living stones . . . built into a spiritual house" (2:5).

This is, at least in part, a dangerous text. How can we bear to listen to words, no matter how powerful, that coach the weak and vulnerable to endure suffering and abuse in silence? How can we bear to listen to words, no matter how beautiful, that endorse restraint in the teeth of brutality? How can we bear to listen to such words? This is a very dangerous text.

But we read it during the octave of the great Sacred Mystery of our Redemption; we read it during the octave of Easter. We encounter this dangerous text in *kairotic* time. And, for the Christian, there is no time in the liturgical calendar more exultant, yet more reverent; more triumphant, yet more solemn. There is no time more steeped in God's power and dark splendor: the battered and crucified body of Jesus of Nazareth, made so luminous in the resurrection, is the seed of a new people adopted by his God and Father and led by the Spirit into new life and hope. We read this dangerous text in *kairotic* time in order to discern and cooperate with the work of the Spirit in history, "to preserve the dangerous memory of the messianic God."[1] We read this dangerous text in *kairotic* time in order to learn something about ourselves as Christians, and something about the work and mission of what is called black theology.

We know the academic mission and lineage of black theology: Like all Christian theology, black theology strives to understand and interpret the word of God and its meaning. But black theology explicitly confronts the historical, cultural, and structural subordination of black peoples within societies dominated by white supremacist rule. Black theology contests the heretical use of the Bible, of doctrine and practice to justify the subordination of black peoples and to sanctify the hegemony of white supremacy. Black theology is Christian theology—real Christian theology—alive and alert to the signs of the times, vigorous and wrestling against the powers and principalities of this world.

Yet, black theology has another, an even longer, more opaque lineage: black theology be here; black theology been here. Black theology was here before there was a Harvard; black theology was here before there was a Yale, before there was a Georgetown, before there was an Andover, before there was a Garrett Biblical Institute. Black theology come from the old heads, come from the wise hearts!

Black theology was born in the moans of the Middle Passage; it protected the weak, suckled the orphan, and comforted the dying. Black theology was reared in slavery and weaned in Reconstruction: its first word was freedom; its first memory the rhythms of Africa; its first step prayers rising from the Gulf and St. Helena, from New Orleans and Bardstown, Kentucky, from New York and Baltimore; its first triumph the ecstasy of the ring-shout and the spirituals.

Black theology's first rebellion snatched God back from the abyss in which the slaveholders had imprisoned the Creator. Black theology demanded freedom before there was a Maria Stewart, faced down the overseer before there was a Frederick Douglass, armed for liberation before there was Henry Highland Garnet. Black theology mourned the "strange fruit" that swung from Southern trees before Billie Holiday cried, shouted before Mahalia knew gospel, and announced God's own signifying self before Louis Armstrong.

Black theology been here; black theology still here! Black theology is the Spirit's gift: Black theology takes us down, lifts us up, carries us over! Black theology been here; black theology still here; black theology be here! Black theology is the Spirit's gift. And in 1969 black theology became a natural, walking man in James Hal Cone. What the Spirit showed him and through him showed us is that black theology is the daring deep black, blue-black, black and blue protest of the "wretched of the earth"! What the Spirit showed him and through him showed us is that black theology must meet the anguish of *chronos* with the power of *kairos*.

Black theology, the deep black desire of our ancestors, has something to say to the scripture at the beginning of this chapter, and that scripture has something to say to black theology.

First, as a *prophetic theology*, in its reading-dialogue with scripture, black theology puts on the lens of liberation: nothing is more sacred to our God than our authentic liberation, our freedom. Black theology prophesies a deliverance: a deliverance from our inattention and passivity, from our sexism and homophobia, from our self-hatred and viciousness. Black theology can help us to understand just how serious the consequences of social suffering and persecution can be.

Black theology's community is under siege: more than 33 percent of black families in the United States live below the poverty line, and of these families nearly 75 percent are headed by single mothers;[2] each day nearly 1,200 black teenagers are victims of violent crime, and nearly 1,500 black children are arrested.[3] More black women will die by homicide than either white women or white men.[4] Black people in the United States have a "three times greater chance than whites of dying from a policeman's bullet."[5] The United States has the world's highest rate of incarceration and imprisons black males at a rate almost five times higher than did South Africa at the peak of apartheid.[6] We cannot be surprised to learn that the federal prison population is over half black and Hispanic, the state prison population about 46 percent black.

Black theology must meet head-on this massive social suffering; our community is being crucified. Black theology can turn and fix our eyes and hearts and minds on the prize—not the house in the Atlanta suburb, not the Mercedes Benz, not the Armani or Versace, but the authentic life that Jesus of

Nazareth offers. Black theology has to fight for our youth, embrace the alien-ated, correct and admonish those of us who have grown smug and biased and self-righteous. What the Spirit showed James Cone and through him showed us is that black theology must meet the anguish of this *chronos* with the power of God's *kairos*.

Second, as *the theology of a crucified community,* black theology must face up to the cross. This is a dangerous task. The message of the cross of Jesus of Nazareth and its reception have never been nor ever can be personally, theo-logically, or socially neutral, nor can that message undermine or mock the great dignity of humanity and human freedom.

Scripture attests to the revulsion that crucifixion provoked in both Jews and Gentiles. Paul's message of the cross countered not only Roman political thinking but the "whole ethos of religion in ancient times."[7] We can imagine the shock experienced by the disciples and the crowd gathered around Jesus when he said, "If any want to become my followers, let them deny themselves and take up their cross and follow me" (Mark 8:34). Such a message would scarcely have been attractive; this was an invitation to something frightening and new, something unimaginable. The ordinary people of the ancient world were well aware of what it meant to be flogged, shamed, and brutalized, to bear a cross through the city and then to be nailed to it. Surely, they feared crucifixion and wanted no part of it; neither do we. But the stone that was rejected by human beings was precious in the sight of God (1 Peter 2:4). Death did not, does not have the last word: our God is able. Our God makes Jesus' cause a divine cause; our God raises Jesus from the dead. In his suffer-ing, death, and resurrection, Jesus discloses our God's compassionate and lib-erating presence in the suffering and pain of our community. What the Spirit showed James Cone and he showed us is that black theology is the daring deep black, blue-black, black and blue protest of the God of the Oppressed!

As a *prophetic theology of a crucified community in a crucified world,* black theology consciously and intentionally affirms black personhood and black humanity. Indeed, black theology affirms and values *all* personhood as God's sacred gift that can never be surrendered or usurped. Black theology is a rest-less theology that can "never be content until the full personal and social implications of the eschatological reality" of our relationship with God and with other human beings are realized in word and deed.[8]

Black theology orients us all and orients our work toward the desires of the Spirit. But we black theologians must be careful. Black theology is a danger-ous theology; it ought not to be domesticated. Black theology is an urgent theology, it must not be made polite. We black theologians must take our bearings by the prompting of the Spirit. We must orient our work to the demands of the Spirit. We must be serious and worthy of our calling. To paraphrase scripture: "Let us not presume to say to ourselves, 'We have Abraham as our Father'! God is able from stones to raise up children to Abraham" (see Matt. 3:9). Only in prayer and in study, in commitment and in humility, in unsparing honesty and in passionate self-control can we, thus, be built up into the precious living stones, an edifice of the Spirit, the precious household of God.

What the Spirit showed James Hal Cone and through him showed us is that black theology is the daring deep black, blue-black, black and blue protest of liberation for oppressed and oppressor! What the Spirit is showing him and is showing us is that black theology must meet the chaos of imperial globalization with the order of divine truth. What the Spirit is showing him and showing us is that in embracing the cross black theology must address the suffering of our people. What the Spirit is showing him and showing us is that standing before the cross of our people's suffering, black theology must resist evil. This is our mandate for black theology's community; this is our hope for ourselves and our students. Yet, first and foremost, always, this is God's doing: it is a wonder to behold!

18 / On Keeping Faith with the Center

Emilie M. Townes

i think it telling that in this late modern/postmodern theological
   world
      academic
      denominational
      local church
that the work of men and women of african descent
      the work of other racial ethnic women and men
remains off the radar screen of so many who declare what is perfect
   and imperfect
      in theological thought
      church doctrine
      and righteous living
our lives
      our experiences of God
      our strivings to understand the nature and work of the
         church
      our yearnings for the spirit
      our cries and shouts to Jesus
oddly enough
      remain categorized as drama or theater or
         "interesting"
some have noticed our absence in their thought
      but have faulted us for not using the masters' and
         mistresses' tools
      with the same kind of ghastly precision they do
         to annihilate or obscure the vastness of God's ongoing
            revelation
         and God's eternal and unrelenting call to all of us to grow
            in grace from right where we have been planted

to celebrate the richness found in being created in the
image of a god who is
quite simply
limitless
they have forgotten a cardinal rule
that many of us learned in nursery school
or perhaps kindergarten: sharing

Faith and Life in the Spirit

as people of faith, we find ourselves wrapped in a postmodern
culture that is a place of increase of political polarizations along
the lines of
nation
race
gender (which for me means sex, sexuality, sex roles, sexual
orientation, sexism)
class
denomination
faith traditions
in our world, culture is sanitized and then commodified
this process of changing aesthetic tastes
domestication of the once exotic or feared other
uncontrolled appropriation
market-driven refiners' fires
mass production
and marketing
are for our enjoyment at the expense of people's lives and shrinking
pay checks
and often the solution is placed in the hands of lottery games
games of chance
rather than challenge and debunk master narratives such as the u.s.
as the city on the hill
the lone heroic self-made man or woman
or inevitable and unalterable progress as good and civilized
our fashionable narratives are
nationalist and xenophobic
with strong religious, racial, patriarchal, homophobic,

heterosexist, ageist, and classist overtones and bell tones
in our postmodern culture, the structural inequalities that form the
superstructure of U.S. society
are alive and well
despite various warnings of postmodern thought with
its critique of modernity's excessive focus on individualism
universals
ahistorical reason
universal knowledge
the elevation of science as sheer objectivity
the social contract and morality organized around civil
rights
and the liberties of the free individual
our postmodern culture has
thus far
has only made a creative and sociocultural space
in which racial
gender
and so-called subclasses
now have *theoretical* entree into the emerging global
marketplace of
power
privilege
and pleasure
this entrée may be imperative for these groups that have been
until recently
among the dispossessed
but too many of our postmodern conversations
do not move us beyond reform to transformation of social
systems and practices
that model justice for all peoples and a respect for
creation beyond human skin
and the violence that circumscribes our lives
this turn has been taken, in part i believe
because postmodernisms have omitted
until recently, with the development of social
post-modernism,
a concern for institutions, social classes, political organization,

        political economic processes and social movements
and it is here where my work as a christian ethicist seeks to
        understand the absurd metaphors encircling our lives
for me, womanist ethics helps us remember and explore the fact
  that
        inclusion does not guarantee justice
        and access to an inequitable and grossly maldistributed social
           order does not mean the transformation of fragmented
           communities or of whole ones
but i am getting ahead of myself just a bit
because, for me, little of what i do
        and less of what i'm able to articulate
        would be possible if james hal cone had not stood up and
           then sat down to write
           if he did not have the courage of his anger and rage
               at injustice
           and the persistently demonic ways it lodges itself in
           racism
                and then refused, for over 30 years, to keep
                  quiet about it
        he has been, to me and to countless others, the thorn in our
           theological flesh
           who has refused to allow us the comfort of our titles or
           positions or notoriety or even obscurity
for what he says each day of his life is true
        there are those out there who despise you just because you are
           black or a woman or gay or lesbian or poor or HIV positive,
           or working class, or from continents outside of europe, or...
they may say that they love you
        but you can feel the blood flowing from the knife
           wounds they inflict with their indifference
              and unwillingness to change their ways
              or even include you in their prayers
they may say we are all brothers and sisters under the skin
        but you can see them checking and tugging
           at their skin
        while looking warily at yours
they may say that the kingdom of God is near

but they shout "look, it's right over there!"
and point in one direction
while they make a mad dash for another
no, no, no
james cone's work calls all of us on our unwillingness to share
God
and our troubling tendency to treat God as a possession
our penchant, in academic circles, to pontificate in ways
that suggest
that only a few of us have the right or the
ability to feel and reason our way
into articulating the complexities *and*
the simplicities of faith and life in the spirit

Cone and Black Theology

Cone's early and enduring articulation of black theology is one of the con-temporary foundations for womanist theological reflection on the nature of black faith and witness. Womanist thought can and does also stand in the theological streams of evangelicalism, liberalism, neo-orthodoxy, and libera-tion theologies. Certainly, as foundational texts, James Cone's *Black Theology and Black Power* (1969) (along with *God of the Oppressed* [1975] and *A Black Theology of Liberation* [1970]) have had and continue to have a profound effect on all of the liberationist social postmodern theologies of which womanist thought is only one. Cone recognized and reformulated W. E. B. Du Bois's most prophetic words that "the problem of the twentieth century is the problem of the color line"; Cone forged his restatement with both an appreciation for and critique of black nationalism and the ways in which African Americans experience the religious. Thus, Cone pushed womanist theological reflection to consider and reconsider the ways in which build-ing an interstructured theo-ethic requires patience, hard work, persever-ance, and a relentless commitment to rigorous critical and analytical scholarship that addresses the general public, the religious communities, and the academy.

As black theology has matured from the firm foundation laid by Cone, it has taken, in these very early days of the twenty-first century, a measured look at the quest for human freedom and justice. One of the major method-ological linchpins of black theology has been this quest for the equality of all persons under God. Indeed, ethicist Peter J. Paris calls this *the* fundamental principle of the black Christian tradition in which human equality under God is understood as categorical, absolute, unconditional, and universally applicable.

Black theology has articulated a strong doctrine of sin in relation to racism and an equally strong doctrine of virtue on the part of those who oppose racism. Black theology is forged from the moral conviction that God cares about the poor and the oppressed. Cone and other black theologians in the liberationist tradition understand that God is deeply involved in the human condition—God understands and knows human suffering and will deliver us from suffering. However, there is not an otherworldly impulse in this. This is the yoking of prophetic and apocalyptic eschatology to deal with the concrete and tangible situatedness of human suffering in our world. Because God is the highest source of moral good, God in Jesus Christ identifies with the poor and outcast as liberator *and* redeemer.

Black theology also has biblical roots. There is, as is the case for many other theologies, the search for moral laws, wrestling with the Ten Commandments, and seeking to understand the ethical mandates in scripture from deontological and teleological frameworks. For many black theologians, loyalty to God means discerning the meaning of existence and the moral truths of the universe primarily in light of scripture. However, there is a profound search for recovering the African presence in the Bible. This is not, to my mind, a revisionist search, for the revisionism began when Eurocentric thought misapprehended the biblical world and refused to see it and its peoples in their richness. As scholarship emerged out of this misapprehension, so did the loss of the African presence in the biblical world. Somehow Egypt was taken out of Africa as European biblical scholarship, from the fourth century to the eighteenth century, recast the Bible into what Cain Hope Felder calls the "saga of European people."[1]

There is a strong emphasis on community. Community is more than a place or a common territory where people meet. It is more than a social organization or a collection of individuals living in close quarters to each other. In black theology, community is the exploration of a "we" relationship through seeking to understand the dynamics of belonging, group identification, and social solidarity. There is a consideration of the black family as the center of values-shaping that can be both orthodox and heterodox in its understanding of the composition of the family. There is a concern for moral achievement in collective life of the black community and the social advancement, growth, and improvement of the condition of African Americans in the United States.

Within black theology today, various motifs have appeared with some regularity, although not with the same emphasis. There has been a concern for inclusive community. This community is both intra- and intercommunal in nature. As such, it is more precise to name these communities (with an emphasis on the plural). There has been the ever-present interest in the worth and dignity of all persons. The *imago dei,* the creation, the fall, the cross, and the resurrection all have varying sites of prominence in this. There has been the concern for just political, economic, and social systems. As such, black theology is rarely "simply" theology. It has within it a strong impulse toward ethics—philosophical, theological, and social. More recent motifs include the equality of women, intersections with the third world, globalism, the environment, war and peace, class, and poverty.

Cone and Womanist Theology

In my reading and rereading of James Cone's work, I am drawn to the last chapter of *Black Theology and Black Power,* "Revolution, Violence, and Reconciliation," in which Cone issues a critical reminder to womanist thought: the problem of racism will not be solved through talk but action.[2] As womanist theo-ethical reflection features an interstructured look at class, gender, and race, Cone's message contains a striking methodological warning about the challenge of holding fast to a praxis-based analysis in ethical and theological discourses that often feature abstraction and nuance. His most recent work, *Risks of Faith,* continues to hold us all accountable to do meaning-filled scholarship rather than academic macarenas and two-steps.

Yet as much as womanist theology and ethics have gained from Cone's probing foundation *and* his continued growth as a scholar, teacher, and man of faith, the very rise of womanist thought signals methodological omissions that Cone himself notes in the introduction to the twentieth anniversary edition of *Black Theology and Black Power.*[3]

The words that were so true more than a decade ago remain true today. Sexism, a bias toward Western theological perspectives, a latent (and at times blatant) Christian triumphalism, an inability to link in concrete and tangible ways with the liberation struggles of peoples outside of the United States, and a sometimes stubborn unwillingness to deal with the class and caste structure of black life in the United States still find a much too comfortable home in many African American churches and in many articulations of black theology.

All of us have much to learn from how hard Cone works to eradicate these drawbacks in his own life and work. It is not so much that he gets it right all the time—he *is* human. What I admire is that he has a commitment to continue to grow his scholarship, teaching, and witness large, and he takes this on with vigor—he holds himself accountable and responsible for his ideas and God-talk. This abiding gift that he shares with the academy should not be underestimated or overlooked.

As Cone put it so well in 1989, "African American theologians and preachers must develop the courage to speak the truth about ourselves, saying to each other and to our church leaders what we have often said and still say to whites: *Enough is enough! It is time for this mess to stop!*"[4] I have no doubt, after reading *Risks of Faith,* that Cone includes all of us in that call for today.

Therefore, taking my cues from Cone's challenge for himself and for all of us to develop and maintain and grow a creative self-critique of black theology, the black church, as well as white churches and dominant theologies, I want to reflect on what Cone's work means for womanist thought and this womanist in particular. Cone's work and its ongoing scholarly evolution has convinced me that womanist theology and ethics cannot and must not merely accept methodologies or constructs of theological reflection that do not consider with rigor the experience of African American women and the diversities found within black womanhood and the larger African American community.

In both an intercommunal dialogue with other racial and ethnic groups and an intracommunal conversation among black folks, womanist thought seeks to explore the nature of oppression as it has a peculiar impact on the lives of black women. This is done with an eye toward the nature of how this may or may not manifest itself in the lives of men, children, the aged, differing sexualities, persons of various class locations, and so forth. What this means is that race is only one consideration for womanist theo-ethical thought. Race is joined with a host of other materialities of black life in a hermeneutic of liberation and transformation.

This requires that womanist theo-ethics accept the challenge to be as self-critical as it is rigorous and analytical in its methodology.

Marginalization and Liberation

I begin with a quotation:

> She was one of the blackest of her race; and her round shining eyes, glittering as glass beads, moved with quick and restless glances over everything in the room. Her mouth, half open with astonishment at the wonders of the new Mas'r's parlor, displayed a white and brilliant set of teeth. Her woolly hair was braided in sundry little tails, which stuck out in every direction. The expression of her face was an odd mixture of shrewdness and cunning, over which was oddly drawn, like a kind of veil, an expression of the most doleful gravity and solemnity. She was dressed in a single filthy, ragged garment, made of bagging; and stood with her hands demurely folded before her. Altogether, there was something odd and goblin-like about her appearance—something, as Miss Ophelia afterwards said, "so heathenish," as to inspire that good lady with utter dismay; and turning to St. Clare, she said, "Augustine, what in the world have you brought that thing here for?"

This representative snippet (from Harriet Beecher Stowe's *Uncle Tom's Cabin*) of the cartel of ideologies that reify our too often multilayered oppressive social order can cause contemporary womanist theo-ethical thinkers and practitioners to paraphrase Miss Ophelia: "What in the world have we been brought here for?" Rather than an impertinent and cavalier question, this is one hemmed with the precision stitch of outrage, historicity, and agency and a critical eye toward justice.

Stowe's description of Topsy is troubling. It is a swill pot of caricature—Topsy is a slave girl who perfectly fits the black stereotype of the time. Stowe's description of Topsy contains imagery of a barely human young girl. In all that Stowe attempts to do in speaking out against the institution of slavery, she clings to imagery that never allows Topsy to be seen as fully human or humane. The reader never comes to know Topsy (or any of the black females in the novel) as a person, for her character (both in print and as a person) is never developed. Stowe repeats the very dehumanizing process she seeks to critique.

This cursory look at Topsy and *Uncle Tom's Cabin* underscores a major challenge that womanist theo-ethical reflection offers: what happens when

Topsy speaks? What happens when Topsy moves from a literary character functioning as metaphor to the material history and lives of African American children, men, and women? What does it mean when the one (now One and containing multiplicities) who has been described and categorized by others starts to carve out and speak out of an identity in which she is an active agent? What does it mean that womanist thought signals a commitment to *conscious* reflection on the interplay among culture, identity, community, theory, practice, life, and death?

It is small wonder that Topsy often becomes lost in the larger sociocultural matrix of U.S. society and the intracommunal dynamics of African American communities. Even in the communities of resistance that seek genuine diversity and equality, the worldviews of Topsy are often muted if not negated. Rather than avoiding the reinscription of conventional oppressive hierarchies of class, gender, and race, black marginalized communities have often fallen victim to hegemonic forces with Topsy and her sisters and brothers as the casualties.

As Cone's work demonstrates so well, marginalization, though not desirable, *can* function as a site of resistance. It can birth spaces of respite and judgment:

Baby Suggs's clearing
Mama Day's lightening powder
Celie's "till you do right by me"
Sanchez's lions
Baby's veil
Danticat's krick krack

Although marginalization can be a lonely place, it can also be a place that encourages creativity in thought, word, and deed. It can push the marginalized into pithy analysis and trenchant cultural critiques. The spirituals, gospels, blues, work and protest songs, jazz, R&B, soul, hip hop all have within them segments that have taken a long, hard look at the nature of subjugations in our lives and had something to say about them and ways to lessen, if not eradicate, the many wounds inflicted on black lives on a minute-by-minute basis.

From a womanist liberatory perspective, the hope was and remains that theo-ethical reflection and sociocultural critique should not further erase and exclude women of color in racial analysis, the multiplicity of sexualities among men and women, the stratification of socioeconomics within and without black culture, the genuine valuing of age—young and old, the continuing impact/fall out/beat down of colonial and neocolonial mentalities on peoples of the African diaspora.

New formulations of identity politics in theo-ethical discourses must avoid the earlier patterns of essentialism and avoid new forms of essentialism to be true to the struggles of exploited and oppressed groups in their attempts to critique the dominant structures from positions that give meaning and purpose for this struggle. This intracommunal analysis is crucial for woman-ist reflection. For it is in this in-house conversation and challenge to the forms of essentialism within the African American church, theological acad-emy, and larger black culture as these locations seek to produce and practice liberatory ethics that womanist ethical reflections address their first audi-ences. Womanist ethical thought does not deny the importance and power of identity-making and shaping but explores the magnitude and scope of the diversity of black identities so that *we* do not commit the gross errors of stereotype and sentimentalization that are often forced on our communities. In the process, we may well neglect accountability and responsibility within our own communities and fall into a warped and inarticulate rhetoric of vic-timization that does little to craft justice.

The interplay between identity and essentialism is not only intracommu-nal, it is intercommunal as well. The challenge here is to maintain the rigor-ous pursuit of identity as a form of resistance to hegemony. This pursuit of the authentic and varied identities in black lives in the United States com-bines the experiential with the analytical (often in this order) to question many of the epistemological and ideological assumptions found in the larger culture and its social institutions. There may be times when the assertion of an exclusive essentialism is a strategy to undercut and destabilize hegemonic forces. Yet great care must be taken to avoid creating a monolithic identity that fails to represent the true heterogeneity of black life in the United States.

To take on the challenges found in the firm foundation laid by Cone's work is to value identity even as we analyze and critique the formation and practice of identity. It is to question the label of essentialism when it is always applied to the people who are dispossessed, yet to be empowered enough to demand that their personhood is valuable and should be valued, those who are cast as being essentialist.[5] Why is it, we must ask, that the ones who have for decades, if not centuries, practiced hegemony with precision are never guilty of collapsing reality into their own image? If this checkered legacy is what we consider to be normal and whole, what a misbegotten notion of normal and wholeness we live. May God help us.

The struggle has always been for womanist theo-ethical reflections to name, analyze, and critique the simultaneous subordinations of class, gender, and race as *lived experiences* as well as theoretical constructs. Further, it is to name the ways in which these forms of subordination and oppression are carried out within the African American community as well as by men and women in other racial ethnic groups. Within this struggle is the recognition that accountability is paramount. This accountability functions on the individual and the communal level. Womanist ethicists are held accountable by the African American community for the ethical, theological, social, and political choices we make as we straddle academy, church, and community. In this vein, womanist religionists can never forget that we stand within a community as active members and participants. The community functions to remind us that we may have lapses within our analysis and critique that demand we reassess our perspectives.

On the communal level, accountability means being open to the width and breadth of the community. It also means remaining vigilant to the forces of hegemony that can and do co-opt authentic black life and replace it with stereotypes and innuendoes that pathologize African American resistance struggles against a dehumanizing hegemony concocted from ideologies of elitism and repression. The question becomes how to implement accountability without reinscribing hierarchies endemic to African American culture and its social institutions. Answering this question is one of the enduring challenges of womanist ethics and to all forms of ethical and theological reflection that focus on black religiosity and African American liberation that is spiritual and social.

Perhaps if we enflesh Topsy by looking around us—at this very moment and in our everyday lives—we can begin to see the elements necessary to make this accountability tangible and long-lasting. Let me offer, as I close, three places to begin.

First, we have to address what I believe to be a major flaw: black theology has not had a sustained and integrated impact on the black church in all its manifestations. Though I suspect that the reasons for this are complex, let me point to what I believe to be the major reason: folks refuse to give up whatever privilege they have to help craft a better day for the African American Christian church and the black societies of the United States. We are caught in whirlpools of individualistic narcissism. Even though black theology is largely ignored by the majority of adherents and practitioners of dominant academic discourses, it appears that this weary state of affairs is even more so in the majority of black Christian churches. I do not hear, witness, or see a groundswell of calls for liberation from most black churches. I do hear calls for living the dream and making a way out of no way. What troubles me about this is that we have little biblical or theological anchor in this. It is as though we in the academy and we in the church are ships passing in the night and we are not even looking for one another. Our continued arrogance and hoarding of our meager privileges must stop, or we need to find another name for ourselves because we have ceased being Christian. We must repeat kindergarten and nursery school over again and practice sharing. We must reject the deadly dualism we have adopted—that you are either a thinker or a doer. The reality is most of us are both and all of us need to learn how to do both better and more faithfully.

Second, many African Americans are the Topsy in the big house of our institutions—be that academy, agency, church, denominational office, local church, or seminary. If we are lucky, we may have some company. But whatever the conditions may be, how do we, in our life and work, help carve a space, however large or small, for ourselves and others to obtain more than just a glimpse of the richness of African American life and thought? As I watch the great care and concern Cone takes as he mentors students (and even new colleagues), I become more convinced that a key part of my work as a womanist ethicist who also dares cultural critique is that I remember that I did not get where I am all by myself, I will not stay where I am all by myself, I will not grow intellectually or spiritually all by myself. I have a responsibility to open the door that was opened for me even wider so that even more folks can not only enter the big house I inhabit but infiltrate farther and start opening those doors even wider as well. (Of course, we can always try to dismantle that damned big house all together and craft institutions that value learning and refuse to be gigantic holding pens for the mind and the intellect.)

Finally, we must never soar so high into the stratosphere of academia or religious hierarchies that we forget to ground our work in realities, not abstractions. As Cone's work reminds us, black culture is real and it is made by people loving and struggling their way into tomorrows. Black culture is also suffering gross commodification and commercialization. And sometimes we participate in its co-optation. Those spaces in which we search for and yearn for home are not up for philosophical or theological justification. We exist in the breathing spaces of our hopes and realities. To do our work in religious bodies means that we do so with an intimacy that feels the rise and fall of each others' chests, that smells the sweat of living and dying, that tastes the sorrow and joy found in the pots simmering on cook fires. In short, accountability means that we keep looking for ways to live into God's ongoing revelation. We put down the temptation to make lists, set quotas, craft exclusive standards of specious excellence, and fight like hell to keep from allowing our work and our lives from becoming monuments of irrelevance and domination. From my colleague and friend Jim Cone, I am reminded every time I walk into the classroom, talk with students during office hours, research a topic, or sit down at my computer to write that it is little help if in our cultural and theo-ethical critiques, we replace the forms of supremacy we know so well with a postmodern black slow drag of annihilation.

19 / The Vocation of a Theologian

James H. Cone

When Professor Linda Thomas invited me to come to Garrett-Evangelical Theological Seminary to speak about my vocation as a theological teacher and scholar, I could not decline. You could wake me up at 3:00 AM and I would be ready to talk about my calling to do theology for the church in America and the world. I like talking about tough, challenging, and unsettling issues about God, ministry, and the church, and I do it every opportunity I get.

Being an effective teacher demands that I also become a good writer. How can I teach any subject and not also place my perspective alongside the texts that I ask students to read? While I can imagine an excellent writer who is not motivated to teach in a seminary or university classroom, I cannot imagine a great teacher in graduate school who is not motivated to write. Writing is teaching. I often say to my doctoral students at Union, "If you plan to teach in graduate school, you also must plan to be a competent and creative writer of essays and books in your discipline. No one should be teaching in graduate school who does not have the talent and discipline to organize his/her ideas into a persuasive argument and narrative. If you do not love teaching and writing, the challenge and the excitement of intellectual debate, then you should find another vocation and stop wasting your time and that of others. By your presence here at Union, I assume that you are already persuaded that theological teaching and research are valuable for the church and society." With that speech, it quickly dawns on my students that I mean business. They shape up or find another advisor who will tolerate their mediocrity.

This essay gives me the opportunity to share with you something about my theological journey. As I thought about what to write for this volume, I reflected back to four key events in my academic career: (1) six years as a graduate student at Garrett-Evangelical Theological Seminary and Northwestern University, 1958–64; (2) another six years of teaching religion at Philander Smith College in Little Rock, Arkansas, and Adrian College in

Michigan, 1963–69; (3) writing *Black Theology and Black Power*[1] in a month's time during the summer of 1968; and (4) thirty-one years of teaching systematic theology at Union Seminary—1969 to the present. I can hardly believe that it has been forty-two years since I first entered seminary and thirty-one years since the publication of *Black Theology and Black Power* and my arrival at Union. I will say a word about how each of these moments influenced my vocational self-understanding as a teacher and scholar.

My vocation as a scholar and teacher was first shaped by my theological studies at Garrett—both positively and negatively. On the positive side, Garrett introduced me to the study of theology. My teachers taught theology in a way that made me unable to resist the intellectual excitement of the discipline. I loved studying the Bible, theology, and the history of the church. Theological debates with professors and graduate students were my favorite pastime. After I completed the B.D. degree (which we call M.Div. today) I entered the joint M.A. and Ph.D. programs at Garrett and Northwestern. I was determined to acquire enough theological knowledge that would enable me to debate anybody in the world about the truth of the Christian gospel.

On the negative side, Garrett and Northwestern assumed that black people's history and culture had nothing to contribute to theology as a discipline. During my six years there, no essay or book about black people or by a black person was assigned as required reading. While I wrote many theological essays, a master's thesis, and a doctoral dissertation on Karl Barth, I did not learn how to write until I left graduate school. Graduate school took me away from the only source that could empower me to write—the history and culture of black people.

After I left seminary, I went back to my cultural roots in Arkansas—the black world that gave birth to me. There I found my theological voice in the songs, prayers, and sermons of black churches and in the political context of the civil rights and Black Power movements. It did not take me long before I got really angry about the 350 years of white supremacy and white theology's silence about it. I decided to channel my anger into theological reflection. The time had come for me to kick some white theological butt. That was when I discovered how to express myself in writing. It was either write or be consumed by my rage—write or go crazy. I turned to James Baldwin for style and to Malcolm X for content. These two black prophets—along with a few others like Richard Wright and Martin Luther King Jr.—became my guides for clear thinking and artful expression. My book, *Black Theology and Black Power* (1969), was my first public theological cry. It was like a baby coming to voice at birth, screaming in response to hurt. I will never forget what I felt back then—the excitement and self-confidence one feels when seized by the Spirit that refuses to let go until the truth is spoken bluntly and without compromise. I thought of the prophet Jeremiah because the experience felt like "a burning fire shut up in my bones" (20:9), an experience so unforgettable that I can retell it at a moment's notice and feel the energy surge again.

Sometimes, as I wrote a sentence or paragraph or chapter, I would look at it and then reread it slowly to see how well it was written, focusing on content and style, so that the language would express both the depth of my rage and the truth of my convictions. I would often sit back in my chair and smile—amazed at how well I expressed a point. I knew that there had to be a divine power at work in the history and culture of black people, a power greater than me or my people. How else could I explain the ease with which I wrote and the skill and courage found in the writing? Even today, I am still amazed at the gift of literary expression God gave me for theology. I am no genius by any stretch of intellectual imagination. I was not a brilliant student in graduate school. Being the first black to be accepted on the joint Ph.D. program at Garrett and Northwestern, I was often regarded by many of my seminary professors as wading in theological waters too deep for my intellectual ability. I was never given any kind of scholarship and had to work as a janitor at Garrett to pay for my room, board, and tuition. When I asked the President of Garrett to sign a document so I could get a federal loan to pay for my tuition at Northwestern, he initially refused to believe that I had been accepted to the doctoral program, since all doctoral students are fully supported. "All but me," I said. I did not get one penny of support while I was pursuing my Ph.D.

In writing *Black Theology and Black Power* and all the essays and books that followed, I did not care what white people thought about what I was saying. Since I was not looking for any kind of award or fellowship from them, I was free to write and say what I believed to be the truth of the gospel. I just turned myself over to the Spirit of black liberation and said, "Do with me what you will." As when I preached, I tried hard to keep God in the forefront and myself in the background. The truth of the gospel is accessible to anyone humble enough to receive it. According to Matthew's Jesus, God has "hidden these things from the wise and the intelligent and [has] revealed them to infants" (11:25). Jesus did not say, "blessed are the intelligent," people with great intellectual ability. On the contrary, Luke's Jesus said, "Blessed are you poor," people who are hungry and oppressed (6:20, 21), the "little people," as Malcolm X called them. When you realize that God does not share the value system of this white supremacist culture, you will not apologize to anyone for being who God created you to be. We black people must not let anybody intimidate us by appealing to an intellectual and spiritual tradition that enslaved and colonized our people. We must not let the descendants of slaveholders and colonizers make us think we are stupid.

I thank God for my mother and father, Lucy and Charlie Cone, who were the smartest woman and man I ever met, even though their formal education did not go beyond the ninth and sixth grades respectively during my childhood. Daddy's life gave me an example of what it means to have the courage to speak the truth, and Mother showed me how to develop the language to articulate it. They were powerful intellectual and spiritual examples—like a one-two knockout punch. As a child I watched my father with only a sixth-grade education stand up to the white folks in Bearden and listened to my mother with only a ninth-grade education articulate the spiritual significance of my father's courage.

Watching and listening to my parents, I soon discovered that God's Spirit makes you say things you would rather not say because the truth is hard-hitting. It makes people angry because it exposes their hypocrisy. While writing *Black Theology and Black Power*, I often said to myself, "Oh, shit, white folks ain't going to like that." When I got to the chapter on the black church, it broke my heart to have to make public what everybody knows to be the truth about it. "The bishops ain't going to like this book anymore than white theologians." In fact some bishops are still angry with me today because of what I wrote many years ago about the African Methodist Episcopal Church. Every time I thought about taking the edge off of what I was writing, an inner voice said, "Don't do it—write the truth!" Whatever we do as teachers, scholars, and ministers, we should never let people make us compromise the gospel. We should put ourselves in a position so we can always speak the whole truth and not a facsimile thereof.

Because I knew that what I was saying would not be received with joy by the white and black theological and church establishments, I had to say it well. Nothing kills a good idea like bad writing. Writing is a craft, a creative skill that one must work hard and daily at perfecting. I felt like I had taken on the whole theological world. The greater the challenge the more persuasive the argument if one succeeds. If there is no challenge, no risk, one is not likely to write anything of significance.

I accepted a teaching post at Union because of the great challenge it posed for me as a young black theologian from rural Arkansas. I had about five job offers—all of which offered me an associate professorship with tenure, and nearly three times the salary of the Union offer. Union tendered an assistant professorship with no tenure or promise of it. Since Union symbolized the epitome of white theological scholarship in 1969 and was located near Harlem, I could think of no better place to test the intellectual worth of my theological convictions. If I could carve out a place for black theology at Union, then I could do it anywhere in the world.

I can remember all the distractions—"ain't no such thing as black theology"; "theology does not come in colors"; "black theology has no intellectual substance." No one ever said these things directly to me. I heard them from black students who reported on what white seminary professors were saying. I also read similar comments in journals and newspapers. Once a *Time* magazine reporter asked me directly whether I thought black theology was a fad. "Absolutely not!" was my emphatic reply. "Black people are no fad. Black theology is an intellectual development defined by the black religious experience."

I knew that white theologians and a few black ones too expected black theology to disappear soon from the theological scene. In 1975, John C. Bennett, then president emeritus of Union and well-known scholar of ethics and theology, referred to black theology as "an ephemeral explosion. I have no doubt that it, like most white theologies, will soon be dated."[2]

John Bennett's condescending comments made me even more determined not to let that happen. Bennett was the president who invited me to teach at Union and should have been supportive. Nothing fires up my intellectual determination like arrogant white people who think that they possess the whole truth and others have nothing to contribute of lasting value. Seminaries and university departments of religion are loaded with such people. Nothing pleases me more than uncovering white theological mediocrity so the world can see it in the raw. There is so much of it in our seminaries, and they are the main obstacles to diversity in theological education. I have fought them at Union for thirty-one years, but they always outnumber me and I usually end up defeated. If Union has declined in academic excellence, it is not because of its black professors and students. Check out white mediocrity. As long as I am at Union, black excellence is the only black presence I will permit to grace its academic halls. I wish I could say the same for white presence.

Two things, I believed, would guarantee black theology's survival for many years to come. First, I had to keep on writing—publishing essays and books. As long as I published books and essays about black theology, it would not die. Since people were criticizing black theology in both white and black theological and church circles, I had a lot of questions to answer and many issues to write about. Less than a year after *Black Theology and Black Power* was published, my second book, *A Black Theology of Liberation*,[3] appeared. The second book was an even harsher indictment of white theology than the first. Bennett, as president of Union, called me into his office and asked whether my second book was theological hyperbole. "You don't really believe that the white church is the antichrist, do you?" I looked John in the eye and told him that I was not dealing with theological exaggeration. "If you really believe that the white church is the antichrist, why are you teaching at Union?" he asked. "My dad was a woodcutter," I said, "and I work at Union. I see little difference between the two workplaces since whites control both. As long as I seek justice in the system, I might as well work at Union. There is no more spiritual significance to working at Union than any other white supremacist institution." John Bennett was a little surprised that I meant what I said in my theological texts and that I was not simply engaging in shock therapy. I was not kind to white theologians who wanted to dismiss black theology as overstatement.

Black scholars were often as critical as whites but in a different direction. When black scholars said that what I call black theology was nothing but white theology painted black, I was deeply wounded. I responded with *The Spirituals and the Blues*[4] and *God of the Oppressed*.[5] I can remember all of the spirited debates in the Society for the Study of Black Religion, the American Academy of Religion, and other academic contexts where we gathered. I felt alone. Even my brother, Cecil, attacked me in his book, *The Identity Crisis in Black Theology*.[6] He claimed that I was more accountable to the academic standards of white theology than to the spiritual life of the black church. That was absurd—almost too silly to warrant a serious response. But I refused to give up my theological convictions. I used my anger to express in writing what I believed to be the truth about God's solidarity with the oppressed.

Embattled, the most important thing I realized was never to stop writing. Writing is therapeutic. It heals the soul and empowers the mind. Words, as Malcolm said, are like theological and philosophical bullets. When they hit their target, enemies are rendered silent—speechless. When I was criticized in print or at a public meeting, I went home and wrote about it. My opponents liked to run off at the mouth in public, but they seldom had the discipline or the conviction to engage in serious theological debate.

Writing is also power. It enables you to define the world, to set limits on a discipline and then to broaden it. I was determined to leave my mark on the discipline of theology. Why spend six or more years learning the ins and outs of a discipline and not put your stamp on it? Why assign other people's writings for students to read and have nothing of your own to contribute to the discussion? If you have nothing to contribute that is worthy of publication, why then are you teaching in graduate school?

Writing enables you to teach the world. You can reach people you've never seen and make an impact on their lives. Many people have thanked me for the books I wrote—some even saying I kept them in the church and influenced their vocation to enter the ministry. The Korean Church in Japan invited me in 1975 to lead workshops and to deliver many lectures and sermons on the theme "The Church Struggling for the Liberation of the People." Dalits in India invited me to do a similar task there. About ten thousand people heard me in India—the largest group I've ever spoken to in one setting. I never will forget my experience in South Africa in 1985, when I was first allowed in the country. It was like going home. I just did not realize how widely I had been read and the influence on their theological imagination and struggle for human dignity. My books have been translated into ten different languages, enabling grassroots people to read about black theology in their native language.

No one writes unless he or she is faced with a challenge. The greater the challenge, the more profound and influential the message if one succeeds. I faced the challenge of making sense out of the black experience in a theological world that did not regard black people's history and culture as having theological value. The more I thought about that white assumption the angrier I became. I was determined to demonstrate its racist nature. It reminded me of what many of my professors assumed about my intellectual ability when I was in graduate school. They said I was in over my head, trying to get a Ph.D. when, as a Negro with limited intelligence, I should be satisfied with a B.D. As a student and scholar, I refused to accept white judgments about black intelligence. When I no longer needed their approval, I challenged all comers to theological debate. That meant that I had to write in order to answer the charges leveled against black theology. If you read my eleven books and about 150 essays, all of them responded to a challenge. No challenge, no writing.

I tell my doctoral students that their challenge today is to complete their Ph.D. degree as expeditiously as possible. They will never become creative thinkers writing papers for professors. Graduate school is an organized effort to crush creativity. To be sure, it lays the intellectual foundation for creative thinking. It is the place to study hard, learn as much as possible from every source available, and then get the hell out of there so you can do your own thing and not simply repeat what someone else tells you. Nothing is more important in graduate school than completing the degree.

I challenge my students to think about what their challenge will be after graduate school is over and they begin teaching. Most people don't write anything after the Ph.D. because they have no challenge to inspire them. Life is not worth living without challenge.

The second thing I did to ensure black theology's survival was to mentor doctoral students who would extend black theology far beyond anything I could imagine. Twenty-seven people have received their Ph.D. degrees with me as their advisor. All but two are persons of color. Nineteen are black, two are Native American, and four are Asian. I have ten doctoral students who are currently working with me. That makes a total of thirty-seven past and current doctoral students. With these people writing and teaching about black theology, it will not die—at least not as soon as my detractors had hoped.

Many of my former students are not only writing about black theology but also mentoring doctoral students who will follow in their steps as they are following in mine. I am not worried about black theology's survival. It inspired and was inspired and challenged by both feminist and womanist theologies; queer theology; the theologies of Native, Asian, and Hispanic Americans; Dalit theology in India; minjung theology in Korea; black theology in South Africa and Britain; and many other theologies among the poor throughout the world. Through mutual inspiration and challenge, black theology stays alive and active in the world. Wherever people of color in the churches have been struggling for justice against white supremacy, black liberation theology has been there.

The third thing I did to ensure the long life of black theology was to create a strong black faculty presence at Union Seminary. I did not want to be the only black professor at Union, which my white colleagues would have gladly accepted. When I went to Union in 1969, C. Eric Lincoln and Lawrence Jones were the only other blacks on the faculty. Within a few years, Lincoln left for Fisk University and Jones for Howard University Divinity School. That left me alone, and whites thought I wanted it that way. I had to fight hard to change their misguided perception. The late professor James Washington came, then James Forbes, Cornel West, and Samuel Roberts. In a few years they also left, but I refused to let Union relax and kept the pressure on. Today, there are a total of seven black professors at Union—three men and four women—Vincent Wimbush in New Testament, Michael Harris in American church history, Delores Williams in theology and culture, Emilie Townes in ethics, Edwina Wright in Old Testament, Annie Powell in practical theology, and me in systematic theology. That is not bad for a faculty of twenty-five. Since five of us are full professors in areas with strong doctoral programs, black students are also developing academic competence in areas other than theology and with people other than me. Diversity in fields of interest and perspective are important in black religion.

I am here today because of the theological challenge to interpret the meaning of the gospel for the church and world in the twenty-first century. I want to urge professors and graduate students to be the best scholars you can possibly be in your discipline. We must not forget the awesome task and great responsibility that our vocation places upon us. We must not be second rate. Give scholarship and teaching all your intellectual power. Write, my brothers and sisters, as if the future of oppressed people and the salvation of your souls depend on it.

To write well, we must also become voracious readers. If you do not read, you will not have much to say. I read for content and style, always conscious of not only what is said but also how well it is expressed. I read everybody, especially my enemies. You must know well the opposition in order to make a persuasive counterargument. I have not met a white theologian who could make an effective argument against black liberation theology because most know so little about it or the black world out of which it comes. I can whip white theologians intellectually anytime and anywhere because they are so ignorant about black history and culture.

I read a variety of writers—especially black theologians, historians, biblical scholars, the whole field of religion. Read as widely as you can. Don't let a day go by without reading a serious book or essay. Reading is food for thought. I try to read and write about eight hours per day. In my younger days, it was about fourteen to sixteen.

What I am saying to you today I've said to all my doctoral students. We meet at least twice per year in my apartment for a little chat about our vocation and scholarship. I have no patience for sorry doctoral students. Ph.D. work is serious business, and few in the African American community have the educational preparation, time, money, and ability to study at the doctoral level. If you are one among the elect few, don't misuse this great opportunity.

Don't blow it. Don't jive me with phony black talk. There is no excuse for doing substandard academic work. I don't tolerate it.

Even being smart is not enough. I know people are smart. Anybody can be smart. Crooks are smart. For me the crucial question is, are you committed to the truth—the truth that will make you free even when it sends you to the cross? Have you found that something so precious, so important that you are willing to give your whole being to it? If you have found it, you will work eight, ten, twelve, and even fourteen hours a day to bear witness to it.

There is nothing so satisfying as doing what you love. It is as erotic as sex, as exciting as making a game-winning shot, and as intellectually satisfying as writing a classic. I experienced all these things before I was even aware that I had written something in theology that would be read in much of the theological world.

I still wake up in the morning as excited about my writing projects as I was when I wrote *Black Theology and Black Power*. I still walk into my classroom at Union as challenged as I was the first day. The adrenaline is running, the eager students are waiting, and I feel compelled to make sense out of the discipline that has been entrusted to me so that the uninitiated will get turned on and find their voice in it. I don't want students to reject theology because of my poor teaching. My certainties and ambiguities are revealed in my teaching and writing. I try to teach theology in a way that students are challenged and empowered—believing that they too can do theology.

A good graduate education is indispensable for a creative theological career. What we do in seminary, how we conceive and execute our vocation as teachers and scholars will have a profound effect on theology, the church, and the world. Becoming a first rate scholar and teacher is 2 percent brains and 98 percent hard work. I challenge all my current and would-be colleagues to be the best we can be. Don't let it be said that we did not work hard at our craft. We must give it the best we've got. That is all anyone should expect of us. God will do the rest.

Notes

1. Calling the Oppressors to Account

1. Francis J. Grimké, *The Works of Francis J. Grimké,* 4 vols., ed. Carter G. Woodson (Washington, D.C.: Associated Publishers, 1942), 1:354.

2. Cited in Albert J. Raboteau, "'The Blood of the Martyrs Is the Seed of Faith': Suffering in the Christianity of American Slaves," in *The Courage to Hope: From Black Suffering to Human Redemption,* ed. Quinton H. Dixie and Cornel West (Boston: Beacon, 1999), 31.

3. James Baldwin, *The Fire Next Time* (New York: Dell, 1964), 46.

4. Martin Luther King Jr., "Letter from a Birmingham Jail," in *Why We Can't Wait* (New York: Harper, 1963), 90–91.

5. Martin Luther King Jr., *A Testament of Hope: The Essential Writings of Martin Luther King, Jr.,* ed. James M. Washington (San Francisco: Harper & Row, 1986), 233.

6. Ibid., 286.

7. Martin Luther King Jr., "Thou Fool," Sermon, Mount Pisgah Baptist Church, Chicago, Ill., August 27, 1967.

8. Malcolm X, *The Autobiography of Malcolm X,* with the assistance of Alex Haley (New York: Grove, 1965), 222.

9. Martin Luther King Jr., "Religion's Answer to the Problem of Evil," in *The Papers of Martin Luther King, Jr.,* 4 vols., ed. Clayborne Carson et al. (Berkeley: University of California Press, 1992–2000), 1:432.

10. W. E. B. DuBois, *The Souls of Black Folk* (Greenwich, Conn.: Fawcett, 1961), 23.

2. Doing Black Theology in the Black Church

1. Chancellor Williams, *The Destruction of Black Civilization: Great Issues of a Race from 4500 B.C. to 2000 A.D.* (rev. ed.; Chicago: Third World, 1987).

2. See Cornel West, *Race Matters* (Boston: Beacon, 1993), and Michael Eric Dyson, *Race Rules: Navigating the Color Line* (Reading, Mass.: Addison-Wesley, 1996).

3. James H. Cone, *Risks of Faith: The Emergence of a Black Theology of Liberation, 1968–1998* (Boston: Beacon, 1999).

4. Albert B. Cleage Jr., *The Black Messiah* (New York: Sheed and Ward, 1968), and *Black Christian Nationalism: New Directions for the Black Church,* ed. George Bell (New York: Morrow, 1972).

5. See William Julius Wilson, *The Declining Significance of Race: Blacks and Changing American Institutions* (2nd ed.; Chicago: University of Chicago Press, 1980).

6. Jacquelyn Grant, *White Women's Christ and Black Women's Jesus: Feminist Christology and Womanist Response* (American Academy of Religion 64; Atlanta: Scholars Press, 1989).

7. Delores S. Williams, *Sisters in the Wilderness: The Challenge of Womanist God-Talk* (Maryknoll, N.Y.: Orbis, 1993).

8. Kelly Brown Douglas, *Sexuality and the Black Church: A Womanist Perspective* (Maryknoll, N.Y.: Orbis, 1999).

9. E. Lynn Harris is the author of several novels, including *Invisible Life* (Atlanta: Consortium, 1991) and *Just As I Am* (New York: Anchor, 1995), that address the theme of African American men and sexuality.

3. Testimony as Hope and Care

1. James H. Cone, *My Soul Looks Back* (Nashville: Abingdon, 1982).

2. Cone, *My Soul Looks Back,* 11–12.

3. Ibid.

4. Selected portions of these topics as presented in the following pages have been excerpted from my book *A Loving Home: Caring for African American Marriage and Families* (Cleveland: Pilgrim, 2000).

5. Excerpt from the second stanza of "Lift Every Voice and Sing" by James Weldon Johnson.

4. Black Theology and the Black Church

1. James H. Cone, "Black Theology and the Black Church," in *Risks of Faith: The Emergence of a Black Theology of Liberation, 1968–1998* (Boston: Beacon, 1999), 43.

2. James H. Cone, *God of the Oppressed* (New York: Seabury, 1975), 152.

3. Cone, "Christianity and Black Power," in *Risks of Faith,* 7.

4. James H. Cone, *My Soul Looks Back* (Nashville: Abingdon, 1982), 68.

5. Cone, *Risks of Faith,* 3.

6. Cone, "Christianity and Black Power," in *Risks of Faith,* 7.

7. James H. Cone, "Black Spirituals: A Theological Interpretation," in *Risks of Faith,* 18.

8. Cone, *God of the Oppressed,* 145.

9. Cone, "Christianity and Black Power," 8.

5. Womanist Theology, Epistemology, and a New Anthropological Paradigm

1. Alice Walker, *In Search of Our Mothers' Gardens: Womanist Prose* (New York: Harcourt Brace Jovanovich, 1983).

2. bell hooks, *Talking Back: Thinking Feminist, Thinking Black* (Boston: South End, 1988).

3. Margaret L. Andersen and Patricia Hill Collins, eds., *Race, Class, and Gender: An Anthology* (Belmont, Mass.: Wadsworth, 1992), 1.

4. Ibid.

5. See Renato Rosaldo, *Culture and Truth: The Remaking of Social Analysis* (Boston: Beacon, 1989), x, for details about Stanford University's "Western Culture Controversy."

6. Andersen and Collins, *Race, Class, and Gender*, 2.

7. Amilcar Cabral, *Return to the Source: Selected Speeches*, ed. Africa Information Service (New York: Monthly Review Press, 1974).

8. Ibid., 142–43.

9. R. Thornton, "Culture," in *South African Keywords*, ed. E. Boonzaier and E. Sharp (Cape Town: David Philip, 1988), 24.

10. See George E. Marcus and Michael M. J. Fischer, *Anthropology as Cultural Critique: An Experimental Moment in the Human Sciences* (Chicago: University of Chicago Press, 1986), 25, for an analysis of interpretive anthropology.

11. For an explanation for how anthropological theory has accented the subject's own life story, see Marcus and Fischer's discussion of the "native point of view" (ibid.).

12. Ibid., 44. The authors summarize two approaches to anthropological methodology (ibid., 25–44). One deals with interpretation that accents culture (i.e., values) and the other underscores the relationship between particular ethnographies and global economies.

6. A White Feminist Response to Black and Womanist Theologies

1. MTS evaluation paper by Sara Moslener, quoted with permission of the author.

2. Published by Paulist Press in 1972.

3. See Audre Lorde, "Open Letter to Mary Daly," in *The Bridge Called My Back: Writings by Radical Women of Color*, ed. Cherrie Morago and Gloria Anzaldua (New York: Kitchen Table, 1983), 94–97.

4. *Christianity and Crisis* (April 29, 1985): 164–65.

5. Mary Farrell Bednarowski, *The Religious Imagination of American Women* (Religion in North America; Bloomington: Indiana University Press, 1999), 138.

6. See *Religious Feminism and the Future of the Planet: A Christian-Buddhist Conversation* by Rita M. Cross and Rosemary Radford Ruether (New York: Continuum,

2001). Also Mary John Mananzan et al., *Women Resisting Violence: Spirituality for Life* (Maryknoll, N.Y.: Orbis, 1996), 27–35.

7. See Rosemary Radford Ruether, *Women and Redemption: A Theological History* (Minneapolis: Fortress Press, 1998), 241–43.

7. What I Learned from James Cone and Black Theology

1. As C. Eric Lincoln put it, "Ironically, the white Church in America is the principle raison d'être for the Black Church, for just as the white Church permitted and tolerated the Negro Church, it made the Black Church necessary for a new generation of Black people who refuse to be 'Negroes' and who are not impressed by whatever it means to be white." *The Black Church since Frazier* (New York: Schocken, 1974), 110.

2. Cone's posture toward sociology in this early work would seem to be able to find common cause in Milbank's *Theology and Social Theory: Beyond Secular Reason* (London: Basil Blackwell, 1990). For very different reasons, both Cone and Milbank recognize that sociology renders theology indifferent to theology's direct political relevance, and this is not because theology has no direct political relevance.

3. These quotes come respectively from *Black Theology and Black Power* (Maryknoll, N.Y.: Orbis, 1997), 21, 24, 40, 53, 20 and *A Black Theology of Liberation* (Maryknoll, N.Y.: Orbis, 1986), 9.

4. *Black Theology and Black Power*, 27.

5. Ibid., 63.

6. This theological indifference is similar to the reaction of the Klan to Malcolm X. They misunderstood him and were favorably disposed to their perception of some of X's political statements and so they approached him with a political "compromise"—you take New York; we'll take Montana.

7. *Black Theology and Black Power*, 41.

8. Ibid., 24.

9. Ibid., 26.

10. The significance of survival is a constant theme in Cone's theology, if not a central theme. "Black theology is a theology of survival because it seeks to interpret the theological significance of the being of a community whose existence is threatened by the power of non-being." Cone, *A Black Theology of Liberation*, 16.

11. Ibid., 5.

12. Ibid., 30.

13. *Black Theology and Black Power*, 42.

14. Ibid., 40.

15. See *A Black Theology of Liberation*, 90–91.

16. "The close identity of American theology with the structures of society may also account for their failure to produce theologians comparable in stature to Europeans like Bultmann, Barth and Bonhoeffer." *Black Theology and Black Power*, 85; see also *Black Theology of Liberation*, 4.

17. *Black Theology and Black Power,* 112.

18. The preface to *God of the Oppressed* (Orbis, Maryknoll, New York: 1997), xiv. See also the 1986 preface to *A Black Theology of Liberation* where Cone distances himself from Barth arguing that when he originally wrote this work he was "intellectually comfortable . . . with the centrality of Jesus Christ in the black church community" but would now structure black theology differently, no longer beginning with "a methodology based on divine liberation" (xviii–xix).

19. The 1986 preface to *A Black Theology of Liberation,* xviii.

20. *Spirituals and the Blues,* 19.

21. John Milbank, *Theology and Social Theory,* 84, 97.

22. *Spirituals and the Blues* (Maryknoll, N.Y.: Orbis, 1995), 5–6.

23. Ibid., 43.

24. "Through the blood of slavery, black slaves transcended the limitations of space and time. Jesus' time became their time, and they encountered a new historical existence. Through the experience of being slaves, they encountered the theological significance of Jesus' death: through the crucifixion, Jesus makes an unqualified identification with the poor and the helpless and takes their pain upon himself. If Jesus was not alone in his suffering, black slaves were not alone in their oppression under slavery. Jesus was with them! He was God's Black Slave who had come to put an end to human bondage. Herein lies the meaning of the resurrection. It means that the cross was not the end of God's drama of salvation." Ibid., 49.

25. *For My People* (Maryknoll, N.Y.: Orbis, 1996), 71.

26. Friedrich Nietzsche, *The Will to Power,* 3, quoted in David Toole's *Waiting for Godot* (Boulder: Westview, 1999), 3.

27. See Cornel West's "Genealogy of Modern Racism," in *Prophesy Deliverance* (Philadelphia: Westminster, 1982).

28. Paul Tillich, *The Courage to Be* (New Haven: Yale University Press, 1952), 161.

29. Cone, *Black Theology and Black Power,* 6.

30. See Luther's "On Secular Authority," in *Martin Luther: Selections from His Writings,* ed. John Dillenberger (Garden City, N.Y.: Doubleday, 1961), 373. For a discussion of this see my *Divine Economy* (New York: Routledge, 2000), 163–71.

31. Cone, *Black Theology and Black Power,* 56.

32. James H. Cone, *Malcolm and Martin and America* (Maryknoll, N.Y.: Orbis, 1991), 305. Oddly enough this reading of the nonviolence of Martin Luther King Jr. seems more indebted to Reinhold Niebuhr's explanation of the civil rights movement than to that of Dr. King.

8. Reconsidering Evangelism

1. James H. Cone, *Black Theology and Black Power* (New York: Seabury, 1969), 71; similar themes are echoed in Cone's more recent statement, "There is a credibility gap

between what we say and what we do [as the church]," in James H. Cone, *Risks of Faith* (Boston: Beacon, 1999), 111.

2. Cone, *Risks of Faith*, 136, "Silence is racism's best friend."

3. James Cone, *God of the Oppressed* (New York: Seabury, 1975), 47; see also Cone, *Risks of Faith*, 130–37, "It is amazing that racism could be so prevalent and violent in American life and yet so absent in white theological discourse," 133.

4. Jacquelyn Grant, "Womanist Theology: Black Women's Experience as a Source for Doing Theology, with Special Reference to Christology," in *Black Theology: A Documentary History*, eds. James H. Cone and Gayraud Wilmore (Maryknoll, N.Y.: Orbis, 1993), 2:273.

5. Albert Cleage, "The Black Messiah," in Cone and Wilmore, *Black Theology*, 1:101–2.

6. Gayraud Wilmore, "Pastoral Ministry in the Origin and Development of Black Theology," in Cone and Wilmore, *Black Theology*, 2:123.

7. David O. Moberg, *The Great Reversal* (New York: Lippincott, 1977).

8. For more detailed historical discussion see Doug Strong, *They Walked in the Spirit: Personal Faith and Social Action in America* (Louisville, Ky.: Westminster John Knox, 1997); Timothy Smith, *Revivalism and Social Reform* (Nashville: Abingdon, 1957); Jean Miller Schmidt, *Souls or the Social Order* (New York: Carlson, 1991); and Michael Taylor, *Not Angels but Agencies* (Geneva: WCC Publications, 1995), among others.

9. H. Hoekstra, *Evangelism in Eclipse: World Mission and the W.C.C.* (London: Paternoster, 1979), 69; see also Taylor, *Not Angels but Agencies*. The concept "holistic evangelism," first mentioned at the 1963 gathering of the W.C.C. in Mexico City, was developed in 1973 at the W.C.C. in Bangkok. Holistic evangelism linked evangelistic and social concern inextricably together asserting that every genuine Christian act has its evangelistic dimension.

10. Cone makes a similar observation regarding the welcome of Latin American liberation theology by North Americans generally while ignoring black theology in *My Soul Looks Back* (Nashville: Abingdon, 1982), 123, and *Risks of Faith*, 133: "It was not until Orbis Books published the translated works of Latin American liberation theologians that white North American male theologians cautiously began to talk and write about liberation theology and God's solidarity with the poor. But they still ignored the black poor in the United States, Africa, and Latin America. . . . African-Americans wondered how U.S. whites could take sides with the poor out there in Latin America without first siding with the poor here in North America. It was as if they had forgotten about their own complicity in the suffering of the black poor."

11. George Cummings writes from the black perspective in North America (while also including a Hispanic perspective) in his paper "Who Do You Say That I Am?— A North American Minority Answer to the Christological Question" presented at the First Conference of Evangelical Mission Theologians from the Two Thirds World

held in Bangkok in 1982. Cummings reiterates the arguments of black theology, including Cone, regarding Christology. The conference papers were compiled into a volume that emphasizes the place of "Two-Thirds" World Christian voices particularly from Latin America, Asia, and Africa. Orlando Costas offered the plenary remarks. Vinay Samuel and Chris Sugden, eds., *Sharing Jesus in the Two Thirds World* (Grand Rapids: Eerdmans, 1983).

12. See Cone, *My Soul Looks Back,* chapter 4; Cone and Wilmore, *Black Theology,* vol. 1, part 4 and vol. 2, part 5.

13. David Bosch, *Transforming Mission: Paradigm Shifts in Theology of Mission* (Maryknoll, N.Y.: Orbis, 1991), 432.

14. Ibid., 437.

15. Ibid.

16. Cone, *God of the Oppressed,* 128.

17. Bosch, *Transforming Mission,* 437.

18. Cone, *God of the Oppressed,* 53.

19. Orlando Costas, *Liberating News: A Theology of Contextual Evangelization* (Grand Rapids: Eerdmans, 1989), 131.

20. Ibid., 149.

21. James Cone, *A Black Theology of Liberation* (New York: Seabury, 1970), 157. Jacquelyn Grant in *White Women's Christ and Black Women's Jesus* (Atlanta: Scholars Press, 1989), 214, makes a similar observation, "For Black women, the role of Jesus unraveled as they encountered him in their experience as one who empowers the weak."

22. Cone, *Black Theology and Black Power,* 49.

23. Carlyle Fielding Stewart, *African American Church Growth* (Nashville: Abingdon, 1994).

24. John Perkins, *Beyond Charity: The Call to Christian Community Development* (Grand Rapids: Baker, 1993), chapter 7.

25. Mortimer Arias and Alan Johnson, *The Great Commission: Biblical Models for Evangelism,* (Nashville: Abingdon, 1992); Priscilla Pope-Levison, *Evangelization from a Liberation Perspective* (New York: Peter Lang, 1991), a study based on Orlando Costas's work; Ronald Sider, *One-Sided Christianity* (San Francisco: HarperSanFrancisco, 1993), Ben Campbell Johnson, *Rethinking Evangelism: A Theological Approach* (Philadelphia: Westminster, 1987); Donald Moberg, *Wholistic Christianity,* (Elgin, Ill.: Brethren, 1985).

26. Grant, *White Women's Christ and Black Women's Jesus,* 209.

27. The following works include many of the most recent scriptural and theologically based studies on evangelism. However, the list is overwhelmingly Methodist and certainly not exhaustive. Walter Brueggemann, *Biblical Perspectives on Evangelism* (Nashville: Abingdon, 1993); Lesslie Newbigin, *The Open Secret: An Introduction to the Theology of Mission* (Grand Rapids: Eerdmans, 1995); William Abraham, *The Logic of Evangelism* (Grand Rapids: Eerdmans, 1989); Walter Klaiber, *Call and*

Response: Biblical Foundations of a Theology of Evangelism (Nashville: Abingdon, 1997); James Logan, *Theology and Evangelism in the Wesleyan Heritage* (Nashville: Abingdon, 1994); James Logan, *Christ for the World* (Nashville: Abingdon, 1996).

28. Cone, *Risks of Faith,* 112.

29. Cone, *Black Theology and Black Power,* 83.

30. Ibid., 59.

31. Cone, *A Black Theology of Liberation,* 89.

32. Ibid., 46.

33. Cone, *God of the Oppressed,* 54. Delores Williams corroborates: "It is no wonder that a theology of liberation has been birthed by Black American theologians and that a theology with emphasis upon survival and quality of life has been spawned by some Black Christian women naming their theological movement, 'womanist.'" Delores S. Williams, "Straight Talk, Plain Talk," in *Embracing the Spirit,* ed. Emilie Townes (New York: Orbis, 1997), 118.

34. Cone, *God of the Oppressed,* 63; Exod. 2:24-25; 15:1-2. According to Cone, *A Black Theology of Liberation,* 19, "The consistent theme in Israelite prophecy is Yahweh's concern for the lack of social, economic, and political justice for those who are poor and unwanted in the society."

35. Cone, *God of the Oppressed,* 64; Exod. 19:4-5; 20:3; 22:21, 23-24.

36. Cone, *God of the Oppressed,* 75–76; Cone, *Risks of Faith,* 114–17.

37. Cone, *God of the Oppressed,* 77.

38. Ibid., 55.

39. Cone, *A Black Theology of Liberation,* 220.

40. John Howard Yoder, *The Politics of Jesus* (Grand Rapids: Eerdmans, 1972), 64.

41. Cone, *God of the Oppressed,* 80.

42. Ibid., 141.

43. "To claim that the Spirit is needed to understand what the gospel is, is to say that our resources alone are not enough to know who Jesus is. To speak of Jesus and his gospel is to speak of his Spirit who opens up dimensions of reality that are not reducible to our intellectual capacity" (Cone, *Risks of Faith,* 113).

9. Black Theology and the White Church in the Third Millennium

1. W. E. B. DuBois, *The Souls of Black Folk* (Greenwich, Conn.: Fawcett, 1961), 15.

2. Roger Bastide, "Color, Racism, and Christianity," *Dædalus* (spring 1967): 327.

3. See James H. Cone, *The Spirituals and the Blues: An Interpretation* (Maryknoll, N.Y.: Orbis, 1972).

4. See, for example, his choice, in the twenty-fifth anniversary edition of his first book, *Black Theology and Black Power* (Maryknoll, N.Y.: Orbis, 1997), to let his original language stand while in the Preface acknowledging criticism and endorsing the multiple "corrections" he received from various womanist, Marxist, and third-world theologians and historians of religions.

5. James H. Cone, *God of the Oppressed* (New York: Seabury, 1975), 134.

6. Ibid., 137.

7. Cheryl Harris, "Whiteness as Property," *Harvard Law Review* 106 (1993): 1709–91; Stephen Nathan Haymes, *Race, Culture, and the City: A Pedagogy for Black Urban Struggle* (Albany: State University of New York Press, 1995), 4; David Roediger, *The Wages of Whiteness: Race and the Making of the American Working Class* (New York: Verso, 1991), 11–13; Richard Dyer, "White," *Screen* 29 (1988): 44.

8. One of the revelations of the Truth and Reconciliation Commission in post-apartheid South Africa was that of a leading Afrikaner scientist, Daan Goosen, to the effect that significant "progress" had been made toward a race-specific germ-warfare agent that would target only certain genetic combinations (that is, black people) (Trevor A. Coleman, "When Racism Reaches for Genocide," *Detroit Free Press* [Sat. June 27, 1998]: 10A).

9. Recent research suggests that the power of stereotypes to erode confidence and constrain consciousness in clearly measurable ways is not just limited to their operation in action (Claude Steele, "Thin Ice: 'Stereotype Threat' and Black College Students," *Atlantic Monthly* [August 1999] 44). The mere anticipation that they might color perception in certain situations such as education tests is enough to affect outcomes.

10. Michael Hudson, for instance, tracks the 1990s development of a $300 billion per year "shadow banking" industry, rearranging resources out of already strapped low income communities (primarily of color) and into the coffers of Fortune 500 companies by way of corporate bankrolling of various alternative credit enterprises (rent-to-own stores, check cashing outlets, pawnshops, finance companies, etc.) charging as much as 240 percent interest per year. See Michael Hudson, *Merchants of Misery: How Corporate America Profits from Poverty* (Monroe, Maine: Common Courage, 1996).

11. Victor Anderson, *Beyond Ontological Blackness: An Essay on African American Religious and Cultural Criticism* (New York: Continuum, 1995, 157–58); Madhu Dubey, *Black Women Novelists and the Nationalist Aesthetic* (Bloomington: University of Indiana Press, 1994), 3.

12. Earl Shorris, "Our Next Race Question: The Uneasiness between Blacks and Latinos," *Harper's* (April 1996): 55.

13. John Hartigan Jr., *Racial Situations: Class Predicaments of Whiteness in Detroit* (Princeton, N.J.: Princeton University Press, 1999), 19.

14. Rita Nakashima Brock, *Journeys by Heart: A Christology of Erotic Power* (New York: Crossroad, 1988), 66–70.

15. Cone, *God of the Oppressed,* 136.

16. The task here would be one of learning from the experience of being "signified upon"—being put at issue and confronted (see Henry Louis Gates Jr.'s *The Signifying Monkey: A Theory of Afro-American Literary Criticism* [New York: Oxford University Press, 1988]). I have explored this possibility for whiteness in a previous

article, "On Being 'Doubled': Soteriology at the White End of Black Signifyin(g)," *Koinonia Journal* (fall 1994): 176–205.

17. See Susan Brooks Thistlethwaite, *Sex, Race, and God: Christian Feminism in Black and White* (New York: Crossroad, 1989), and Sharon D. Welch, *Communities of Resistance and Solidarity: A Feminist Theology of Liberation* (Maryknoll, N.Y.: Orbis, 1985).

18. Charles Long, *Significations: Signs, Symbols, and Images in the Interpretation of Religion* (Philadelphia: Fortress Press, 1986), 194–95.

19. Michel Foucault, *Power/Knowledge: Selected Interviews and Other Writings, 1972–1977,* ed. and trans. C. Gordon (New York, Pantheon, 1980), 92–108.

20. Dwight N. Hopkins, *Shoes That Fit Our Feet: Sources for a Constructive Black Theology* (Maryknoll, N.Y.: Orbis, 1993), 100–28.

21. Paul Gilroy, *There Ain't No Black in the Union Jack: The Cultural Politics of Race and Nation* (Black Literature and Culture; Chicago: University of Chicago Press, 1991), 199–202.

22. Stuart Hall, "What Is This 'Black' in Black Popular Culture?" in *Black Popular Culture,* ed. G. Dent (Seattle: Bay Press, 1992), 27.

23. Jon Michael Spencer, *The Rhythms of Black Folk: Race, Religion and Pan-Africanism* (Trenton, N.J.: Africa World Press, 1995), 145; Frantz Fanon, *The Wretched of the Earth* (New York: Grove, 1963), 57.

24. See Delores S. Williams, *Sisters in the Wilderness: The Challenge of Womanist God-Talk* (Maryknoll, N.Y.: Orbis, 1993), and Toni Morrison, *Beloved: A Novel* (New York: Knopf: 1987).

25. Cited in a talk given by Joe Feagin, "Racism and the Coming White Minority," on April 20, 2000, at Wayne State University, Detroit, Michigan; see also Joe Feagin, *Racist America: Roots, Current Realities, and Future Reparations* (New York: Routledge, 2001).

26. Feagin again, in the talk cited above, based on research he conducted as a sociologist.

27. Noam Chomsky, in a talk titled, "Containing the Crisis at Home and Abroad," given at Loyola University on October 18, 1994, cites the research of criminologist William Chambliss of George Washington University, who regularly sent students with police on their patrols to take transcripts later published in criminology journals. The transcripts detailed the way "black males are simply considered a criminal population." Chomsky revises that summary to say that the "situation is more like that of a military occupation": criminals under the law have constitutional rights, but this is a population for whom the laws are not considered even to apply— a "population targeted for destruction." Of course, "DWB" (driving while black) and racial profiling are the new wrinkles on the old tactic, and the kind of brutalizing received by Rodney King is a brief revelation of a continuing practice (the litany in New York alone in the last couple of years has continued with Abner Louima, Amadou Diallo, and Patrick Dorismund).

28. Eric Schlosser, "The Prison Industrial Complex," *Atlantic Monthly* (December 1998): 51–77.

29. The term is bell hooks's way of keeping the complexity of the social formation we find ourselves imbedded in sharply in focus (bell hooks and Cornel West, *Breaking Bread: Insurgent Black Intellectual Life* [Boston: South End, 1991], 160).

30. James H. Cone, *Black Theology and Black Power* (New York: Seabury, 1969), 1–4.

31. Michael Omi and Howard Winant, *Racial Formation in the United States from the 1960s to the 1990s* (2nd ed.; New York: Routledge, 1994), 84–91.

32. Ibid., 95–112.

33. Foucault, *Power/Knowledge,* 92–108.

34. Thomas Kochman, *Black and White Styles in Conflict* (Chicago: University of Chicago Press, 1981), 57.

35. Ibid., 5.

36. Gilroy, *There Ain't No Black,* 114, 150.

37. Ibid., 156–60.

38. Aloysius Pieris, *An Asian Theology of Liberation* (Maryknoll: Orbis, 1988), 62–63.

39. Cone, *God of the Oppressed,* 36–37.

40. James Scott, *Domination and the Arts of Resistance: Hidden Transcripts* (New Haven: Yale University Press, 1990), xi.

41. DuBois, *Souls of Black Folk,* 15, 20.

10. Black Theology's Impact on the Ecumenical Association of Third World Theologians

1. EATWOT was created in the 1970s and is the only global network comprised of liberation theologians from Africa, Asia, the Caribbean, Latin America, the Pacific Islands, and U.S. minorities. I am the coordinator of the United States Minorities' Region of EATWOT and a member of its executive committee.

2. For the contributions of Kelly Delaine Brown-Douglass, J. Deotis Roberts, and Cornel West in this area, see James H. Cone and Gayraud S. Wilmore, *Black Theology: A Documentary History,* vol. 2: 1980–1992 (Maryknoll, N.Y.: Orbis, 1993), 355–425. Another valuable contribution to this topic is Jacquelyn Grant, "Doing Theology Out of Minority (Black) Women's Experience," in *Third World Theologies: Commonalities and Divergences,* ed. K. C. Abraham (Maryknoll, N.Y: Orbis, 1990), 90–92.

3. James H. Cone, *My Soul Looks Back* (Nashville: Abingdon, 1982), 93.

4. Ibid., 15.

5. Ibid., 93–103.

6. This awareness was also painfully expressed by James Cone to fellow and sister third-world theologians at the Second General Assembly of EATWOT in Oaxtepec, Mexico, in a statement urging their recognition of the oppression to which United States ethnic minorities are subjected in North America: "We, the U.S. minorities,

have more in common with the Third World peoples of Africa, Asia, and Latin America than we do with the ruling classes and races in the United States. For we must not forget that the great majority of U.S. minorities come from Africa, Asia, and Latin America. We are your brothers and sisters and feel hurt when you reject us. We are culturally, politically, and economically Third World people living in the First World. Being Third World in the First World creates a hyphenated identity: we are African-Americans, Hispanic-Americans, Asian-Americans, and Native-Americans." James H. Cone, "Cross-fertilization: A Statement from the U.S. Minorities," in *Third World Theologies,* 129–30.

7. James H. Cone, "Reflections from the Perspective of U.S. Blacks: Black Theology and Third World Theology," in *Irruption of the Third World: Challenge to Theology,* ed. Virginia Favella, M.M., and Sergio Torres (Maryknoll, N.Y: Orbis, 1983), 236.

8. In this regard Cone mentions that at an earlier stage both third-world and even some North American black theologians had been so influenced by first-world theological reflection that they ignored and even disregarded his contributions and those of black theology "because they do not think that they could have anything of theological value to say" (ibid., 237). To his credit, Cone admits to having been led by this weakness in his earlier writings, but he argues that since being made aware of this fact by his black colleagues and third-world theologians, he has struggled to affirm and incorporate the experience and culture of the oppressed in his writings (ibid., 237–38).

9. Cone, *My Soul Looks Back,* 102.

10. Cone also notes that the Spanish edition of Gustavo Gutiérrez's book *A Theology of Liberation* was published one year after the publication of his second book. "Reflections from the Perspective of U.S. Blacks," 238.

11. Ibid., 239.

12. Ibid.

13. Ibid., 240.

14. Ibid., 240–41.

15. Ibid., 242.

16. Ibid., 242–43. Cone provides an important assessment of this dialogue in his article "From Geneva to São Paulo: A Dialogue between Black Theology and Latin American Liberation Theology," in *The Challenge of Basic Christian Communities,* ed. Sergio Torres and John Eagleson (Maryknoll, N.Y: Orbis, 1981), 265–81.

17. Cone, "Reflections from the Perspective of U.S. Blacks," 243. For an interesting consideration of Cone's exploration of this topic, see his article "A Black American Perspective on the Asian Search for a Full Humanity," in Cone and Wilmore, *Black Theology,* 2:358–70.

18. Cone, "Reflections from the Perspective of U.S. Blacks," 244. Given the response of participants at the first session of the first EATWOT Inter-Continental

Dialogue held at Union Theological Seminary in New York (July 12–15, 1994), the improvements taking place in this dialogue are very encouraging. See James H. Cone, "First EATWOT Inter-Continental Dialogue," in *Search for a New Just World Order: Challenges to Theology* (Papers and Reflections from the Fourth Assembly of the EATWOT, December, 1996, Tagaytay, Philippines), ed. K. C. Abraham, 179–88.

19. Cone, *My Soul Looks Back,* 24.

11. The Outsider's Role in Socially Engaged Scholarship on African Religion

1. Native American George E. Tinker raises similar concerns about researcher's interpretations of Native American traditions in his book *Missionary Conquest: The Gospel and Native American Cultural Genocide* (Minneapolis: Fortress Press, 1993).

2. George E. Marcus, "Contemporary Problems of Ethnography in the Modern World System," in James Clifford and George E. Marcus, eds., *Writing Culture: The Poetics and Politics of Ethnography—A School of American Research Advanced Seminar* (Berkeley: University of California, 1986), 165–93; George E. Marcus and Michael M. J. Fischer *Anthropology as Cultural Critique: An Experimental Moment in the Human Sciences* (Chicago: University of Chicago Press, 1986), 33–44; James Clifford, *The Predicament of Culture* (Cambridge: Harvard University Press, 1988), 21–54; Renato Rosaldo, *Culture and Truth: The Remaking of Social Analysis* (Boston: Beacon, 1989), 25-45; Mamphela Altetta Ramphele, "Participatory Research: The Myths and Realities," *Social Dynamics* 16/2 (1990): 1–15.

3. David Westerlund, "'Insiders' and 'Outsiders' in the Study of African Religions: Notes on Some Problems of Theory and Method," in Jacob K. Olupona, ed., *African Traditional Religions in Contemporary Society* (New York: Paragon, 1991), 20.

4. Okot p'Bitek, *African Religions in Western Scholarship* (Nairobi: Kenya Literature Bureau, 1970), 15.

5. African Independent Churches, *Speaking for Ourselves: Members of African Independent Churches Report on Their Pilot Study of the History and Theology of Their Churches* (Braamfontein: Institute for Contextual Theology, 1985), 5.

6. During my fieldwork, I traveled throughout the country with informants to cultural and church rituals as well as to religious festivals in urban and rural settings. However, my primary research base and location for data collection on healing rituals was St. John's in Guguletu. Since St. John's members lived in Nyanga, Crossroads, New Cross Roads, and Khayelisha, fieldwork was also conducted in those townships, which are located in the Western Cape. I conducted interviews with eighteen of St. John's forty-eight members. These interviews detail illnesses described by members, their accounts of treatments received at St. John's, and their descriptions of the social situation in which they live.

7. G. C. Oosthuizen, *Post-Christianity in Africa* (London: Hurst, 1968); Jean Comaroff and John Comaroff, *Ethnography and Historical Imagination* (Boulder:

Westview, 1992); and J. P. Kiernan, *The Production and Management of Therapeutic Power in Zionist Churches within a Zulu City* (Studies in African Health and Medicine 4; Lewiston, N.Y.: Mellen, 1990).

8. For additional demographic material and a full textual treatment on informants, see Linda E. Thomas, *Under the Canopy: Ritual Process and Spiritual Resilience in South Africa* (Columbia: University of South Carolina, 1999). Space does not permit the material to be presented in this chapter. Pertinent data is supplied in the larger text.

9. The following information provides salient data about members interviewed: the average age was 43.5 years, and the average level of formal education was 5.7. Seven of the persons interviewed were unemployed, five were employed, four were retired, and one was disabled and not able to work. The average monthly income of those interviewed in 1991–92 was R394 ($141) for a family of 5.6. The average national monthly cost of living for an African household of 5 was R1,217 ($435). As interviews were conducted in members' homes, I observed that all lived in extremely limited space with several other people. Most dwellings were single-room shacks.

10. Pseudonyms are used throughout this chapter.

11. Myira Zotwana was in the original sample; however this interview about her arrest was conducted on September 19, 1996.

12. Interviews were conducted in Xhosa and translated into English by a research assistant.

13. I present direct quotes from structured interviews in order for the voices of informants to speak for themselves. This is out of respect for the request made by members of AICs in *Speaking for Ourselves*. In addition, my goal in this chapter is to have layers of voices in the text to which readers can respond, rather than only my interpretations. The selected quotations were chosen because they are linked to my argument in this chapter.

14. It is important to note that Nozipo says "there are so many things that do not encourage *us.*" Xhosa speakers often refer to themselves in the context of the community to which they are connected in conversations. For example in greetings: Kunjani? (How are *you?*) Response: Sikhona, enkosi. (*We* are well, thank you.)

15. This and the other unattributed quotations that follow are from interviews, field notes, and research diaries of fieldwork conducted in the Republic of South Africa in 1991 and 1992. See Thomas, *Under the Canopy.*

16. Okot p'Bitek, *African Religions in European Scholarship* (New York: ECA Associates, 1990), 7.

17. Ifi Amadiume, *Male Daughters, Female Husbands: Gender and Sex in an African Society* (London: Zed, 1987), 7.

18. Peter Berger, *The Sacred Canopy: Elements of a Sociological Theory of Religion* (New York: Doubleday, 1967), and Robert Towler, *Homo Religious: Sociological Problems in the Study of Religion* (London: Constable, 1974).

19. Thomas Blakely, Walter E. A. van Beek, and Dennis L. Thomson, ed. *Religion in Africa: Experience and Expression* (Portsmouth, N.H.: Heinemann, 1994), 3.

20. Ibid.

21. This is precisely the problem that Robin Horton describes in "African Traditional Thought and Western Science," *Africa* 37/1 (1967): 50–71.

22. Edward W. Said, *Orientalism* (New York: Random House, 1979), 25.

23. Ibid., 10.

24. Ibid.

25. Karen McCarthy Brown, *Mama Lola: A Vodou Priestess in Brooklyn* (Berkeley: University of California Press, 1991), 14.

26. Paul Rabinow, *Reflections on Fieldwork in Morocco* (Berkeley: University of California Press, 1977), and Jean-Paul Dumont, *The Headman and I* (Austin: University of Texas Press, 1978).

27. Rabinow, *Reflections,* 155.

12. Black Theology and Ecumenism

1. Gayraud S. Wilmore, *Black Religion and Black Radicalism: An Interpretation of the Religious History of African Americans* (Maryknoll, N.Y.: Orbis, 1998), 3.

2. Silvia Regina de Lima Silva, "Black Latin American Theology: A New Way to Sense, to Feel, and to Speak of God," in Dwight N. Hopkins, ed., *Black Faith and Public Talk: Critical Essays on James H. Cone's* Black Theology and Black Power (Maryknoll, N.Y.: Orbis, 1999), 199.

3. Iva E. Carruthers, *The Church and Reparations: An African American Perspective* (Chicago: United Church of Christ, 2001), 223.

4. Ibid., 109.

5. Ibid., 92.

6. Cain Hope Felder, *Troubling Biblical Waters: Race, Class, and Family* (Bishop Henry McNeal Turner Studies in North American Black Religion 3; Maryknoll, N.Y.: Orbis, 1989), 99.

7. Gayraud S. Wilmore, "Black Theology at the Turn of the Century: Some Unmet Needs and Challenges," in *Black Faith and Public Talk,* 234.

8. James H. Cone, *For My People: Black Theology and the Black Church* (Bishop Henry McNeal Turner Studies in North American Black Religion 1; Maryknoll, N.Y.: Orbis, 1984), 94.

9. James H. Cone and Gayraud S. Wilmore, eds., *Black Theology: A Documentary History,* 2 vols. (2nd ed.; Maryknoll, N.Y.: Orbis, 1993), 1:157–58.

10. Ibid., 389.

11. Mary R. Sawyer, *Black Ecumenism: Implementing the Demands of Justice* (Valley Forge, Pa.: Trinity Press International, 1994), 133.

12. Cone, *For My People,* 110.

13. From the Black Theology Project brochure.

14. Cone and Wilmore, *Black Theology*, 1:167.

15. Ibid., 173.

16. Jacquelyn Grant, "Black Theology and the Black Woman," in Cone and Wilmore, *Black Theology*, 1:334–35.

17. Cain Hope Felder in Cone and Wilmore, *Black Theology*, 1:157.

18. Gayraud S. Wilmore in Cone and Wilmore, *Black Theology*, 1:9.

19. James H. Cone, *Risks of Faith: The Emergence of a Black Theology of Liberation, 1968–1998* (Boston: Beacon, 1999), 47.

20. Dwight N. Hopkins, "Postmodernity, Black Theology of Liberation and the U.S.A.: Michel Foucault and James H. Cone," in David B. Batstone, Dwight N. Hopkins, and Eduardo Mendieta, eds., *Liberation Theologies, Postmodernity, and the Americas* (New York: Routledge, 1997), 217.

21. Cone, *Risks*, 49.

22. Dennis Wiley, "Black Theology, the Black Church, and the African-American Community," in Cone and Wilmore, *Black Theology*, 2:131, 135.

23. Jeremiah A. Wright Jr., "An Underground Theology," in *Black Faith and Public Talk*, 98, 101.

24. Felder, "Cultural Ideology, Afrocentrism and Biblical Interpretation," in Cone and Wilmore, *Black Theology*, 2:191, 194.

25. Jamie T. Phelps, "Racism and the Church: An Inquiry into the Contradictions between Experience, Doctrine, and Theological Theory," in *Black Faith and Public Talk*, 59.

26. Cone, *Risks*, 134.

27. Ibid., 137.

28. Ibid., 133.

29. Ibid., 143.

30. Ibid., 142–43.

31. Emilie M. Townes, *Womanist Justice, Womanist Hope* (American Academy of Religion 79; Atlanta: Scholars, 1993), 84.

32. Wilmore, "Black Theology at the Turn of the Century," in *Black Faith and Public Talk*, 242.

13. American Indian Religious Traditions, Colonialism, Resistance, and Liberation

1. See Paul Chaat Smith and Robert Allen Warrior, *Like a Hurricane: The Indian Movement from Alcatraz to Wounded Knee* (New York: New Press, 1996); and Russell Means with Marvin Wolf, *Where White Men Fear to Tread: The Autobiography of Russell Means* (New York: St. Martin's, 1975).

2. I make this argument for the community-centered nature of American Indian ceremonial structures in spite of the persistent attempt of white scholars (the recognized "experts on Indians") to twist Indian cultural values into a more Euro-compatible form of individualism. See, for instance, Clyde Holler, *Black Elk's Religion: The Sun*

Dance and Lakota Catholicism (Syracuse, N.Y.: Syracuse University Press, 1995), but also note Dale Stover's insightful critique in his review of Holler's book, "Eurocentrism and Native Americans," *CrossCurrents* (1997): 390–97. Stover particularly addresses the tendency of Holler and others to impose an individualist interpretive overlay on the Indian cultures they purport to describe with "old fashioned . . . scholarly objectivity" (Holler, *Black Elk's Religion,* xvi).

3. Perhaps there is a connection here between the Indian sense of *doing* and liberation theology's notion of *praxis.*

4. *National* is used here in reference to the traditional sovereign communities of Indian peoples. It is used in preference to the usual but derogatory words *tribe* and *tribal.* See the essay by Ward Churchill, "Naming Our Future," *Global Justice* 3 (1992).

5. See Ward Churchill, "Carlos Castañeda: The Greatest Hoax Since Piltdown Man," in idem, *Fantasies of the Master Race: Literature, Cinema and the Colonization of American Indians,* ed. M. Annette Jaimes (Monroe, Me.: Common Courage, 1992), 43–64; and "Spiritual Hucksterism: The Rise of the Plastic Medicine Men," in ibid., 215–28. Also see Wendy Rose, "The Great Pretenders: Further Reflections on White Shamanism," in M. Annette Jaimes, ed., *The State of Native America: Genocide, Colonization, and Resistance* (Boston: South End, 1992), 403–22.

6. See my review of Mails's book in *American Indian Quarterly* 17 (1993): 393–95.

7. See the essay on the "men's movement" by Ward Churchill in this regard, "Indians Are Us: Reflections on the Men's Movement," in idem, *Indians Are Us? Culture and Genocide in Native North America* (Monroe, Me.: Common Courage, 1994), 207–77.

8. Many distinguish between open and closed ceremonies. The Pueblos of New Mexico, for instance, publish a calendar of ceremonies open to the public but also maintain their more critical ceremonies as private community events.

9. Louis F. Burns, *Osage Indian Customs and Myths* (Fallbrook, Calif.: Ciga, 1984), 3ff., discusses the qualifications of the *Nonhonzhinga,* based on the extensive work of Francis La Flesche. See also Garrick Bailey, *The Osage and the Invisible World from the Works of Francis La Flesche* (Norman: University of Oklahoma Press, 1995).

10. See, for example, Neal Salisbury, "Survivors and Pilgrims," in idem, *Manitou and Providence: Indians, Europeans, and the Making of New England, 1500–1643* (New York: Oxford University Press, 1982), 110–40.

11. Already noted by Albert Memmi in the context of 1950s Africa in his *The Colonizer and the Colonized,* trans. Howard Greenfeld (New York: Orion Press, 1965); and further described for the colonial context in India by Ashis Nandy, *The Intimate Enemy: Loss and Recovery of Self under Colonialism* (Delhi: Oxford University Press, 1983).

12. See Ward Churchill, *Struggle for the Land: Indigenous Resistance, Ecocide, and Expropriation in Contemporary North America* (Toronto: Between the Lines, 1992).

13. Don C. Talayesva, *Sun Chief: The Autobiography of a Hopi Indian,* ed. Leo William Simmons (New Haven: Yale University Press, 1942). See a similar ethnographic description for the Osage people in Bailey, *The Osage,* 56.

14. See Anne McClintock, *Imperial Leather: Race, Gender, and Sexuality in the Colonial Contest* (New York: Routledge, 1995).

14. Ecology as Experience in African Indigenous Religions

1. Lynn White Jr., "The Historical Roots of Our Ecological Crisis," *Science* 155 (1967): 1203–7.

2. David E. Cooper, "The Idea of Environment," in *The Environment in Question: Ethics and Global Issues,* ed. David E. Cooper and Joy A. Palmer (New York: Routledge, 1992).

3. Jürgen Moltmann, *God in Creation: A New Theology of Creation and the Spirit of God,* trans. Margaret Kohl (Minneapolis: Fortress Press, 1993), 12.

4. David Anderson and Richard Grove have noted, as have many others, that the introduction of European models of ecological conservation was often based on ignorance of indigenous methods of environmental protection. See their essay "The Scramble for Eden: Past, Present, and Future in African Conservation," in *Conservation in Africa: People, Policies, and Practice,* ed. David Anderson and Richard Grove (Cambridge: Cambridge University Press, 1987), 1.

5. Terence Ranger, "Whose Heritage? The Case of the Matobo National Park," *Journal of Southern African Studies* 15 (January 1989): 222.

15. A Theological Reflection on the Korean People's *Han* and *Hanpuri*

1. By becoming a shaman in the Confucian Korean society, one is automatically made an outcast, as she or he belongs to "the eight categories of the outcast *(pal-chun).*"

2. "The direct translation of 'minjung' is 'people.' But minjung is not a neutral term. Minjung implies a specific people. According to a Korean Minjung theologian, Suh Kwang-sun, minjung are 'the oppressed, exploited, dominated, discriminated against, alienated and suppressed politically, economically, socially, culturally, and intellectually, like women, ethnic groups, the poor, workers and farmers, including intellectuals themselves." Hyun Kyung Chung, "'Han-puri': Doing Theology from Korean Women's Perspective," in Virginia Fabella and Sun Ai Lee Park, *We Dare to Dream: Doing Theology as Asian Women* (Maryknoll, N.Y.: Orbis, 1989), 138–39.

3. Suh NamDong, "Towards a Theology of Han," *Minjung Theology* (Singapore: CCA, 1981), 65.

4. Chung, "Han-puri," in *We Dare to Dream,* 138.

5. Ibid.

6. Rita Nakashima Brock and Susan Brooks Thistlethwaite, *Casting Stones: Prostitution and Liberation in Asia and the United States* (Minneapolis: Fortress Press, 1996), 284.

7. Chung, "Han-puri," in *We Dare to Dream.*

8. NamDong, *Minjung Theology,* 54.

9. Chung, "'Han-puri,'" in *We Dare to Dream,* 143.

10. Brock and Thistlethwaite, *Casting Stones,* 284.

11. Korean culture has been dominated by Buddhism, Confucianism, and Christianity during the last 1,700 years. But no matter which foreign religion Korea has taken, the Confucian culture's impact upon Korea was the overlaying cultural, moral, and ideological authority and influence. It is this ruling Confucian culture that mostly damaged and marginalized the status of the shamanic minjung believers.

12. Sarah Nelson, "Gender Hierarchy and the Queens of Silla," in Barbara Miller, ed., *Sex and Gender Hierarchy* (Cambridge: Cambridge University Press, 1993), 304ff. According to her archaeological works based on Tomb 98 in Kyongju, Korea, gender equality was apparent in the ancient Silla before the significant Chinese presence (during 108 B.C.E.–313 C.E.). She suggests that the Silla queen in the more luxuriously decorated mound of the dual tomb might have been the actual royal and priestly ruler as her belongings (gold bracelets, earrings, crowns, and necklaces) in the mound seem to symbolize. Her husband, who might have been the co-ruling warrior of his wife king, has the military belongings in the less decorative mound of the double-mounded Royal Tomb 98.

13. Nung-wha Yi, *Chosun Musok-ko (The History of Korean Shamanism),* trans. Cahe-gon Lee (Seoul: Dongmunsun Dosuh, 1927), 32–33.

14. See the mythic creation story of Korea called Tangun Myth: (1) in ibid., 10–11, or (2) in Sob Zong, *Folk Tales from Korea* (New York: Grove, 1953), 3–4.

15. In terms of psychological and cultural assimilation, Korea was not so much influenced by the thirty-six-year-long period of Japanese political and economic colonialism. It could be partly because of the severity of oppression and brutality of Japanese colonialism. In addition, Japan was not a real political influence on Korea before it suddenly gained political power during the late nineteenth century.

16. Korea has its own language, Hangul, that was created in 1446 C.E. But the Confucian scholars and officials had continuously used Chinese for their writing until the early twentieth century, while regarding their own language as designed only for lowly commoners and women.

17. Brock and Thistlethwaite, *Casting Stones,* 39–40: "Estimates of 20 to 40 percent are given for the number of Korean Christians, and the overwhelmingly vast proportion belong to a conservative Presbyterian-rooted evangelical Protestantism whose sexual attitudes and practices are virtually indistinguishable from Confucian ones."

18. Ibid.

19. This summary is from the numerous sources of the myth, written or spoken and performed in the rituals. For a psychoanalytical approach to the concept of *han* and the myth of Princess Bari, see Lee Jaehoon, *The Exploration of the Inner Wounds—Han,* ed. Susan Thistlethwaite (Atlanta: Scholars Press, 1994), 99–119.

20. This is the exact fashion by which the colonial and neocolonial religious, cultural, and social power of Confucianism from China was brought to Korea during the Yi dynasty. Protestant Christianity followed the same method as Confucianism in its intrusion into Korea. By this oppressive form of colonialism, it further aggravated the already existing class and gender hierarchy and built a strong religious and cultural

hierarchy between the indigenous religion and the dominating foreign religions. Thus the *han* of the Korean shaman minjung women grew as the minjung in Korea, and the power and desire for their *hanpuri* grew as well. Korean minjung shaman women have come to be the most powerful wounded healers among all healers in Korea.

21. In Korea, the ordinary minjung women were not encouraged to pursue education. At a rough estimate, far less than 0.1 percent of Korean women were educated beyond high school level in the late nineteenth century.

22. Jung Young Lee, *Korean Shamanistic Rituals* (New York: Mouton, 1981), 153–66; Tong-sik Yu, *Hanguk Mukyo-ui Yuksa-wa Kujo (A History and Structure of Korean Shamanism)* (8th ed.; Seoul: Yunsei University Press, 1992), 110–12. According to their studies, Princess Bari was a shaman woman of a new style of Korean shamanism that seems to have emerged around the ninth century C.E. This new style of Korean shamanism is called "the cult of mudang (meaning 'shaman')," which differs from the traditional Korean shamanism. In my unpublished paper, "A Historical Analysis on Minjung Shaman Women and Social Change in Korea," I argue for the Princess Bari's new shamanic style as a liberative revolution that the shaman minjung women have accomplished in order to survive as the outcast shamans in the oppressive Korean society. While the Korean shamans of the Princess Bari tradition are charismatic and enter into ecstasy through the process of spirit possession, the traditional priestly Korean shamans basically remain the same, that is, priestly and liturgical. The traditional Korean shamans were mostly males who held a relatively higher status than the charismatic female shamans. The traditional priestly shamans perform, with the authority originating from the first divine ruler shaman (Tangun), very artistic and elaborate rituals. Nonetheless, they do not have ecstatic possession, through which the gods of the charismatic shamans manifest their supernatural power and help believers. The ninth century was a transitional period during which the Korean people of the late Silla dynasty suffered the numerous occasions of the external and internal turmoil. It seems that the society's hostility directed against Korean shamanism grew greater as the impact of Chinese Buddhism on the lives of Korean people grew much stronger under the increasing pressure of Tang China's colonial auspices. The religious conflict intensified between the newly dominating foreign religion and the indigenous religion, whose shaman priests held relatively high social and religious authority and prestige among the commoners. It is this period when the core dynamics of Korean shamanism shifted from priestly to charismatic under the new female minjung leadership. The myth of Princess Bari is an outstanding example of this effort shown by the new Korean minjung shaman women to overcome challenges to survival. They needed direct divine intervention, and the dynamics of ecstatic possession had newly appeared. These charismatic shamans have been known as more determined and compassionate than the priestly shamans in serving people for *hanpuri*. While the traditional priestly shaman role is handed down from generation to generation by the training received from their predecessors, the charismatic shamans are called by shamanic gods and become ordained directly

by the divine through spirit possession. Princess Bari demonstrated her supernatural power in the myth by spiritual birth and the journey taken in the form of death— "the journey through the western world of death, *suhbang segeh.*" Like Jesus, Princess Bari's own charismatic resurrection and her power to resurrect her loved ones required her own death and the death-thriving journey through the netherworld.

16. A Black American Perspective on Interfaith Dialogue

1. Gustavo Gutiérrez, "Two Theological Perspectives: Liberation Theology and Progressivist Theology," in *The Emergent Gospel: Theology from the Underside of History,* Sergio Torres and Virginia Fabella, eds. (Maryknoll, N.Y.: Orbis, 1978), 241.

2. Ibid.

3. Aloysius Pieris, *An Asian Theology of Liberation* (Maryknoll, N.Y.: Orbis, 1988), 87.

4. Esau Tuza, "The Demolition of Church Buildings by the Ancestors," in *The Gospel Is Not Western: Black Theologies from the Southwest Pacific,* ed. G. W. Trompf (Maryknoll, N.Y.: Orbis, 1987), 84.

5. Pieris, *An Asian Theology of Liberation,* 70.

6. Gabriel M. Setiloane, *African Theology: An Introduction* (Johannesburg, South Africa: Skotaville, 1986), 40.

7. Manuel M. Marzal, "The Religion of the Andean Quechua in Southern Peru," in *The Indian Face of God in Latin America,* eds. M. M. Marzal, E. Maurer, X. Albo, and B. Melia (Maryknoll, N.Y.: Orbis, 1996), 69.

8. Ruth M. Stone, "Bringing the Extraordinary into the Ordinary: Music Performance among the Kpelle of Liberia," in *Religion in Africa,* Thomas D. Blakely et al., eds. (Portsmouth, N.H.: Heinemann, 1994), 392.

9. Aruru Matiabe, "General Perspective: A Call for Black Humanity to Be Better Understood," in *The Gospel Is Not Western: Black Theologies from the Southwest Pacific,* ed. G. W. Trompf (Maryknoll, N.Y.: Orbis, 1987), 17.

10. Quoted in V. T. Rajshekar, *Dalit: The Black Untouchables of India* (Atlanta: Clarity, 1987), 41.

11. Rosario Battung, "Indigenous People's Primal Religions and Cosmic Spirituality as Wellsprings of Life," in *Springs of Living Water,* eds. Marlene Perera and A. Nunuk P. Murniati (Nagasandra, Bangalore: St. Paul's Press for EATWOT, 1997), 121.

12. Eugenio Maurer, "Tseltal Christianity," in *The Indian Face of God in Latin America* (Maryknoll, N.Y.: Orbis, 1996), 25.

13. Anne Pattel-Gray, *Through Aboriginal Eyes: The Cry from the Wilderness* (Geneva: WCC Publications, 1991), 6–7.

17. Living Stones in the Household of God

1. Johann Baptist Metz, "Theology in the Struggle for History and Society," in Marc H. Ellis and Otto Maduro, eds., *The Future of Liberation Theology: Essays in Honor of Gustavo Gutiérrez* (Maryknoll, N.Y.: Orbis, 1989), 167.

2. Andrew Hacker, *Two Nations: Black and White, Separate, Hostile, and Unequal* (New York: Scribner, 1992), 73; also Iris Marion Young, *Justice and the Politics of Difference* (Princeton, N.J.: Princeton University Press, 1990), 122–55.

3. Eugene F. Rivers III, "Beyond the Nationalism of Fools: Toward an Agenda for Black Intellectuals," *Boston Review* 20, no. 3 (summer 1995): 16.

4. Deborah Prothrow-Stith, *Deadly Consequences: How Violence Is Destroying Our Teenage Population and a Plan to Begin Solving the Problem* (New York: HarperPerennial, 1993), 16–17.

5. Hacker, *Two Nations,* 189.

6. Holly Sklar, "Young and Guilty by Stereotype," *Z Magazine* 7, no. 8 (July/August 1993): 60.

7. Martin Hengel, *Crucifixion,* trans. John Bowden (Philadelphia: Fortress Press, 1977), 1.

8. David and Elouise Fraser, "A Biblical View of Women: Demythologizing Sexegesis," *Theology, News, Notes* [Fuller Theological Seminary] (June 1975): 14-18, cited in Clarice J. Martin "The *Haustafeln* (Household Codes) in African American Biblical Interpretation: 'Free Slaves' and 'Subordinate Women,'" in Cain Hope Felder, ed., *Stony the Road We Trod: African American Biblical Interpretation* (Minneapolis: Fortress Press, 1991), 229.

18. On Keeping Faith with the Center

1. Cain Hope Felder, "Introduction," *The Original African Heritage Study Bible, King James Version* (Nashville: Winston, 1993), viii.

2. James H. Cone, *Black Theology and Black Power* (New York: Harper & Row, 1989), 135.

3. Cone, *Black Theology,* vii–xiv.

4. Ibid., x.

5. bell hooks, *Teaching to Transgress: Education as the Practice of Freedom* (New York: Routledge, 1994), 81.

19. The Vocation of a Theologian

1. New York: Seabury, 1969.

2. John C. Bennett, *The Radical Imperative: From Theology to Social Ethics* (Philadelphia: Westminster, 1975), 124.

3. Philadelphia: Lippincott, 1970.

4. *The Spirituals and the Blues: An Interpretation* (New York: Seabury, 1972).

5. New York: Seabury, 1975.

6. Cecil Wayne Cone, *The Identity Crisis in Black Theology* (Nashville: AMEC, 1975).